Hidden Dangers

Hidden Dangers

Railway Safety in the Era of Privatisation

STANLEY HALL, MCIT

Ian Allan PUBLISHING

Preface

This book examines the causes of the more serious accidents on the main line railways of Britain in the last 10 years, beginning with the Clapham accident in December 1988, and it takes up the story where the two previous volumes Danger Signals (1987) and Danger on the Line (1989) left off. It concludes by examining the current state of railway safety.

As was the case with those two books, it attempts to discover and examine the underlying causes of accidents, which are so often obscured. The immediate cause of an accident is almost always quickly established, but it is the impact of other forces which provides much of the interest. Weaknesses and changes in railway organisation, unreliable and variable investment levels, the Treasury's endless (but understandable) demands for economies, coupled with vacillation and uncertainty in every government's transport policies, or lack of them, all play an important part, and most accidents can be traced back to a combination of these factors. It is too easy to blame the driver or the signalman or the technician; there are others, well hidden, who ought to suffer some of the blame, but rarely do so. This book attempts to put the record straight.

The last 10 years have seen greater and more sweeping changes in safety organisations, both within the industry and externally in the government's regulatory bodies, than in the previous century and a half, whilst during that decade the industry itself has been reorganised and converted from a state-owned monolith to a multi-faceted conglomeration of privately-owned companies. It is a paradox in the highest degree that whilst all this activity was taking place, and whilst managers' attentions were elsewhere, safety standards did not deteriorate. The only explanation available is that the men out on the line continued to do their jobs with their customary care and attention as good railwaymen should, whilst in the higher reaches divorced from day-to-day realities things changed out of all recognition. There are intriguing precedents for this — following the upheaval of the Grouping which created the 'Big Four', there were no passenger deaths in train accidents in 1925; following nationalisation there were no deaths in 1949, and now, after the biggest upheaval in railway history, there have been no passenger deaths in train accidents in 1998; remarkable parallels.

I have been fortunate during the last 10 years to have had the opportunity to make a thorough study of the subject of railway safety and accidents, to attend public inquiries, Coroners' inquests, court proceedings and to discuss questions of safety and organisation with a variety of railwaymen of all grades, both active and retired, including former colleagues whose opinions and experience I respect. The views expressed in the following chapters and the criticisms made represent a distillation both of their own judgements and of mine, and are therefore very broadly based and, I trust, well founded.

Many people have helped me with information, criticisms, ideas and their own views, but I would particularly like to thank John Whitehouse MBE, my guide and mentor for many years; Roy Bell MBE and Robin Nelson, both very senior signal engineers now retired from the railways, for their technical advice; Arthur Lowe, of the Friends of the National Railway Museum, for running his practised eye over the script; and all those who have supplied photographs for the book, particularly Brian Morrison, who has been most helpful and generous.

This book is not an attack on privatisation. Quite the opposite; BR was far from perfect and something had to be done to reduce the impact of government control. Whilst the government's chosen method of privatisation is also flawed, it does at least provide hope for the future. But vigilance will be required to ensure that growing financial demands on the companies are not allowed to imperil safety. HM Railway Inspectorate has a vital role to play to ensure that they do not.

Stanley Hall
Skipton, North Yorkshire, August 1999

LIST OF ABBREVIATIONS

ATC	Automatic Train Control
ATP	Automatic Train Protection
AWS	Automatic Warning System *(of train control)*
BR	British Rail*(ways)*
BRB	British Railways Board
BTC	British Transport Commission
BTP	British Transport Police
CSR	Cab Secure Radio
CWR	Continuous-Welded Rail
DEMU	Diesel-Electric Multiple-Unit
DMU	Diesel Multiple-Unit
DOO	Driver-Only Operation *(no guard)*
DOS	District or Divisional Operating Superintendent
DRA	Driver's Reminder Appliance
EMU	Electric Multiple-Unit
ETD	Extension Trunk Dialling
HMRI	Her Majesty's Railway Inspectorate
HSE	Health & Safety Executive *(or H&SE)*
HST	High Speed Train *(a specific type of train)*
ICI	Imperial Chemical Industries
LMS(R)	London, Midland & Scottish Railway
LNER	London & North Eastern Railway
NRN	National Radio Network
SPAD	Signal Passed at Danger
TPWS	Train Protection & Warning System

Front Cover
Collision at Southall on 19 September 1997, between an HST and a train of empty wagons (see Chapter 13).

Back Cover (upper)
The result of vandalism at Greenock. An obstruction on the line derailed the train, which then collided with a bridge abutment, killing the driver. The culprits were caught and prosecuted.

Back Cover (lower)
The devastating result of a head-on collision at Cowden between two passenger trains in fog on 15 October 1994 (see Chapter 13).

Half Title
A possible case of a signal passed at danger resulted in this collision between a Class 87 and 'Pacer' (see Chapter 13).

Title Page
On 23 January 1975 the electric locomotive and first vehicle of the 22.15 sleeping car express from Euston to Glasgow plunged down an embankment at Watford (see Chapter 12).

First published 1999

ISBN 0 7110 2679 3

All rights reserved. No part of this book may be reproduced or transmitted in any form or by any means, electronic or mechanical, including photocopying, recording or by any information storage and retrieval system, without permission from the Publisher in writing.

© Stanley Hall 1999.

Published by Ian Allan Publishing

An imprint of Ian Allan Publishing Ltd, Terminal House, Shepperton, Surrey TW17 8AS.

Printed by Ian Allan Printing Ltd, Riverdene Business Park, Hersham, Surrey KT12 4RG.

Code: 9910/B2

Contents

CHAPTER 1

The Prologue:
Setting the Scene

THE BACKGROUND

Railways are, and always have been, in a state of conflict: politically, with governments; with economic and competitive pressures (often government influenced); with their staff and trade unions; and through internal, organisational in-fighting. Safety of operation is only one of many aspects of the running of railways and, it might be argued, not necessarily the most important. Whilst safety of operation is an essential component, the survival of the industry might be thought to rank even higher; it is always important to bear that in mind, and empires which have been built on the single concept of safety might find that hard to accept.

THE 19TH CENTURY

Railways were brought into existence to enable industrialists to increase their profits, through being able to move their raw materials and finished products more cheaply, efficiently and quickly. However, it was not long before railways became an industry in their own right, dedicated to making a profit for the shareholders (ie the owners) in the transport of goods and passengers. The directors had two aims — to maximise their profits and to ensure the enduring prosperity of the company. The fulfilment of both those aims was essential to avoid bankruptcy on the one hand and to be attractive to potential investors on the other.

These economic aims brought the railways into conflict with the government at a very early stage, and those conflicts dominated the 19th century. Although it was the great era of laissez-faire, when industrialists in general were left unconstrained by the government in the pursuit of profit, the railways were seen as being in a position to hold both industry and the travelling public to ransom, to charge extortionate rates and fares and provide an inadequate service with, incidentally, little regard for safety. Governments felt that the railways should not be allowed to abuse their monopoly position, and passed a number of Acts controlling rates, fares and service. Not content with that, governments encouraged the building of competitive railway lines between main centres, as a further attack on monopoly. Thus the railways became heavily over-capitalised, and a major potential weakness in their financial position was created, which was to cause immense problems in the future. It is significant that during the whole of the 19th century (and for most of the 20th) there was only one main Act concerned with safety of operation (the 1889 Regulation of Railways Act), apart from those Acts concerning level crossings.

The end of the 19th century found the main railway companies in a reasonably healthy financial state, despite their affairs being tightly controlled both by legislation and by successive governments' attitudes towards the railways. Other industries were allowed to amass huge profits, but not the railways, despite the fact that it was the railways which had made possible Britain's enormous economic and social growth.

THE 20TH CENTURY, UP TO 1923

The 19th century had seen stability and expansion; the 20th was to be a period of continual upheaval. It started badly with increases in the cost of staff and raw materials which the railways were unable to recover through their legally fixed rates. Trade unions were formed and rapidly expanded, and there were a number of serious strikes prior to 1914. They were to be followed by the most serious upheaval of all — the Great War.

The railways suffered little damage during the war, and traffic levels increased considerably. The government took control of the railways in 1914 under powers contained in the Regulation of the Forces Act of 1871, and that control extended to profits. It might have been expected that surplus profits would be returned to the railways after the war in order to enable them to overcome wartime arrears of maintenance and new building, but that was not the case. In fact the government, which retained wartime control until 1921, so badly handled railway finances after the war, with greatly increased costs of staff and materials on the one hand and inadequate increases in rates and charges on the other, that the railways were in great danger of being unable to balance their books. Once again there was conflict between the government of the day and the railways, to the latter's considerable detriment.

AFTER 1923 — THE GROUPING

The government's answer to this was the enforced merger in 1923 of all except a few very minor railways into what became known as the 'Big Four': the London, Midland & Scottish Railway (LMS), the London & North Eastern Railway (LNER), the Great Western Railway and the Southern Railway. It was undoubtedly a sound decision. Wartime control had demonstrated the benefits of co-operation between the companies (which incidentally was developing despite government opposition before the war!) and it was hoped that the financially sound pre-Grouping companies would thus support the weaker ones. It was a vain hope. The government encouraged the uncontrolled development of road transport to attack the railway monopoly, whilst retaining the

Above
On 10 December 1937 a collision on the LNER at Castlecary station, between Edinburgh and Glasgow, resulted in the deaths of 35 people and injuries to a further 179 passengers. At the time of the accident, this was the highest peacetime casualty list in railway history. *Hulton-Deutsch*

19th century anti-monopoly legislation which handicapped the railways in answering the new competition. In the midst of all this there occurred the world economic slump of the early 1930s. Railways found themselves in the unfamiliar position of an uncertain future. Traffic levels fell, especially on the LNER which was very dependent on heavy industry, and there was little to spend on safety on the railways. Safety investment became secondary to economic survival.

In the interwar years, the state of prosperity of the railways was ruled by economics and politics. Then history repeated itself. When World War 2 began, the railways were again taken under government control and their current preoccupations were set aside. Rates, charges and profits were again controlled. Traffic levels increased enormously, but, as before, the railways were not allowed to retain their surplus profits for postwar rebuilding and renewal. In a postwar settlement they were reimbursed an inadequate portion of those surplus profits. The government simply pocketed the rest. It was of little consequence, because politics were about to intrude yet again in the railways' fortunes.

1948 - NATIONALISATION

The return of a Labour government in 1945 made nationalisation of the railways inevitable. On 1 January 1948 British Railways was born, to become the butt of comedians' jokes for the next 40 years or so. People may have had their grumbles about the 'Big Four', but they were generally regarded with a certain esteem, which BR was never to receive. BR was a political target.

Political interference and economic pressures had long been the lot of the railways; the new nationalised railway now had to contend with staff conflict and organisational in-fighting in addition. Staff conflict had been at a low level since the early 1920s, and it was confidently expected that it would disappear

now that the railways were owned by the nation. The pursuit of profit was no longer an objective and the staff assumed that they would be rewarded with a good standard of pay and conditions of service. The honeymoon did not last long — conflict arose from two sources. Inflation led to annual demands for pay increases which the financial state of the industry was ill-equipped to meet, plagued as it was by its old enemies — road competition and an inflexible rates structure. There were annual conflicts between BR and the railway trade unions, resulting in strikes and go-slows, known inaccurately as 'working to rule'. Each trade dispute resulted in a loss of freight traffic as dissatisfied customers turned to the more reliable road transport. The trade unions had assumed that they would have at least a share of the profits which formerly went to the shareholders, but, as events turned out, there were no profits. Indeed, there were ever increasing losses, and BR's efforts to stem those losses led to more disputes with the trade unions. It was an impossible situation. The Chairman of the British Transport Commission (BTC) during most of the 1950s was Sir Brian Robertson, an ex-army man. He firmly believed that the government, having defined the railway's role, should provide the means, ie the funds. He regarded his duty not as that of a manager or an entrepreneur, but as an administrator, implementing the declared purposes of the 1947 Transport Act. He was to discover that whilst he was prepared to do his part, the government was not willing to do its. There had been a change of government. Successive chairmen spent their energies in trying to square the circle, and in their turn departed, defeated and perplexed.

The railways had been kept in business by an artificial structure known as nationalisation. Only the starry-eyed and dogma-ridden believed that it would succeed, and it quickly became apparent that it could only do so if it were to be supported by large handouts of taxpayers' money, in the face of concerted attacks on its traffic by road haulage, the private car and the aeroplane, and the gradual collapse of its staple freight traffics: coal and steel. Paradoxically, it was the success of the car and the lorry that saved the railways. It became apparent that the unbridled use of cars was leading to unacceptable levels of congestion in towns and cities and that suburban railways should be subsidised to provide some relief. At the same time, technical advance had given the railways the high-speed intercity network which was able to compete commercially. But freight, unsubsidised, continued to decline, and without a large volume of freight traffic the railways could never pay their way, with their high fixed costs.

ORGANISATIONAL CONFLICT

Our fourth area of conflict, organisational, arose directly from nationalisation. Prior to that, the railway companies had a well-established organisation which had been developed and refined almost from the 19th century. Everyone understood it, and everyone knew their position in it. Internal relationships, so important to success, worked smoothly. There had been little upheaval since the aftermath of Grouping in 1923.

The organisation for running the nationalised railways, which was conceived by well-meaning civil servants who unfortunately had little concept of organisational interactions, bordered on the farcical. At the top stood the BTC, itself headed by a former civil servant, which controlled not only the railways, but also London Transport, some road haulage, some buses, canals, docks, and hotels. Beneath that lay the Railway Executive, in charge of railways, but divorced from the private companies' non-railway activities which had been an integral part of the railway business. The Railway Executive stood above what had been the four main line companies, now bereft of their boards of directors. Those four companies became six regions — in general terms the LMS lines in England became the London Midland Region, the LNER lines in England became the Eastern and the North Eastern (which were merged in 1968), the proud Great Western became merely the Western and the Southern remained the Southern. Scotland had its own Region. There were some reshuffles a few years later when the Regions settled old company scores by pinching bits of each other's territory.

The Regions inherited all the proud company traditions and rightly considered themselves perfectly capable of running their own lines without interference from above. Matters common to all Regions could easily have been conducted through inter-Regional committees, as they were between the former companies. However, that would have left the Railway Executive with little to

do, and a war broke out between the Regions and the Executive on questions of responsibilities, authorities and, of course, prestige, position and power. The Executive was also attacked from above by the BTC, which also wanted a slice of the action. There ensued five years of organisational in-fighting before the government, in a rare moment of insight in railway affairs, dissolved the Railway Executive. The BTC then took unto itself much of the Railway Executive's duties, thus ensuring a continuance of the battle, which was now between the Regions and the BTC. The whole episode was a disaster for the railways, resulting in a lack of direction and no firm, progressive policy. Out on the line the railways struggled to move their still substantial freight traffic with a chronic shortage of staff and a lack of investment. Faced with so many problems, the BTC had neither the time nor the money to spend on major improvements in safety, although it should be pointed out that there were no great pressures on the BTC to do so.

THE BEECHING ERA

As the 1950s progressed, the railway's financial situation worsened, its losses increasing year by year. The government, searching for a solution, decided that responsibility for running the railways was a big enough job on its own for anyone, and abolished the BTC, putting the railways under a board, known as the British Railways Board, and writing off much of the accumulated loss. Its first chairman was Richard (later Lord) Beeching, formerly with ICI, who knew nothing about railways but plenty about organisation, which was what was wanted. Railway management temporarily ceased to flounder, but the experiment of nationalisation had wasted hundreds of millions of pounds.

Beeching is remembered in popular mythology as the villain who destroyed our railways, but he quickly discovered that local stopping passenger trains and rural lines made a thumping loss. Half of all passenger stations produced only 2% of all passenger receipts. He asked, in effect, what was the economic sense in keeping them open? But the main thrust of his report concerned freight traffic, which at the time produced almost twice as much revenue as passenger traffic. Sundries traffic (ie traffic in less than full wagon loads) made an even bigger loss, and was eventually handed over to newly formed National Carriers Ltd, part of another newly formed body under the 1968 Transport Act, the National Freight Corporation. On the positive side, dedicated company train freight traffic was extensively developed. But the fond hopes that Beeching's plans would put the railways back on the path to prosperity were soon to be dashed. Nothing could restore the railways to prosperity. Beeching was one of the bogeymen of the Labour Party, and when Labour was returned to power in 1964 he was rapidly replaced. His successors were no more successful. The government finally faced reality and decided that it would financially support those passenger services which were unprofitable but ought to be retained in the public interest.

This was a major step, which has preserved the railway network almost unchanged in the last 30 years, and has led to considerable increases in train services in Passenger Transport Authority areas.

The halving of the railway network in the 1960s, and the continuing decline in freight, led inevitably to changes in railway organisation. The railways had been top heavy with organisational layers since 1948, but paradoxically this caused them to be undermanaged. Beeching recognised this, but his assistants produced even more complex organisational charts. From that time until the present day, railway managers have often spent more time on reorganisations than on actually running the railways. At any one time they were bedding in the previous reorganisation, and planning the next. The priority, as always, was to reduce staff numbers. The government demanded that staff numbers be reduced. The Board told the Regions, and the Regions passed on the message. It was left to local managers to decide how this was to be done. There was no policy guidance. It is fortunate that front-line staff such as drivers, signalmen, inspectors and junior managers continued to run the railways day by day with a proper concern for safety, as indeed they always had done. They were often the recipients of the latest reshuffle, but at least they were not distracted by having to plan and implement it. It is yet another paradox that in such circumstances many front-line staff continued to display a degree of dedication and commitment to the concept of the railway service (not to the Board, be it noted) that is quite astonishing.

THE CONCEPT OF BUSINESS MANAGEMENT

Beeching had tried to introduce a more businesslike approach, but it withered on the vine. Twenty years were to elapse before another chairman, the first Sir Robert Reid, introduced business management. He regarded railway engineers as robber barons who had bled the railways dry and were responsible to no one for their costs, and he set in motion yet another reorganisation, but one that was both essential and long overdue, to establish business-led sectors with full responsibility for the bottom line. Business managers queried the need for the railway to have its own in-house engineering departments with all their associated costs, something which the Board should have done long ago. They quickly appreciated the supreme flaws of railway nationalisation — the lack of financial accountability and discipline: the comfortable knowledge that BR could never become bankrupt and go out of business. It created the begging bowl mentality, with the Treasury always there to prop up the inefficiently run railway, however unwillingly.

There was just one victim — safety. Business managers failed to listen to experienced operators, whom they regarded as hidebound traditionalists unwilling to change, which resulted in several unsatisfactory and potentially unsafe track remodelling and resignalling schemes. There was a lack of firm purpose and direction in the planning of safety improvements such as Automatic Train Protection or an improved Automatic Warning System. Other measures to help drivers were also subjected to delayed development. But that had also happened under previous BR organisations.

SAFETY BECOMES HIGH PROFILE

In the late 1980s, safety suddenly became a high-profile subject. There was no single reason for this. BR created a Safety Directorate mainly because it thought it ought to have one. It was fashionable, but it was also a protective measure. The hidden menace of the Health & Safety at Work Act 1974 was beginning to be appreciated, and a series of non-railway transport accidents, such as the *Herald of Free Enterprise* sinking and the M1 air crash at Kegworth brought the question firmly to public notice, assisted greatly by television coverage and culminating in the massive television response to the 1988 railway accident at Clapham. The subsequent public inquiry, which lasted in all for 65 days, with attendant publicity, heavily criticised the Board, which took fright and declared that safety was its top priority. This sounded good and no doubt pleased politicians and the media but was a nonsense. No doubt the Board knew this, but felt it had to pay lip service. Had it been true, we would already have had nationwide Automatic Train Protection and every other conceivable safety initiative, whether justified financially or not. A cynic might observe that job protection was the top priority.

Right
Devastation at Wembley Central, showing the derailed EMU after its collision with a freightliner train on 11 October 1984. Three passengers were killed in the accident caused by the driver of the passenger train running past a signal at danger. *Mick Roberts*

The aftermath of the Purley collision of 4 March 1989 which claimed five lives. The wreckage of the Littlehampton-Victoria express is shown after it collided with the rear of the preceding train and plunged down the embankment. *Mail Newspapers*

The value of the Health & Safety Executive in other industrial fields is not a matter for this book, but so far as the nationalised railway was concerned it was an irrelevance. The railways were already sufficiently regulated by the Railway Inspectorate, which had always performed that responsibility adequately. One witnessed the supreme absurdity of a publicly funded body (the HSE) prosecuting another such publicly funded body (BR) in the publicly funded courts, and being fined large sums of public money, which could have been better spent on safety projects. Even W. S. Gilbert would have thought the situation too far-fetched to be the subject of one of his satires.

PRIVATISATION

The 1990s introduced changes in the railway industry which were without parallel in its history. The government had denationalised most state-owned industries, but regarded railways as the most difficult subject, mainly owing to the fact that the railways were heavily supported by public funds, a situation that would have to continue for some years until the greater efficiency expected from private ownership began to reduce that demand. In any case, there were considerable doubts as to whether the railways could be sold off at all, other than very cheaply. It was a miscalculation. In the event, there was far more interest in railways than had ever been thought. Fortunes were made overnight, and Railtrack's shares quadrupled in value in a few years.

One of the prime concerns in the privatisation process was the maintenance of a high standard of operational safety in a fragmented railway system. The role of the Railway Inspectorate now became vital. It was charged with producing a report on how safety could be managed on a privatised railway. The report,

Ensuring Safety on Britain's Railways (January 1993), was masterly, and ran to 156 pages, proposing a complex bureaucratic but effective system of safety cases, in which each train operator and every other organisation concerned had to produce a safety case setting out how all risks were to be managed safely. Railtrack was charged with approving these safety cases. Railtrack's own safety case was approved by the Inspectorate.

The railways had always policed their own safety standards and the responsibilities of the Railway Inspectorate had been ones of audit of the results and the investigation of accidents. These were post-facto responsibilities and there were considerable concerns that the new commercial companies running parts of the railway might have lower concerns for safety than had been traditional in the railway industry, especially if there were financial pressures. It was therefore necessary to create an organisation to monitor current safety standards, to ensure as far as possible that safety was not compromised, and these duties are now performed by a necessarily expanded Railway Inspectorate. Regrettable as this external policing may be, it is undoubtedly essential in the present circumstances and has demonstrated its worth. Safety standards have been compromised on several occasions, as these pages will show, both by BR's reorganisation into business sectors in the late 1980s, and by the upheaval of privatisation, and it is now time to examine the events of the past 10 years in more detail.

CHAPTER 2

The Prelude:
The State of Railway Safety Before Clapham

The Clapham accident occurred on Monday 12 December 1988 and killed 35 people. It was not the worst accident in railway history by any means — far more people were killed in the Harrow collision in 1952 and at Lewisham in 1957 — but its impact on the railway's safety culture was unparalleled in its all-embracing severity. In order to measure the extent of the changes which took place, and their justification, it would be helpful to examine the state of safety in the years immediately preceding Clapham.

In the 10 years from 1970 to 1979, 52 passengers lost their lives in 14 train accidents, of which drivers were responsible for no fewer than 10, either through excessive speed or by passing signals at danger.

In the nine years from 1980 to 11 December 1988, 35 passengers were killed in nine train accidents, a reduction (ie an improvement) of roughly 25% in each case. Drivers were responsible for only two of the accidents, both of which were caused by signals passed at danger. It might also be added that the two most serious accidents were caused by circumstances largely outside the railway's control — 13 passengers were killed when a train ran into a cow which had strayed onto the line near Polmont (between Edinburgh and Glasgow) in 1984, and eight passengers lost their lives when a Bridlington to Hull diesel multiple-unit collided with a small van whose driver had driven past the flashing red lights at an automatic level crossing at Lockington in 1986. If those two accidents are excluded, train accidents caused only 14 passengers deaths in almost nine years, which must be considered a remarkably good record and a credit to the railway's safety systems. It certainly provided no justification whatsoever for the safety hysteria and upheaval which followed Clapham.

The high standard of safety which existed before Clapham resulted from the railway's safety culture and its safety management systems, and it would be appropriate to examine

Top
Massive breakdown cranes work through the night clearing the wreckage after the disastrous double collision at Clapham on 12 December 1988. *Jeremy de Souza*

Centre
The collision at Lewisham St John's on 4 December 1957 caused part of the overhead railway bridge to collapse on to one of the trains, resulting in many more fatalities. Altogether 90 people lost their lives, almost three times as many as at Clapham. *British Rail*

Bottom
The collapsed span has been removed, and the line reopened on 12 December. The overhead line was reopened with a temporary bridge on 13 January 1958. *British Rail*

Left
An accident which could have been a repeat of Polmont. A Class 321 electric multiple-unit forming the 18.20 from Liverpool Street to Witham ran into a herd of cows at Hatfield Peverel on 18 June 1996 and was derailed. *Michael J. Collins*

Below
Lockington 26 July 1986. The coaches of the 09.33 diesel multiple-unit from Bridlington to Hull are spread in all directions after the train collided with a small van, the remains of which are in the foreground, at an automatic open level crossing. The van driver had driven past the flashing red traffic signals. Eight passengers in the train were killed and one passenger in the van. *Press Agency (Yorkshire)*

those systems in order to judge whether the severe criticisms which were levelled at them after Clapham were justified or were misguided.

It is perhaps surprising in 1999 to relate that in 1980 there were no railway operating managers or staff with the word 'safety' in their job titles. The reason is quite simple — everyone accepted that safety was their own responsibility and they would have felt insulted to have had the word 'safety' in their title, as though they needed reminding of their safety responsibilities. It would have been equally absurd to have included the word in some titles and not in others; human nature would have resulted in the development of a 'them and us' attitude to safety, and

those excluded would inevitably have regarded safety as someone else's sphere of interest. During the later 1980s transport safety became a higher profile subject and British Railways responded by creating a post of Director Safety with an appropriate backup. Also, by this time organisational changes had resulted in a different command structure, but on the whole the same principles of reporting and investigation of accidents continued.

If we take 1980 as our starting point, it is of interest to note that Lt-Col Ian McNaughton, the Chief Inspecting Officer of Railways at the time, stated in his Annual Report on Railway Safety that:

'The railways of Great Britain have always set their own high standards of safety...and the previously unequalled safety record for 1980 will set a new standard for the future, providing a challenge and an incentive to achieve even better results.'

How were those high standards achieved? The basic requirements for safety are:

1 Safe and reliable equipment — track, signalling and rolling stock.

2 Equipment to guard against the failure of the human element — eg track circuits, signalling controls, automatic train control or warning systems.

3 Safe working methods and procedures, clearly set out in the books of Rules and Regulations.

4 A well-trained staff, so that the safe working methods can be properly applied.

5 A well-motivated staff, who will apply the safe working methods.

6 Effective supervision, to detect lack of knowledge or lack of care, so that remedies can be applied.

7 Effective leadership, to inculcate correct safety attitudes and provide motivation.

Improvements in safety stem from a number of sources, but the primary source is the rigorous examination of every accident to establish the cause and to determine what action, if any, needs to be taken. During their lifetime, the railway companies had evolved a comprehensive system for ensuring that all accidents were recorded and reported to a higher level of authority so that proper investigation could take place, and this organisation was continued by the nationalised railway. There were four levels of authority, and their responsibilities were as follows:

1 The first layer, the bottom layer, was the stationmaster or yard master. His responsibility was to see that operations in his domain were conducted strictly in accordance with the Rules and Regulations and to report, normally by correspondence, any infringements. Accidents were reported on the appropriate forms, but in addition they were reported currently by telephone to the District Control Office so that any necessary alterations to train or traffic working could be instituted. All such reports were recorded in the Control Office log.

2 The second layer was the District Office (subsequently renamed the Divisional Office). The head man of the District Office was called the District Operating Superintendent (or Manager or Controller) and was responsible for what was known as 'the safety of the line' throughout his domain. That phrase really means the safety of train working and anything that might affect the safe working of passenger and freight trains.

The District Operating Superintendent (DOS) supervised operations in his domain through his Control Office and by the use of a number of District Inspectors, who were regarded as his eyes and ears. The Control Office was mainly concerned with the punctual and efficient operation of trains, the expeditious movement of freight traffic, and the most economical use of traction and traincrews. It was not part of the safety organisation, but because it was open continuously it was the natural centre for the reporting of all accidents. If there was a serious accident, the DOS and his inspectors would be alerted and other measures would be taken, including notifying the emergency services and calling out breakdown cranes. Headquarters would also be notified if necessary.

The DOS was responsible for ensuring that all accidents were fully investigated and the cause established. Where engineering departments were involved (eg a defective wagon or piece of track) a formal joint inquiry would be held, chaired by the DOS, with the engineering departments concerned being represented on the panel. Those involved in the accident, or who could help with technical evidence, were then interviewed by the panel and a formal report was drawn up, including a conclusion as to the cause, based on the evidence. A copy of the report was then sent to Headquarters. Recommendations, if any, were sent separately.

3 The next layer was at Railway or Regional Headquarters level. Responsibility at this level was mainly to ensure that satisfactory safety standards were maintained and that any necessary system-wide remedial action was taken. Another important function was the reporting of accidents to the Railway Inspectorate, and arranging public inquiries if requested to do so by the Railway Inspectorate.

4 In pre-nationalisation days Chief Operating Superintendents of the various railway companies or their representatives met each month to discuss matters of mutual interest concerned with the safety of the line and to agree changes to the Rules and Regulations. After nationalisation this committee continued in being, chaired by the Board's Signalling Officer, with each Region being represented by a senior operator.

Engineering departments were also structured in a manner to ensure as far as possible that accidents did not arise from errors or malfunctions in rolling stock, the infrastructure and the signalling system.

This very comprehensive system ensured that all matters of importance were considered at the highest level, and that any necessary remedial action was instituted throughout the railway system. It resulted in a very high standard in the safety of train working. Subsequent reorganisations changed job titles and layers, but the principles remained the same.

Remedial action following accidents is a continuous process, and accidents from a cause which has not previously been experienced are relatively rare and confined to the impact of new technologies. However, remedial action is not automatically applied; it has to be considered against a number of factors:

▪ Is the cause of the accident sufficiently serious to justify changes in procedures?

▪ Would any change impact unacceptably in the ability to operate trains efficiently?

▪ Is the cost of any proposed change justified?

Cost is a factor in any proposed change and a moment's consideration will show that this must be the case. It applies throughout human activities in whatever field, and it is instructive to hear what an eminent Queen's Counsel had to say on the subject. That QC was Mr E. B. Gibbens, and he had been appointed by the Minister of Transport under Sec 7 of the Regulation of Railways Act 1871 to hold a formal inquiry into a collision at Hixon (Staffs) automatic half-barrier level crossing on 6 January 1968. On that date a massive road transporter lorry carrying a 120-ton transformer was proceeding very cautiously over the level crossing when the red lights started to flash and the barriers began to descend. The lorry was moving so slowly that it was unable to get clear before a train, a Manchester to Euston express which had caused the lights to flash and the barriers to fall automatically, arrived at the crossing travelling at almost full speed. The electric locomotive struck the transformer and hurled it aside, becoming derailed in the process. Several coaches were also derailed and 11 passengers were killed. BR should have been informed beforehand of the proposed movement of the lorry over the level crossing, but no such prior notice was received.

Mr Gibbens wrote in his report:

'Safety is a relative concept varying in proportion to its opposite, danger. It is almost impossible to remove absolutely the risk of accident from any form of human activity, and it is a truism that many forms of progress, though producing greater safety than of old, are all liable to produce serious loss of life but they have been accepted by the public because the advantages they bring outweigh the inescapable risks. Safety can, in a sense, be bought like any tangible commodity — the higher the price paid, the better the safety; and, in assessing the degree of safety to be acquired, one must put into the balance, on the one side, the magnitude of the danger to be eliminated and, on the other, the sacrifice in money, time, convenience, material resources (and the neglect of other pressing safety needs elsewhere) involved in eliminating that danger... There

is no such thing as unbounded resources for every desirable reform.'

How beautifully phrased, cogently argued and sensibly put. One might hope to be defended by Mr Gibbens if one ever found oneself in the unfortunate position of facing a criminal charge.

Mr Gibbens refers to the public acceptance of safety and it is a phrase that comes to mind when considering how safe the railway should be. There is no absolute standard and in a realistic world there is no prospect of a completely safe, 100% accident-free railway. It is simply not affordable and to attempt to achieve it would be an enormous waste of resources. In the absence of such a standard, public acceptance is a useful yardstick, but the public's view needs to be uninfluenced by media hysteria of the type which is so common nowadays. It is an oddity of modern life that a railway accident resulting in one or two deaths receives far more media attention than a road traffic accident resulting in several times as many. In a strange kind of way it is a compliment to the railways for their high safety standards and astonishment at any lapse. Serious railway accidents are always news because they are so rare; road accidents are not because they are commonplace.

In the last Annual Report on Railway Safety to be written by a Chief Inspecting Officer of Railways who had many years' experience of working in the field of railway safety and knew what he was talking about (there has not been one of such experience since, which is an odd state of affairs and will be examined in a later chapter) Major C. F. Rose stated:

'1986 was a year which showed little overall change from the generally satisfactory situation of recent years. Whilst a few adverse trends will need watching...the majority of the long-term trends remain favourable. The railways continue to provide a very safe form of transport and to maintain their traditionally high standards.'

Throughout the 1980s up to Clapham there were several safety initiatives in progress, developed from investigations into accidents and the need to deal with adverse trends. Some were long-term projects, others were one-off, but almost all were dependent on the provision of funds to a railway industry which was increasingly under pressure from the government of the day to reduce its need for Treasury support. Such pressure inevitably lengthened the timescale for improvements to be achieved. It also resulted in schemes being reduced in scale or content, making them less effective. Government ministers could confidently comment that reduced financial support for the railways did not cause any reduction in safety levels because BR could not point in response to any accidents which would have been avoided if the cuts had not been made. In any case, governments always had a get-out clause — their oft-repeated assertion that it was up to BR to decide how and where to spend the money that was available. This was true, but unhelpful.

It is now time to review the safety initiatives which were in progress in the 1980s up to Clapham:

Top Left
Automatic Warning System equipment, consisting of a permanent and an electro-magnet fixed between the rails. *British Rail*

Centre Left, Below Left & Bottom Left
Automatic Warning System train equipment, consisting of a receiver located at the front of, and below, the bogie. This detects the message relayed by the track equipment. The AWS 'Sunflower' in the driving cab is seen in the black and yellow segmented display, which is provided to remind the driver that he has acknowledged a warning by pressing a button on the control desk and has cancelled the automatic application of the brake. It is now his responsibility to do so. *Author*

1 The programme to equip most routes and traction on BR with the automatic warning system of train control had started in 1958 and had proceeded mainly hand in hand with the modernisation of signalling. Progress was generally, but not entirely, limited by the availability of funds. By 1980 BR had equipped 4,972 route miles of its total route mileage of just over 10,000, and by 1988 the mileage equipped had increased to 7,013. This was one of the most significant safety initiatives undertaken this century and has been of incalculable value.

2 New rolling stock with improved crashworthiness (ie resistance to deformity in collision) continued to be introduced. Higher standards of fire resistance were incorporated and most new coaches were equipped with power-operated sliding doors under the control of the guard.

3 Multiple-aspect signalling with continuous track circuiting, replacing traditional manually-operated signalboxes, continued to be extended throughout BR.

4 The track mileage equipped with continuously-welded rail (CWR) increased from 10,380 in 1980 to 12,143 in 1988. CWR is generally safer than jointed track and easier to maintain.

5 Radio communication between drivers and signalmen or train control centres began to be introduced as quickly as funds could be spared.

6 Improvements in safety standards at automatic level crossings continued to be made.

7 Electrical signalling controls continued to be installed in manually-operated signalboxes to guard against human error on the part of signalmen.

8 Steps were taken to reduce the number of cases of drivers departing from stations and wrongly passing platform starting signals at danger. Changes in train working procedures were introduced and 'Off' indicators were provided on station platforms to inform guards and station staff when platform starting signals had been cleared (ie had shown an 'Off' [proceed] indication).

This list is not intended to be all-inclusive, but gives an indication of the considerable extent of ongoing safety initiatives. There were others, and there were many improvements of only local significance. However, there were two areas where either questionable decisions were taken or necessary action failed to be taken, and which caused a significant proportion of serious accidents in the years following Clapham. These two areas concern what became known as 'single lead junctions', and an improved automatic warning system. They will be examined in detail in subsequent chapters, but they have their genesis in the years preceding Clapham.

SINGLE LEAD JUNCTIONS

A single lead junction is the term given to a section of track layout where train movements onto and from a secondary route are made over a piece of track which is common to both directions. Such a layout became popular with the spread of power signalling and the demand for higher speeds through junctions. Its advantages are:

■ The need for a fixed diamond piece of track where one line crosses another is eliminated. Fixed diamonds are expensive to maintain and a potential source of derailment.

■ Fixed diamonds would be inappropriate at high speed junctions, because the diamond would be elongated in one direction, resulting in severe wheel/track interface problems.

■ High speed junction layouts can be installed.

The disadvantages of single lead junctions are:

■ Simultaneous train movements onto and from the secondary route cannot be made, leading to a loss of operational flexibility.

■ A ladder of single leads (ie two or more crossovers following in succession) requires more space laterally.

■ In common with all sections of line used by trains in both directions there is a real risk of head-on collision if a driver wrongly passes a signal at danger.

■ The safety feature of flank protection is removed (see sketch). The points at a traditional double line junction are interlocked in such a manner that the trailing points leading from the secondary route cannot be moved to allow a train to travel from that route onto the main line until the parallel facing points have been set towards the secondary route. This ensures that if a train approaching the junction in the facing direction accidentally runs past the junction signal No 1 at danger it will be diverted on to the secondary route out of harm's way instead of crashing headlong into the train coming off that route.

Modern signalling controls should make single lead junctions perfectly safe, but to be absolutely sure there must be 100% obedience by drivers to signals. This is not always the case and collisions at single lead junctions have not been uncommon in the years since Clapham, especially where they are located immediately beyond a station platform. This question will be studied in greater detail in Chapter 7.

THE BRITISH RAILWAYS AUTOMATIC WARNING SYSTEM (AWS)

British Railways' Automatic Warning System, inherited by Railtrack, was developed in the 1950s to give a driver a visual and audible warning as a reminder that he was approaching a caution signal (or a severe speed restriction) and that he needed to be ready to slow down or stop. It might be thought that drivers should not need such reminders and that observance of, and obedience to, the lineside signal should be sufficient. However, some of the worst disasters in railway history proved otherwise, and the installation of the Automatic Warning System was one of the most important safety measures taken by the railways this century.

The Automatic Warning System was based on the absolute block signalling system of manually-worked signalboxes, where each signalbox had a distant signal on the approach to the first stop signal. The distant signal was the fundamental safety signal and drivers had to maintain a very careful lookout when approaching such signals. If it was at caution they had to be prepared to stop at the first stop signal; if it was in the clear position it indicated that all the stop signals worked from that signalbox were also clear (the interlocking ensured that) and that the line was clear as far as the first stop signal of the succeeding signalbox. The distant signal was therefore the critical signal, and it had only two indications — caution and clear. The AWS concept was almost (but not quite) foolproof in such an application.

When the AWS concept was applied to multiple-aspect colour-light signalling there was an immediate conflict, because in such signalling installations each signal is, in effect, a signalbox, and each signal can show green (clear), two yellows (double yellow, preliminary caution), one yellow (caution) and red (stop). The decision was taken at that time (in the early 1950s) to use the same AWS warning indication for every signal aspect except clear, because the top priority at the time was to be able to install an AWS system as quickly as possible and it was felt that if the system were to be refined to provide different indications for two yellows and one yellow, valuable time amounting to several years would be lost. It had already taken several years to produce the very simple AWS system and it is

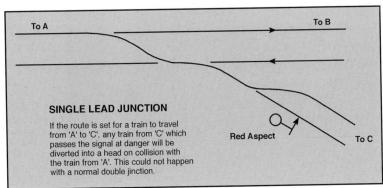

SINGLE LEAD JUNCTION

If the route is set for a train to travel from 'A' to 'C', any train from 'C' which passes the signal at danger will be diverted into a head on collision with the train from 'A'. This could not happen with a normal double jinction.

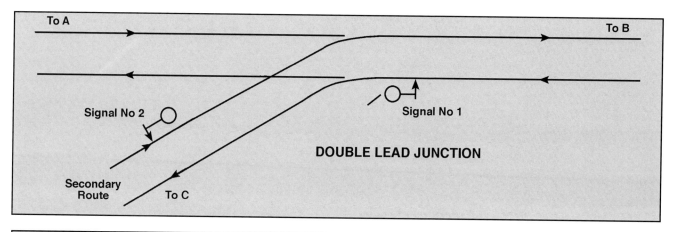

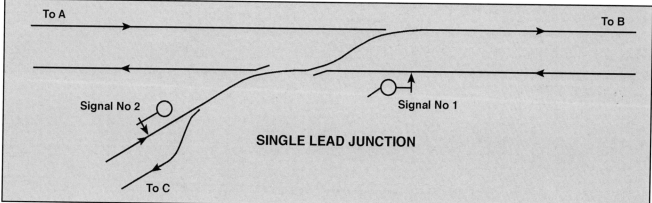

quite possible that between five and 10 years of development might have been needed to refine the system, during which time the whole of the railway network would have been unprotected. One cannot say that the wrong decision was taken.

However, the Southern Region immediately saw the problem clearly, because much of its inner suburban, and some outer suburban, signalling had been modernised using four-aspect colour-light signalling, and on its intensively worked lines drivers were likely to encounter a whole series of double yellow aspects, at which it was quite possible that they needed to take no action to apply the brake. It was therefore vital that they should be alerted to the fact that after running through a series of double yellow aspects they were approaching a signal showing a single yellow aspect, and that required a different AWS warning. Some development work was done on the Southern Region in an attempt to achieve this, but it was inconclusive and was abandoned.

As the years went by, and as more and more of the railway system became equipped with multiple-aspect colour-light signalling, it was perhaps inevitable that there would be cases where drivers failed to react to an AWS warning at a signal displaying a single yellow aspect, and so it turned out to be. The Southern Region's development work should have been taken over

An illustration of flank protection.
If a train wrongly passes signal No 1 at danger when a route is set to allow a train to travel from 'C' to 'B', it will be diverted out of harm's way at a double junction (upper layout), but into head-on collision at a single lead junction (lower layout).

by the Railways Board in the late 1970s, but it was a victim of the financial squeeze. It was felt to be too expensive. But by the mid-1980s it was quite evident that something needed to be done. All that can be said at this stage is that by 1999 very little has been done so far as additional assistance to the driver is concerned, and that the railway passenger is correspondingly little better protected. The reasons for this will be explored in more depth in Chapter 5.

And so to 1988. By December no passenger had been killed in a train accident that year, and it looked as though the fine safety record of the previous three years was to be maintained. But it was not to be, and when Nemesis struck it was not because a driver had wrongly passed a signal at danger, or a train had become derailed at high speed, or indeed from any previously known cause. What happened at Clapham Junction on 12 December 1988 forms the subject of our next chapter.

CHAPTER 3

Nemesis? The Clapham Accident:

The Formal Inquiry and its Findings

Above
The approaches to Clapham Junction station from Woking and Wimbledon. The line to Croydon and Brighton curves away to the right. No fewer than five trains are to be seen in this photograph, taken on 7 August 1975, which fully justifies Clapham Junction's claim to be the busiest station in Britain. *Kevin Lane*

1 DESCRIPTION OF THE ACCIDENT

On the morning of Monday 12 December 1988, trains on the up road into Clapham Junction and Waterloo were running more or less normally after the weekend signal engineering work. It is true that there was some problem with a signal on the approach to Clapham Junction — several drivers had noticed that it was exhibiting an unusual series of aspects, but none of the drivers had considered the matter sufficiently serious for them to stop at the next signal and report to the signalman what they had seen (the trains were not equipped with radio).

Shortly after 8am several commuter trains were approaching Clapham Junction in close succession on the up main through line and heading for Waterloo. They were:

- The first train — the 07.18 from Basingstoke
- The second train — the 06.14 from Poole
- The third train — the 06.53 Waterloo circular via Hounslow and Weybridge, and back to Waterloo

The up main through line on the approach to Clapham Junction station lies on a moderate left-hand curve in a shallow cutting containing altogether four tracks. It is on the left-hand side approaching Clapham Junction, the other three tracks being, from left to right, the down main through, the up main local and the down main local. The signalling is of the modern four-aspect colour-light type, and the series of signals approaching Clapham Junction on the up main through line is as follows:

- Signal WF152 — an automatic signal approaching Earlsfield station.
- Signal WF148 — an automatic signal past Earlsfield station, 523yd from the previous signal.
- Signal WF142 — an automatic signal, 757yd from the previous signal.
- Signal WF138 — an automatic signal, 719yd from the previous signal.
- Signal WF46/47 — controlled from Clapham Junction 'A' signalbox, 776yd from the previous signal. This signal controls the entry of trains into platforms 7 and 8 at Clapham Junction station.

The sequence of signal aspects if signal WF46/47 were at red would be as follows:

■ Signal WF138 — one yellow, meaning 'caution - be prepared to stop at the next signal'.

■ Signal WF142 — two yellows (known as double yellow), meaning 'preliminary caution — be prepared to find next signal exhibiting one yellow light'.

■ Signal WF148 and all preceding signals - green, meaning 'Clear - next signal exhibiting a green light or two yellows'.

The 07.18 train from Basingstoke was being driven by Driver McClymont. He passed Earlsfield at about 60mph with all signals green, and as he came round the bend approaching signal WF138 he could see that it was showing green. However, when he was almost about to pass the signal it suddenly changed to red and he immediately made an emergency brake application, bringing his train to a stand at the next signal WF46/47, which changed from red to one yellow as he stopped. The driver had no means of knowing why signal WF138 had suddenly changed to red, but it was his duty to stop his train as quickly as possible and report to the signalman. Telephones are provided at all signals in colour-light areas.

Signalman Cotter in Clapham Junction 'A' signalbox answered the telephone and replied that there was nothing wrong with signal WF138 so far as he could tell from the indications on his signalling equipment. In actual day-to-day experience a signal changing to red in front of a driver is usually caused by a malfunction of the signalling equipment or a defect on the track. Such equipment is designed to 'fail-safe', ie switch signals to red,

Above
The black and white diagonal sign indicates the location of a telephone giving communication with a signalbox. The telephone cabinets are fixed to signal posts and the telephones are mainly for the use of drivers. The number plate above the telephone cabinet is the identification number of the signal. Drivers quote this number at the beginning of a message to the signalman so that the latter can identify the train and its location. *Author*

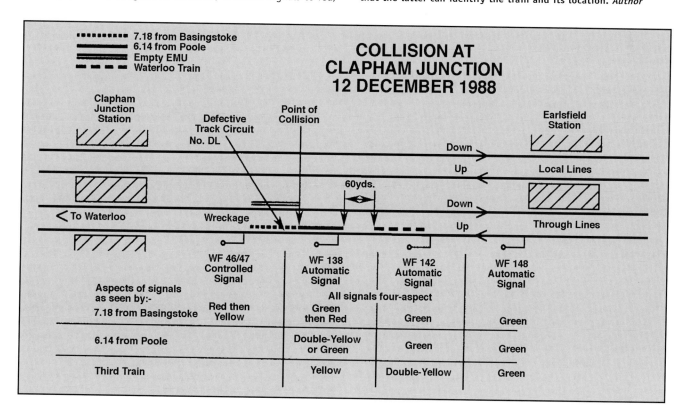

COLLISION AT
CLAPHAM JUNCTION
12 DECEMBER 1988

Aspects of signals as seen by:-	WF 46/47 Controlled Signal	WF 138 Automatic Signal	WF 142 Automatic Signal	WF 148 Automatic Signal
		All signals four-aspect		
7.18 from Basingstoke	Red then Yellow	Green then Red	Green	Green
6.14 from Poole		Double-Yellow or Green	Green	Green
Third Train		Yellow	Double-Yellow	Green

Left
Clapham Junction 'A' signalbox and relay rooms, looking towards Waterloo and Victoria, on 7 August 1982. *Colin J. Marsden*

in the event of any defect and such occurrences are not uncommon, but the driver must also react in 'fail-safe' mode and treat the incident as if it were a true emergency.

When the Basingstoke train stopped at signal WF46/47, the Poole train was close behind, but there should have been no danger of collision. The signal in rear of the Basingstoke train, WF138, should have been at red, with the previous signals at one yellow and two yellows respectively, giving the Poole driver plenty of time in which to stop safely at signal WF138, a perfectly normal and routine situation. However, things were not normal. The peculiar behaviour of signal WF138 observed by previous drivers had a sinister and hidden cause, as we shall see.

As Driver McClymont replaced the telephone handset he had a grandstand view of the horror that was unfolding. The Poole train had not stopped at signal WF138 but had passed it and crashed at some speed into the back of his own train, just as a train of empty coaches was passing in the opposite direction on the next line. Nemesis had struck. It could have been worse — signal WF138 was still showing one yellow instead of red — and a third train came along (the Waterloo circular). Fortunately, the collision had caused electrical power to the third rail to be cut off and the driver of the Waterloo Circular train realised this. He decided to coast as far as Clapham Junction station if possible and he ran past signal WF138,

which was showing one yellow. He then saw, to his astonishment and horror, the rear of the Poole train, made an emergency brake application and could do more than sit tight and keep his fingers crossed. To his immense relief his train ground to a halt only 60yd from the rear of the Poole train.

2 THE CAUSE

People's first thought was: 'Why didn't the Poole train stop at WF138?' The emergency services swung into action and simultaneously British Rail's accident investigators began their search for the cause. It was not long before the Signal Engineering Department found it: a 'rogue' wire (specifically, a redundant wire) in the relay room at Clapham Junction 'A' signalbox which was causing a 'wrong-side' failure of the signalling equipment, specifically a track circuit between signals WF138 and WF46/47.

A track circuit is a simple electrical device in widespread use throughout British Railways. Sections of line are electrically insulated from each other and a low-voltage electric current is passed along one rail of a section and back along the other rail. So long as the current is flowing, the switch in a piece of equipment known as an electrical relay is held closed. If current ceases to flow through the relay because it has been short-circuited by the presence of a train and returns to source through the wheels and axles of the train, the switch opens and, through electrical circuitry, causes signals to switch to, or be held at, danger. It may operate other controls too, especially at points, and indicates to the signalman the presence of a train. It is a simple, reliable piece of equipment and has been in use for a century.

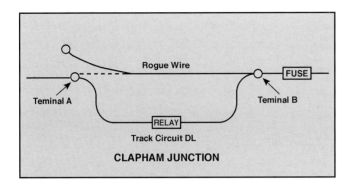

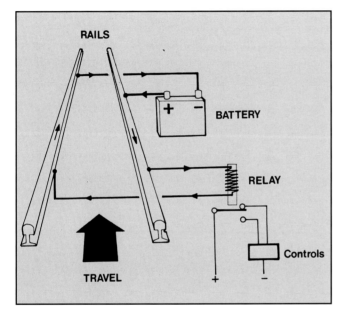

Above
A track circuit. When no train is present, a weak electric current flows from the battery (or other power source) through one rail to a relay, and returns to the battery through the other rail. When a train enters the section of track its wheels and axles short-circuit the current, which no longer flows through the relay. The presence of a train is then detected and acts upon point and signalling controls, as well as the train running information base.

The redundant wire had been left with the metal terminal tag at its loose end too close to the terminals of working relays. It came into contact with one such terminal and allowed current to flow direct to the coils of the relay that controlled WF138 signal. The track circuit controls for WF138 were overridden by the redundant wire and this had the effect of causing current to flow in the relay when it should have been short-circuited and the current cut off by the presence of the Basingstoke train. Trains on the track circuit between signals WF138 and WF46/47

Facing Page Far Left
Work to clear the line proceeds through the night after the Clapham accident. Coaches of the passenger trains lie against the cutting wall. On the adjacent line, next to the breakdown cranes, are the coaches of the empty stock train which happened to be passing at the precise moment of the collision. *Jeremy de Souza*

Facing Page Left
Damaged coaches are removed from the site by road transport for convenience. *Jeremy de Souza*

were therefore 'lost' to the system. The system did not know they were there, therefore it did not switch signal WF138 to red. Even when there were no fewer than three trains between the two signals, WF138 remained stubbornly at yellow. The question then was: 'Why was the rogue piece of wire there?'

3 WHAT WENT WRONG?

It is necessary to go back to events a fortnight earlier, on Sunday 27 November 1988. Signalling modernisation work was taking place as part of the major Waterloo Area Resignalling Scheme and the wiring in the relay room at Clapham Junction 'A' signalbox affecting the operation of track circuits was being changed. New wires were connected and the redundant wire should have been removed, ie physically detached from the terminals at each end, or, if left attached at one end, the metal terminal tag at the loose end should have been cut off and the end should have been taped with insulating tape so that it could no longer make accidental contact with its former terminal, and indeed with any other terminal. However, the technician did not do this; he merely detached the wire from one terminal, bent it back out of the way, and applied insulation to the loose end. For the next fortnight it did no harm, but it was a hidden danger.

Two weekends later, further signalling modernisation work was taking place in the same relay room and this required the replacement of a relay very near the redundant wire. It appears that during this work by the technician's assistant and unknown to the technician himself (the same person as a fortnight earlier) the rogue wire was accidently disturbed and sprang back to its original shape. The insulation at its loose end was dislodged and the bare wire made contact with its previous terminal. Current commenced to flow continuously, irrespective of the presence of trains, which were therefore 'lost' to the system.

It would be odd, and potentially dangerous, if such errors could be allowed to go undetected. There should be checking and testing procedures to ensure safety, and of course there were, but they were not applied. Why not? A sorry tale emerged at the subsequent public inquiry, whose findings will be discussed later in this chapter.

4 THE MECHANICS OF THE ACCIDENT, AND THE CASUALTY LIST

The Basingstoke train was formed of three four-car electric multiple-units type VEP (vestibule coaches with the electro-pneumatic brake). It had seating capacity for 840 passengers and there were known to have been at least 700 on board, although the actual figure may have been nearer 900. Certainly, some passengers were standing in the front coaches, although they may have done so from choice even though there may have been vacant seats further back along the train, so that they could be first through the ticket barriers at Waterloo and thus avoid the crush.

The Poole train was formed of a four-car REP (restaurant car and electro-pneumatic brake) electric multiple-unit plus two

sets each of four unpowered vehicles. The restaurant vehicle was a buffet car and was the second vehicle on the train. The buffet was closed. There was seating capacity for 610 passengers and the train was known to have been carrying at least 519 passengers, but probably there were more.

All the coaches of both trains were of Mk 1 construction with slam doors.

The Poole train collided with the rear of the Basingstoke train and the leading coach 'bounced off' to its right into the side of a train of empty coaches which was just passing in the opposite direction on the next line. The empty coaches formed a barrier to any further sideways movement and the first two coaches were therefore forced to make their way between the rear of the Basingstoke train and the empty train — a space of only a few feet. The last two coaches of the Basingstoke train were thrown to the left up the embankment. The driver of the Poole train and 34 passengers lost their lives, whilst 69 were seriously injured. The location of casualties is quite significant:

■ Nearly all the deaths and most of the serious injuries occurred in the first coach of the Poole train, where 29 people died, including the innocent driver. Sixteen passengers in that coach suffered only minor injuries or shock.

■ The other six passengers who died were in the seating portion of the second coach of the Poole train. Standing passengers in the buffet area were protected by the longitudinal bulkhead, which remained largely intact and saved their lives. The pattern of deaths did not seem to have been influenced by whether passengers were standing or sitting.

Above
A Class 423 electric multiple-unit of the type which formed the train from Basingstoke. It is seen ex-works at Eastleigh on 29 January 1988. *Chris Wilson*

Below:
A Class 432 (REP) electric multiple-unit of the type at the front of the train from Poole enters Southampton station on 4 July 1981. *David Maxey*

There were no fatalities in the Basingstoke train, but nine passengers were seriously injured in the last coach and two more in the next one. Casualties in the Basingstoke train were remarkably light compared with those in the Poole train, and this requires some explanation.

The speed of impact was not particularly high, estimated to be about 35mph, and if only the Basingstoke and Poole trains had been involved, one would not have expected there to have been more than a handful of fatalities, if indeed any at all. There have been collisions at higher speeds than 35mph with no fatalities. But there were two critical factors:

1 There was a 10ft high concrete retaining wall on the left-hand side of the Basingstoke train at the foot of the cutting slope. This effectively prevented any sideways movement to the left of either the Basingstoke train or the Poole train as a means of absorbing at least some of the forward momentum of the Poole train and providing a controlled deceleration.

2 The second factor was the involvement of the third train — the train of empty coaches. If it had not been there, the Poole train would have bounced to the right off the rear of the Basingstoke train, as it actually did, and would have continued unimpeded over clear tracks until all its momentum had been exhausted.

The Poole train could escape neither to the right nor to the left and had to dissipate its momentum as it forced its way forward into the narrow, virtually rigid, gap between the two other trains, tearing itself to pieces in the process. The involvement of more than two trains inevitably inflates the casualty list, and was a piece of outright misfortune of a type against which there is little practical defence, but it is also inevitable that there will occasionally be a collision in which more than two trains are involved.

5 THE PUBLIC INQUIRY PROCEDURE — WHY WAS A FORMAL INQUIRY CHOSEN?

In 1988 the holding of public inquiries was governed by the 1871 Regulation of Railways Act. This provided for two types of inquiry:

1 Sec 3 of the Act provides for the Board of Trade to appoint a person to be an Inspector for the purpose of making any inquiry into the cause of any railway accident. In practice the person appointed had always been an already appointed Inspecting Officer of Railways of considerable experience.

2 Sec 7 of the Act provides that the Board of Trade may direct that a more formal investigation of an accident be held, and may appoint a person possessing legal or special knowledge to assist an Inspector. Alternatively, the person

possessing legal knowledge may hold the inquiry, assisted by an Inspector. These formal inquiries are required to be held in open court.

Since the 1870s, there had been only two instances of the provisions of Sec 7 of the Act being applied to an accident on a main line railway and in each case there were special features. The two instances were the Tay Bridge collapse in 1879 and a collision between an express passenger train and an abnormal load on a lorry at an automatic half-barrier level crossing at Hixon (Staffs) in 1968, described in Chapter 2. In each case the

Below and Bottom
Clearing the line at Hither Green after the derailment of the 19.43 from Hastings to Charing Cross on 5 November 1967. Also illustrated is the broken rail which caused the derailment.
Author's collection

Railway Inspectorate had been previously involved and it was necessary for the person holding the inquiry to be seen to be independent. It was also an advantage to be able to call non-railway staff as witnesses, ie the designers and builders of the Tay Bridge in the one case, and the Department of Transport officials, road haulage people and police on the other. These two accidents were exceptional in that they were not train accidents of a conventional nature. Clapham was an entirely conventional accident. Only railway staff were involved. An inspecting officer of the Railway Inspectorate could quite adequately have held a public inquiry. Why, then, did the Secretary of State decide on a Sec 7 investigation?

The Railway Inspectorate had held public inquiries into far more serious accidents than Clapham — eg Harrow & Wealdstone in 1952, when 108 passengers were killed, Lewisham St Johns in 1957 (89 passengers killed) and Hither Green in 1967 (49 passengers killed). All these took place within the London area, so one cannot accept the view sometimes expressed that accidents within the London area are regarded as more important than those occurring elsewhere. A feature of the Clapham accident was the intense media interest, the impact upon public opinion (and MPs) being consequently magnified. It was unfortunate for British Rail that Clapham followed in the wake of several other serious transport accidents, including the loss of the cross-Channel ferry *Herald of Free Enterprise* and the fire at King's Cross London Transport station. The whole issue bears all the marks of an over-hasty reaction by the Secretary of State of the day under political pressure from his parliamentary shadow, who was demanding a full public inquiry. Note that the political opponent probably knew nothing about Sec 7 — he merely demanded a full public inquiry, which could quite properly have been held under Sec 3 by a Railway Inspecting Officer.

The fact of there having been only two Sec 7 inquiries in the last 100 years would appear to indicate that the provision was to all intents and purposes superfluous. It is suspected that it was inserted at the time by legal pressure, and indeed several Sec 7 inquiries were held for a few years after 1871, but they were held by a Railway Inspecting Officer assisted by a barrister-at-law. The practice was quickly abandoned, because it was found to be worse than useless.

The essential differences between the two types of inquiry might be summarised as follows:

■ A Railway Inspecting Officer investigating a serious accident such as Clapham is likely to have held many public inquiries and to be thoroughly experienced. He knows what evidence he requires. He knows what questions to ask and how to evaluate the answers. He knows how to judge how reliable the witnesses are. And he knows what practical measures are needed to reduce the likelihood of further accidents from the same cause, or avoid them altogether. His inquiry will be concluded within a few days.

■ A formal investigation becomes a court of inquiry. The Inspector reaches his conclusions on the evidence put before him, as in a court of law, but there is no guarantee that the evidence is complete. Evaluating evidence requires some technical knowledge, and the Inspector is compelled to rely upon assessors appointed to help him. Witnesses are likely to feel more intimidated by the atmosphere of a court of law, faced with serried ranks of the representatives of all the interested parties (dozens and dozens of them at the Clapham inquiry). Correct, accurate and complete evidence is likely to become more difficult to obtain. Representatives may, and do, ask questions which the witnesses do not understand, and those representatives may not appreciate that they have been given an unintentionally misleading answer. Misunderstandings abound. Railway witnesses use in-house jargon which outsiders may misunderstand.

It is a very imperfect way of arriving at the cause, but it does have the benefit of allowing the Inspector to call for interview whomever he chooses, so that he can get to the very root of those factors which underlie the cause and are hidden from view. However, it is in the field of making recommendations that a person with no practical railway experience or knowledge is most vulnerable, because he is not equipped to weigh the value of his recommendations in the balance of practicality and realism.

The Clapham public inquiry lasted for an incredible 65 days, during which the massed ranks of senior railway managers were absent from their desks. Add to that the time taken on preparation for the inquiry, and one might ask: 'Who was minding the shop and what else was going wrong meantime?'

It is ironic that all this effort went into an investigation into an accident:

■ the cause of which was identified within hours.

■ the cause of which was unique in the history of fatal train accidents. This was the first fatal train accident in the whole history of the main line railways that had been caused by a Signal Department technician making a wiring error.

■ the effects of which were considerably magnified by the unpredictable presence at the crucial moment of a third train.

■ the effects of which were considerably magnified because the Basingstoke train happened to be standing in a cutting next to a 10ft high concrete retaining wall.

The likelihood of those circumstances being precisely re-created at some point in the future must be very small indeed.

6 THE REMIT AND ITS FINDINGS

The remit given to the Inspector, Anthony Hidden QC (later Sir Anthony) was as follows: 'The Secretary of State directs that a formal investigation of the accident and the causes thereof and of the circumstances attending the same be held...'

The findings occupy no fewer than 20 pages and bring forward the following points:

■ The technician made wiring errors on 27 November 1988 and had fallen into bad habits regarding failing to shorten redundant wires and 'cap' them. *However, it must be said that he was regarded within the industry as being both thorough and conscientious, and carried out his work neatly.*

■ He was insufficiently supervised, mainly because the supervisor relied upon him to do his work correctly because he (the supervisor) was heavily engaged elsewhere assisting with other parts of the work in the absence of a sufficient workforce and having to work to a tight timescale. *It might be commented that this situation had applied in most departments throughout the railway industry since World War 2, and was particularly bad in the London area. The vital role that supervisors played in ensuring that jobs were done and that the railway continued to function can only be fully appreciated by someone who experienced it. Even managers were reluctant to admit that the practice existed, but they accepted the situation because they recognised that circumstances gave them no alternative. It was misguided and unfair of the Report to criticise the supervisor.*

■ Checking was inadequate. In particular, instructions about counting the number of wires on terminals, which would have revealed the presence of the redundant wire, were not carried out.

■ The various layers of management did not manage the scheme and the checking and testing effectively.

■ In the London area, there was a shortage of suitably qualified technicians because BR could not afford to pay the market price for such staff. This resulted in existing staff having to work long hours and many weekends. In the main, they were glad to do this because it brought their earnings up to the market level.

■ The adverse effect of frequent reorganisations. The Signal Engineering Dept of the Southern Region was reorganised in 1982, 1984, 1986 and 1988 in order to reduce staff numbers. *The effect of such frequent reorganisations was considerable; line managers were distracted from their normal jobs for months on end preparing for the reorganisations, preparing detailed job descriptions for every job involved, consulting with the trade unions, making any necessary changes, advertising all jobs affected, interviewing staff for new posts and allocating posts to all staff made redundant by the reorganisation. Staff in new posts or who had been transferred had to go through a learning curve before they became fully effective. Other, experienced, staff left the railway. Efficiency and morale both suffered. The Report signally fails to demonstrate the detrimental effect of reorganisations, but in reality it was unable to do so. The effect of reorganisations can really only be fully appreciated by those who have lived through them. A former highly regarded railway general manager once said: 'When you reorganise, you bleed.' Blood was spilt at Clapham; reorganisations were a lot to blame.*

Why was it necessary to reorganise, and so frequently?

1 Partly to reduce staffing costs resulting from government pressure to reduce the degree of financial support. It was perfectly right and proper for the government to do this, because public funds were involved, but the Railways Board failed to spell out sufficiently clearly the consequences, or if it did so, the government ignored them. This assumes that the Railways Board fully appreciated the effects of constant reductions in staffing, which is certainly open to question.

2 The Board decided to introduce a new, business-led, organisation. This was a very necessary change. The railways had traditionally been organised on strong departmental lines, which were appropriate in an unchanging commercial world, but unsuited to modern times. However, in making the change the Board overlooked the need to maintain those parts of the railway organisation which had previously ensured high standards of safety.

3 Industrial change in the heavy industries on which the railways relied so heavily for their traffic led to the need for a simplified management structure.

4 There was, inevitably, the 'New brooms sweep clean' factor.

The measures necessary to deal with the shortcomings revealed in the findings will be discussed in the next chapter.

CHAPTER 4

Clapham:
The Recommendations

WHERE DOES THE BUCK STOP?

Most of the inquiry's findings indicate that the Board's shortage of money was the root cause of this accident. The Board's low-wage policy meant that it could not afford to pay the market rate for the job, therefore it was unable to recruit sufficient staff; it was unable to recruit staff of a sufficiently high calibre; and it was unable to retain staff, particularly the better members of its workforce. The result was an expensive wastage. The Board itself was partly to blame. Traditionally, railway rates of pay were low, but there was plenty of opportunity to increase take-home pay by overtime and rest day working, by weekend working, and by enhancements for night-time working. Traditionally, the railway gave security of lifetime employment.

Those traditions became a millstone in the postwar world, but the Board did not change its policy. It would have been difficult to do so when it employed three-quarters of a million staff, but as staff numbers declined and most of the low-paid labouring-type jobs disappeared an opportunity arose to restructure the grading systems. Why wasn't it done?

No additional funds were available for restructuring. Higher pay rates depended on savings elsewhere, through improved productivity and efficiency, which often meant staff cuts. The trade unions had seen staff numbers decline precipitously since nationalisation in 1948 and considered their main task to be the protection of jobs, even though such a policy was likely to lead to an even greater loss of jobs in the long term as the railways became increasingly uncompetitive. They resisted job cuts in exchange for higher basic rates. It was a situation that required statesmanship from the government, the Board and the unions. There was none.

But eventually the tide turned. The so-called 'continental rostering' (ie weekends being regarded as part of the normal working week) came to be seen as a possible solution to the pay structure of those grades involved in weekend working. Traditionally, the ordinary working week was considered to run from Monday to Friday or Saturday. Weekend work was extra, at an enhanced rate. The solution was to abandon the concept of weekday/weekend working and to consider Saturdays and Sundays as part of the working week, with staff being rostered as most appropriate in relation to the workload. It also required the abandonment of many hallowed working practices which impaired productivity.

Restructuring took place first in part of the civil engineering department, where there was a considerable amount of work which could only be performed during the night or at weekends when rail traffic was light. Civil engineering track work, both maintenance and renewals, had become increasingly mechanised, and it was essential that very expensive machinery be used to the maximum extent. This enabled restructuring to be funded, so that total take-home pay did not suffer, but total hours worked were reduced. Little real progress had been made on restructuring in other departments before the Clapham accident, but in the years before privatisation it was introduced in the Signal Operating Department, in the Signal and Telecommunications Department and among traincrews. It was a long, hard road, punctuated by strikes and other disputes, but the goal was eventually achieved. Basic rates of pay are now relatively high and conditions of service have improved.

But to return to 1988. For some years the government had been demanding that the Board reduce its dependence on public funds, and the Board had been attempting to do so with some success but at the price of constant reorganisations in the administrative layers. The government/Board relationship was a difficult one. The government maintained that it had no responsibility for the running of the railways, which was a matter entirely for the Board, but that was not a tenable stance. In the first place, the government appointed the Board. It set out its duties and responsibilities. It decided how much financial support it could have. It had the last say on major schemes. It was very much akin to the board of directors of a public company and cannot therefore escape much of the responsibility for the Clapham accident, but it appears to have done so, with the assistance of the Inquiry Report.

On the other hand, did the Board make clear to the government the effect on safety of the financial squeeze? Could the Board, pre-Clapham, have done a hypothetical report on an accident such as Clapham, pointing out that among the causes were low wage rates, long hours, staff shortages, constant upheavals of reorganisation, restrictions on investment on safety equipment and new rolling stock of improved crashworthiness? Did it try? No, because it would have been difficult to make a sound case when set against the very high safety levels achieved in the years preceding Clapham. If the Board had suggested that one day there would be a serious accident involving two loaded commuter trains in a cutting with a third train involved because a technician had made a wiring error and testing procedures had not been properly applied, it would have been ridiculed. The government could merely have retorted that the Board should ensure that testing procedures were properly carried out. But the government cannot escape some of the responsibility, even though the authors of the Clapham Report failed to address the issue. Perhaps they failed to appreciate the significance of it. If so, it is a serious failing. And it is not acceptable for the government to reject any element of responsibility.

In defence of the government, it has to be said that it was not satisfied that the Board always used its money wisely, or that its policies were soundly based, and such suspicions date back to the late 1950s, with a review of the then British Transport Commission's 1955 Modernisation Plan. From that date onwards, the government took a much closer interest in railway investment projects, amounting in some cases to second-guessing. Such interference was not an efficient way of running a major industry but was perhaps inevitable. The Board's deficit was growing and public money was being used to support it. But the government wanted it both ways and would say that 'These are matters for the Board' whenever it wanted to deny responsibility for some event, despite the fact that the Board was not a free agent.

THE RECOMMENDATIONS

The scope of the Clapham Inquiry was broadened to include recommendations arising from the Purley collision on 4 March 1989 and whilst this was a tenable decision where there were similar features in the two accidents, it was a mistake to include those which were not. The Purley accident was caused by a signal being passed at danger and had little relevance to the circumstances of the Clapham accident, except that the trains in both accidents were composed of Mark 1 coaches and the Board's financial situation was involved in both. The Clapham Inquiry made recommendations on the former (signals being passed at danger) but not on the latter (the Board's financial position), which was obviously considered to be too political and therefore best left alone; a major omission in view of its implications for the Board's conduct of its business.

The Report contains 93 recommendations. Excluding recommendations directed specifically to the Purley accident, which will be dealt with in the next chapter, and excluding those of a minor character, there are some 50 recommendations in the following groups:

▪	Wiring and testing	15
▪	Administration and training	7
▪	Staff matters	7
▪	BR organisation	5
▪	Operations	8
▪	Driver/signalman radio	3
▪	Mk 1 rolling stock	6

Radio and rolling stock will be discussed separately later in this chapter.

As in any other field of railway activity, in order to achieve high standards of safety, hands-on operatives must know what they have to do, and do it; testers must test, supervisors must supervise and managers must not only manage but must know what is going on at the workface. This is a counsel of perfection

and not easy to achieve when faced with chronic shortage of cash, constant reorganisations, inability to recruit sufficient staff, government turning on and off the investment tap and all the other ills which have beset the nationalised railways ever since day one. The Report fails to pay sufficient regard to these factors, but why should it? Those who have not lived through those years and have not experienced those factors would find it very difficult to visualise the problems.

However, the Board recognised that there was a growing public disquiet about safety and the way that public transport operators ran their businesses. There was, in fact, a developing safety hysteria on the one hand and a fear of prosecution under the Health & Safety at Work Act on the other. A climate of fear arose, which inevitably resulted in an over-reaction by all parties. But some improvements were desirable and this Report helped to create an atmosphere in which it was easier to justify the expenditure and organisational changes which were necessary to achieve those improvements.

There is an interesting philosophical point here. Should those who make recommendations have regard to their cost and the ability of the Board to fund them, or should they ignore such practical issues and concentrate on making whatever recommendations are necessary to avoid a recurrence of such an accident, regardless of cost, the availability of finance and all the other issues of practicality and reality? And in the large grey area between the two extremes who should decide whereabouts the Report and its recommendations should be located? This is one of the major flaws of the Sec 7 formal inquiry procedure. It has no standards against which to set its stance and its choice is bound to be arbitrary and influenced by current opinion, as voiced by the media; a very unsatisfactory basis. Clapham, for all its seriousness, was an island in the sea of history, a snapshot in time. If, on the other hand, the inquiry had been held by an Inspecting Officer of the Railway Inspectorate in the normal way, under Sec 3 of the 1871 Act, he would have had all the standards built up during the 150-plus years of the Railway Inspectorate's history and his own years of experience to assist him when making recommendations, with minimal hysteria and a common-sense outcome. But ought not the government, having willed the end, also have been prepared to will the means? Perhaps it would be too naïve to believe that the government, any government, ever had any intention of doing so.

DRIVERS REPORTING SIGNAL DEFECTS

As already mentioned, several drivers had seen the aspects of signals approaching WF138 suddenly become more restrictive and the question arose as to whether they should have stopped at the next signal to report the irregularity to the signalman. None of them did until a specific irregularity caused the driver of the Basingstoke train to stop at signal WF46/47 in order to report it. Whilst his train was stationary, the collision occurred. Had earlier drivers stopped to report the irregularities it is still possible that a collision would have ensued, because the signalman would have been unaware of the wiring error which was causing those irregularities. The track circuit indications being displayed on his equipment were working normally.

The rule in force at the time of Clapham referred generally to 'irregularities', and it was not clear whether a driver observing an irregular aspect sequence, ie a signal switching to a more restrictive aspect in the face of a driver, should be constituted an irregularity. However, an irregular aspect sequence denotes either that the signalman has turned a signal to red because he wants to stop the train for whatever reason, or that there is some form of equipment failure which the signalman does not know about (if he had known, the driver would have been told about it at a previous signal). In either case, it is clear that the driver should stop at the first opportunity, and it is a pity that the rule did not make this clear. An earlier rule did specify that 'Should a driver observe any irregularity in the working of signals...', which could be construed to cover the Clapham case, but this precision was lost in subsequent Rule Book changes. It has been restored, and the rule now refers to 'an irregular aspect sequence'.

Rules are often referred to as being for the instruction of fools and the guidance of wise men, but in the absence of a specific and clear instruction in the Rule Book, wise men may make different interpretations, which would be unsatisfactory.

DRIVER/SIGNALMAN RADIO COMMUNICATION

Recommendation 43 stated that 'BR shall implement as a priority its programme to install a system of radio communication between driver and signalman on all traction units'. Such communication is, of course, desirable both for day-to-day operations and in an emergency, but to say blandly that it should be implemented as a priority is pointless because it immediately prompts the response 'What degree of priority?' when set against all the other demands on the Board's purse. For some years the Board had been steadily extending the provision of such communication as quickly as finance was available, and it might be appropriate to examine the development of radio communication between drivers and signalmen.

There are two quite distinct train radio systems in use. One is known as 'Cab Secure Radio' (CSR) and the other as the 'National Radio Network' (NRN). (There is a third system, known as Radio Electronic Token Block, but it is not relevant to this case.)

CAB SECURE RADIO (CSR)

This was designed in the late 1970s for use on trains which were to be operated without guards, now known as 'Driver-Only Operation' (DOO). The provision of this type of equipment was one of the safety requirements agreed between the Board and the Railway Inspectorate for the working of trains without a guard. For technical reasons this radio system can be used only on lines controlled by a power signalbox equipped with modern train describer equipment, because it is necessary to interlock the call number of the train's radio system with the signalbox train describer and locate the train, so that the signalman can speak to a driver by using the train's normal four-digit train identity code. Similarly, when the driver calls the signalman an indication of the train identity code appears on a VDU in the signalbox. The signalman can then ascertain at once where the train is, by referring to the signalling control panel or VDU.

Radio messages between the signalman and a driver cannot be heard by other drivers; therefore there is no danger that another driver might act upon an instruction that is not meant for him. That is the nature of the security. The signalman can, if he so wishes, broadcast a general message to all drivers in a particular area.

Left
A Class 423 electric multiple-unit, formed of Mk 1 coaches, pauses at Fleet on a train from Southampton on 14 January 1989. *John C. Baker*

Right
An empty stock working, headed by a Class 423 (4-VEP) electric multiple-unit, passes through Clapham Junction station on 18 July 1988. Clapham Junction 'A' signalbox is in the background. *Brian Morrison*

THE NATIONAL RADIO NETWORK (NRN)

This was first installed in 1973, on the West Coast main line, to provide radio communication between the radio control office and engineering department staff out on the line. It also allowed lineside telephones to the electrical control centre to be removed on ac overhead electric lines. The system has never reached its full potential due to the unreliability of the software, inadequate radio coverage and lack of capacity. The facilities on trains provide radio—radio communication and also allow calls to be made from a train radio to a telephone on the railway telephone network. The driver can make an emergency call by pressing a red button, which immediately connects him with a railway traffic control office. The control office can broadcast a message to all trains within a particular radio base station coverage area, which will be heard over the loudspeaker in driving compartments. By 1996 there were five railway traffic control offices at Crewe, York, Glasgow, Swindon and Waterloo. Owing to the unreliability of the system, drivers on some routes were provided with commercial-type mobile phones.

NRN is not classed as a secure radio system, since there is no correlation between the train's radio call number and the train description number. The signalman is not normally aware of the radio call number of a particular train, therefore the radio traffic is normally initiated by drivers. The system is being developed to enable a driver to speak directly to the power signalbox signalman who controls the section of line on which the train is running or standing.

Such vague references to priority as contained in Recommendation 43 are harmful, because the pressures that they create may have the effect of diverting funds from what are judged to be more important avenues. A more appropriate recommendation would have been to state that the Board should extend the provision of radio as quickly as its resources allowed, but that is what the Board was doing anyway, so the recommendation might be considered to be superfluous.

MK 1 COACHING STOCK

There was some criticism of the crashworthiness of the coaches used in the Basingstoke and Poole trains, which were all of Mk 1 construction, although, sensibly, there was no suggestion that they should all be replaced quickly even before they were life-expired, but that their crashworthiness should be enhanced as far as reasonably practicable. Unfortunately, the issue has become clouded by the Health & Safety Executive's ardent desire to see slam door carriages eliminated unless the opening of the doors can be controlled by the guard, and this subject will be considered in Chapter 8.

We are faced with another philosophical issue. When a new design of coaches is introduced, constructed to the best contemporary standards, should they be withdrawn from service as soon as another design is introduced which embodies further technological advance? If not, at what stage should the earlier coaches be withdrawn? Should they be allowed to remain in service until they are life-expired, even though they may be not quite so safe as later models?

Left and Below
The collision on the Brighton line, between Hassocks and Preston Park, on 19 December 1978, after a signal was passed at danger. The 21.40 from Victoria to Littlehampton ran into the rear of the 21.50 from Victoria to Brighton.
C. Burnham

As an empirical guide, it is instructive to examine the performance of Mk 1 electric multiple-unit (EMU) coaches in accidents on the Southern Region in the years before Clapham. In the 18 years between 1970 and Clapham, there was only one passenger fatality in a train accident (a collision on 19 December 1978, between Hassocks and Preston Park, caused by a signal being passed at danger).

The record of only one passenger being killed in a train accident in an electric multiple-unit on the Southern Region in 18 years might be considered an almost impossibly high standard and worthy of the greatest praise. But, in fact, the hysteria which greeted Clapham and the tenor of the Inquiry Report might lead one to believe that fatal accidents were almost a daily occurrence. However, the Southern's safety record gave no grounds whatsoever for any early withdrawal of Mk 1 EMU stock nor for any expensive modifications. The Mk 1 coaches in the Poole train were criticised because fatalities occurred in them; paradoxically no credit was given to the absence of fatalities in the Mk 1 coaches of which the Basingstoke train was formed. That might have undermined the vendetta against Mk 1 coaches.

A CRITIQUE OF THE REPORT

The remit was very vague and open-ended. It resulted in a Court of Inquiry which sat for 65 days. It resulted in the longest report ever compiled into a railway accident (212 pages, plus appendices). It produced by far the greatest number of recommendations ever made into a railway accident (93). It ranged far and wide and attempted to cover too many issues. Its recommendations attempted to dot every 'i' and cross every 't'. And it failed to give sufficient emphasis to the effects of chronic underfunding.

The size and nature of the inquiry was quite out of proportion to other national disasters. Whilst the Court was sitting, some 600 people were killed on the roads. Was there a major public inquiry? No. The nation at large accepts death on the roads with what amounts almost to indifference. Why should it take a different view with deaths on the railway? That is a conundrum to which there is no satisfactory answer. But the Court did a disservice by magnifying the issue.

The Clapham accident was caused by events and circumstances in one Region of British Railways. There was no evidence that such circumstances existed elsewhere and investigations on the other regions demonstrated that similar bad practices when carrying out alterations to vital signalling equipment as had occurred at Clapham did not occur. What is more, accidents from such a cause were virtually unknown so what grounds did the Court have for its apparent assumption that such an unsatisfactory state of affairs was endemic?

In many ways, the Board had only itself to blame for the scope of the recommendations. It gave the impression that the best course was to admit everything and keep the lowest possible profile. One might have hoped for a more robust stance, but there

was none. Perhaps the spectre of possible prosecution either for corporate manslaughter or under the Health and Safety at Work Act dictated prudence, but in fact the Board was in a panic and it needed a sacrificial lamb. It chose, not one of its own members, nor the general manager, but the Chief Signal Engineer, who had come to the Southern Region in 1982 and was already having some success in eradicating the bad working practices that had developed since the war. The Clapham shortcomings were the outcome of pressurised management trying to maintain an uninterrupted train service on what is widely regarded as one of the busiest suburban train networks in the world, and to carry out major resignalling projects with inadequate staff.

Whether the Board foresaw the financial implications of the recommendations when applied to signal engineering staff is open to question, and they are not capable of accurate costing, but the additional procedures applied to new works require more staff, take longer to implement, cause more interference with ordinary traffic and cost considerably more. The increased pay scales which the Board had to adopt in order to be able to recruit staff to fill vacancies and reduce overtime, and the additional staff needed to implement the new procedures, amount to many millions of pounds annually. Was it all really necessary? It must be pointed out that in the 40 years between nationalisation and Clapham, BR had resignalled almost all its main and suburban lines, many thousands of miles, sometimes twice, with considerable expedition and the minimum of impact on the normal train service, and had done so safely. On those grounds it would be very difficult to justify some of the Clapham recommendations.

And the final verdict — Clapham was the most expensive railway accident of all time. It need not have been so. The government, not BR, was responsible for the waste of funds, in choosing a Sec 7 Court of Inquiry with such a vague remit, instead of leaving the inquiry in the competent hands of an experienced Inspecting Officer.

THE CONSEQUENCES OF THE INQUIRY
POSITIVE

It has to be said that many improvements flowed from the Clapham Inquiry, which could not otherwise have been achieved:

- There was a realignment of culture within BR which recognised the need to pay more attention to safety whilst at the same time still attempting to improve efficiency and reduce costs. A slight shift of emphasis.
- The Signal Engineering Dept produced a comprehensive suite of technical manuals and procedures.
- Technician training was enhanced and became more specific.
- Investment in signalling received an enhanced status. The Clapham wiring error could not have occurred if modern 'plug-in' relays had been in use instead of an obsolete type with exposed terminals.

Top and Above
In memoriam. The sombre memorial to the victims of the Clapham accident, erected in a recess off the roadway overlooking the exact spot in the cutting where the collision took place. *Author (2)*

Licensing of technical staff was introduced by a neutral body, the Institution of Railway Signal Engineers, to ensure that staff carrying out work on vital signalling equipment were properly trained and examined as competent to do so. The system also provides for re-examination of competence at regular intervals.

NEGATIVE

A considerable increase in the costs and the time taken to carry out work on the infrastructure, resulting from the increase in procedures. Staff necessarily spend more time on the track and are accordingly exposed to risk for a greater time. Trains passing work sites are worked under emergency arrangements for longer periods than previously and are consequently more at risk.

A senior well-respected signal engineer was, in effect, compelled to resign. This was grossly unfair; he had already planned a reorganisation to improve testing, but was instructed by the Board to withdraw it and introduce another reorganisation aimed at reducing staff numbers (known as the 'Numbers Game'). He was the scapegoat, but the 'buck' should have stopped elsewhere. Perhaps on a Board member's desk, or even the desk of the Minister of Transport, as happened in France after a particularly serious railway accident. After all, he is in effect the Managing Director.

The police have taken a much higher profile on site in the protection of evidence following an accident, and this can handicap the railway authorities in their search for the cause and in the clearance of the line so that normal services can be restored as quickly as possible.

A rather unpleasant cult has emerged of looking for a scapegoat after an accident, as though that were more important than finding the cause.

An unwholesome safety hysteria within BR was generated, which resulted in some absurd over-reactions to trivial misdemeanours.

The Purley Collision -
4 March 1989

Two Class 423 electric multiple-units leave Clapham Junction for Basingstoke on 7 May 1988. A unit of this class, No 3441, formed the 12.50 from Horsham. *Alex Dasi-Sutton*

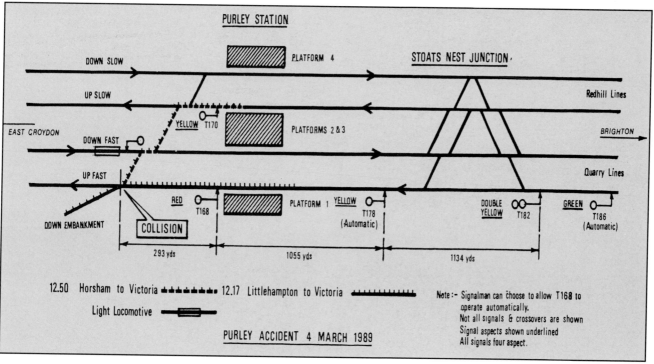

PURLEY STATION

PLATFORM 4

STOATS NEST JUNCTION

DOWN SLOW

UP SLOW

Redhill Lines

YELLOW T170

EAST CROYDON

DOWN FAST

PLATFORMS 2 & 3

BRIGHTON

UP FAST

Quarry Lines

RED T168

PLATFORM 1

YELLOW T178 (Automatic)

DOUBLE YELLOW T182

GREEN T186 (Automatic)

DOWN EMBANKMENT

COLLISION

293 yds

1055 yds

1134 yds

12.50 Horsham to Victoria ▪▪▪▪▪▪▪▪ 12.17 Littlehampton to Victoria ┃┃┃┃┃┃┃┃┃┃┃

Light Locomotive ━▭━

Note :- Signalman can choose to allow T168 to operate automatically.
Not all signals & crossovers are shown
Signal aspects shown underlined
All signals four aspect.

PURLEY ACCIDENT 4 MARCH 1989

DESCRIPTION OF THE ACCIDENT

The Clapham accident was unique; the Purley accident three months later was a classic.

Saturday 4 March 1989 was a perfectly normal day. The 12.50 electric multiple-unit (EMU) from Horsham to London Victoria, a four-car set, made its usual routine stop at the up slow line platform at Purley, and on departure it was crossed from the up slow line to the up fast line. Although a non-stopping train was closely approaching Purley on the up fast line it should have been an absolutely safe movement, because the Horsham train was protected by a red signal, No T168, 293yd in the rear of the crossover from the up slow line.

The signalling in the whole area was controlled from Three Bridges signalbox, one of BR's standard installations, opened on 14 January 1984. Signals were of the four-aspect colour-light type; the lines were continuously track-circuited and were equipped with the BR standard automatic warning system (AWS). It would be difficult to envisage a safer layout.

The non-stopping train was the 12.17 eight-car EMU from Littlehampton to Victoria and it was running at high speed down the four-mile favourable grade from Merstham tunnel. Signal T182, 2,482yd from the crossover, was displaying two yellow lights (double yellow), indicating to the driver that the next signal, T178 1,134yd away, was displaying one yellow light and that signal T168, a further 1,055yd along, would be at red. The driver's visual observation of the signals was reinforced by the automatic warning system. Equipment consisting of a permanent magnet and an electro-magnet is fixed between the rails 200yd before each signal and has the effect of sounding a warning horn in the driving cab whenever the signal shows any aspect other than green. The driver has two or three seconds to press an acknowledgement button on his control desk and if he fails to do so the brakes are automatically applied. AWS has been a very valuable safeguard since it was first introduced in the late 1950s and it is impossible to know how many collisions it has prevented, because no driver is likely to admit that he missed the signal but the AWS horn saved him.

Left
Signal T168 on the up fast line at the north end of Purley station. This signal protects the crossover from the up slow line and was passed at danger by the 12.17 from Littlehampton. *Author*

Below Left
A Class 421 electric multiple-unit stands at Clapham Junction when working a Victoria to East Grinstead service on 30 January 1988. Two units of this class, Nos 1280 (leading) and 1295, formed the 12.17 from Littlehampton. *David Brown*

Below
View northwards from Purley, looking towards the site of the collision. *Author*

Saturday 4 March 1989 soon ceased to be a normal day. The express from Littlehampton passed the double yellow signal and the single yellow signal without the brakes being applied and the driver did not react to stop the train until he saw the red aspect at signal T168. By then it was too late to avoid a collision. The express, still travelling at an estimated speed of 55mph, struck the last car of the Horsham train a glancing blow as it came off the crossover and plunged down a tree-clad embankment, leaving only the last coach of its train on the rails. The first six coaches were strewn almost at random as the train expended its momentum. Five passengers were killed and 32 were detained in hospital.

This Page
Policemen guard the wreckage of the 12.17 from Littlehampton after it collided with the rear of the 12.50 from Horsham and plunged down the embankment just north of Purley station on 4 March 1989. Damaged coaches were taken away by road over a track specially built through the gardens of houses. *Brian Morrison*

THE HISTORY AND DEVELOPMENT OF THE BR AUTOMATIC WARNING SYSTEM

Drivers inadvertently passing signals at danger has always been a common cause of railway accidents and after much experimentation and many false starts (there was no lack of technical knowledge or expertise) the Railway Executive decided immediately following nationalisation in 1948 to equip its more important lines with a form of automatic train control. From a driver's point of view, the system developed by the Railway Executive was very similar to the former Great Western Railway's automatic train control, in that it gave separate audible warnings for green (proceed) signals and for other than green signals. It also had the fail-safe back-up of an automatic brake application if the driver should fail to acknowledge an audible warning.

The system appeared to be foolproof. One could understand a driver missing a signal through lack of concentration, but for him to fail to apply the brakes after acknowledging receipt of the audible warning would have seemed incomprehensible. However, events were to prove otherwise; there were warning signs long before the Purley collision.

There was a serious high-speed derailment on the Western Region at Milton, near Didcot, on Sunday 20 November 1955, when an excursion train from Treherbert (South Wales) to Paddington, hauled by a 'Britannia' class locomotive, entered Milton loop at too high a speed. The driver had failed to react to the ATC audible warning at the distant signal, after either he or his fireman had acknowledged it. Eleven passengers were killed.

A year later there was another, fortunately less serious, accident at Ludlow when the brakes were not applied by the driver after the ATC audible warning had been acknowledged, and there was a third instance at Norton Bridge on the West Coast main line in 1963.

By then the programme to install AWS was in full swing and for many years there were only occasional examples that might have raised doubts (eg at Lenton South, Nottingham, on 16 December 1971 when the driver of a parcels train ran past a red signal and collided with a coal train, having acknowledged AWS audible warnings at a double yellow signal and a single yellow signal and taken no action to apply the brake), but officers on the Southern Region were unhappy with the system when it was proposed to install AWS on its lines. Much of the Southern Region was equipped with four-aspect colour-light signalling which allowed trains to run at close intervals without severe speed reduction, thanks in part to the highly effective electro-pneumatic brake with which electric multiple-units were equipped. Drivers were accustomed to passing double yellow signals with little or no speed reduction because they were satisfied that they could brake safely after sighting a single

Below
The result of a head-on collision on 16 December 1971 on a ladder of crossovers at Lenton South Junction, Nottingham, between a coal train heading west off the Leen Valley branch and a parcels train heading east towards Nottingham station, whose driver had passed a signal at danger despite receiving AWS warnings.
Jack Moore

alternative is to have only one beacon, located on the approach to a signal, but this leads to what may be unacceptable delays in updating the computer, preventing the driver from accelerating when he can see that the signal ahead has changed to a less restrictive aspect. This is not a safety issue, but one of operating convenience and efficiency. It can be alleviated to some extent, at a price, by having one or more intermediate beacons, but is not entirely satisfactory on lines with a very frequent train service.

To return to the narrative, the development process ran into very serious technical difficulties with the fitting of ATP equipment to the High Speed Trains (HSTs) used on the Paddington services, which inevitably called into question the practical possibility of equipping a wide variety of traction units on a national basis. The estimated cost of installing ATP widely rose from £250 million initially, to £750 million. Questions then began to be asked as to whether it was worth it, ie would it be cost-effective, prompted in part by the almost total absence (at mid-1994) of serious accidents caused by drivers ignoring AWS warnings, and it is instructive to examine the record since 1970 of those accidents which occurred to trains equipped with AWS, omitting those which have been subsequently protected by other means. In other words, the list contains those accidents which could recur today in similar circumstances:

Shields Junction (Glasgow) 1973	**driver and four passengers killed**
Wembley Central 1984	**three passengers killed**
Battersea Park 1985	
Colwich 1986	**driver killed**
Purley 1989	**five passengers killed**
Cowden 1994	**driver, guard and two passengers killed**
Watford Junction 1996	**one passenger killed**

(The Southall accident in 1997, in which seven passengers were killed, does not qualify for inclusion in the above list because the train was running with the AWS isolated, ie, not in use.)

Nineteen fatalities in 29 years does not give good grounds for an expenditure of £750 million, even when the cost of those accidents is taken into account. Accordingly the Board, Railtrack and the Railway Inspectorate considered the position and decided that on cost-effective grounds no case could be made for proceeding with ATP, even using calculations of four to six equivalent lives saved per annum (the term 'equivalent lives' includes in the calculation an allowance for both major and minor injuries). The 1994/5 Annual Report of the Railway Inspectorate estimated the cost per equivalent fatality avoided at about £11 million. This proposal was accepted by the Secretary of State for Transport, but it left a major gap for which there was no fallback position.

So far as the two trial sites are concerned, ATP is now fully operational on the Chiltern line and will remain in use in order to obtain its undoubted benefits. However, the situation is not so satisfactory on the Great Western line. Track equipment is in place, but on-train equipment is not yet fully operational, for the reasons given, but it is important, for political reasons, that it should be made so as quickly as possible.

THE TRAIN PROTECTION AND WARNING SYSTEM

It might be argued that when the Board began to have doubts about the viability of ATP it should immediately have commissioned an urgent study to find a way of improving the existing Automatic Warning System, but it is unfortunate that at that very moment the Board was in the turmoil of privatisation. As a result, the railways of Britain approach the 21st century with an Automatic Warning System that has its roots in the 19th and was becoming obsolescent (although still very valuable) 20 years ago. Henceforth, ATP will only be installed when entire routes and associated traction are comprehensively upgraded, as is planned for the West Coast main line.

However, Railtrack began to plan an alternative to ATP which will provide 70% of the benefits at a fraction of the cost. It is therefore considered to be affordable and is estimated to cost £3.3 million per equivalent life saved, utilising the existing AWS equipment. It would have been prudent for the British Railways Board to consider the development of this or any other alternative simultaneously with the development of ATP, because there was always the possibility that ATP would prove too expensive or too technically challenging. The chosen alternative is known as the Train Protection and Warning System (TPWS) and it is based on an intriguing philosophy. It does not set out to avoid all collisions but to avoid most and to reduce the effect of the remainder. It recognises the truth of the old saw that the best is the enemy of the good. Or to put it more bluntly 'half a loaf is better that no bread', but in this case it's three-quarters of a loaf.

Development work started in 1994, with installation planned to begin in 1997. That date was over-optimistic, as has tended to be the case with all such developments (eg AWS and ATP), and general implementation is now unlikely to start before 2000. In the meantime, pilot trials are to be held in the Harpenden and Three Bridges areas.

TPWS will initiate a mandatory brake application if a red signal is approached at excessive speed or is actually passed. This is achieved by means of a speed trap and a train stop feature respectively. The speed trap consists of a pair of loop aerials between the running rails on the approach side of an AWS magnet which enable the train-borne control unit to determine the aspect of the signal and the safe speed at that point. Power is shut off and the brakes are applied automatically if the train is exceeding the safe limit. The system is not designed to bring a train to a halt without fail before it passes the signal, but takes

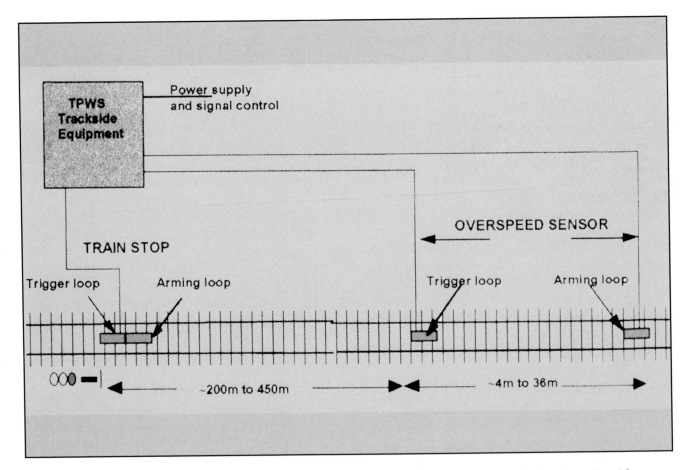

into account the presence of the safety overlap beyond the signal (normally 200yd) and the substantial reduction in the impact speed if there should be a collision. It is not intended to provide the equipment at every signal, but only at those considered to be most at risk, probably at about 40% of the total. Railtrack estimates that this will cost £250 million. Almost all traction units will be equipped.

The Health & Safety Executive is concerned both with the installation of TPWS and the modification or withdrawal of Mk 1 coaches. It appears to have overlooked the fact that TPWS will considerably reduce the extent and frequency of damage to trains, including those formed of Mk 1 coaches, which will correspondingly reduce the already questionable financial justification for such modification or withdrawal.
The campaign against Mk 1 coaches is beginning to resemble a religious crusade.

The train stop feature is a very valuable safeguard against a train starting away from a station platform and irregularly passing a signal at danger. This is a type of occurrence which has plagued the railways for many years and sometimes causes collisions, Indeed, the fact of a platform starting signal being at

danger is likely to mean that signals have been cleared for a conflicting move. On preliminary consideration it might seem unlikely that a driver would set off from a station stop and go straight past a danger signal which is clearly within his view and which has been so all the time that his train has been standing in the platform, but experience proves that it does happen and with distressing frequency.

It has long been considered that drivers are occasionally lulled into a subconscious belief that the road ahead is clear by the psychological impact of the receipt of the guard's 'train ready to start' signal. Station staff and guards have therefore been instructed not to give the 'train ready to start' signal if the platform starting signal is at red, but it has been impossible to prevent them from doing so occasionally, despite the widespread provision at considerable cost of 'off' indicators on the platform, which are illuminated when the signal is cleared. This issue will be examined in greater detail in Chapter 7.

This is not the end of the Purley story. The driver was prosecuted and jailed and that will be the subject of the next chapter.

The Purley Collision:
The Driver as Scapegoat?

On 3 September 1990 Robert Morgan, the driver of the train from Littlehampton involved in the Purley collision, appeared at the Central Criminal Court and pleaded guilty to the charges brought against him of manslaughter and endangering life. He was given a sentence of 18 months' imprisonment with 12 months suspended.

He was the unlucky victim of the media-inspired thirst for vengeance, the feeling that 'someone must pay', which followed in the wake of a number of very serious transport disasters, including the Clapham collision less than three months earlier than Purley.

It is quite rare, but not unknown, for drivers to be prosecuted after an accident for which they are considered to be responsible, and over the years there have been a number of cases. Here are details of some of the more notable ones:

■ 24 June 1984 MORPETH, East Coast main line. At 12.40am the sleeping car express from Aberdeen to King's Cross, the 'Night Aberdonian', consisting of seven almost brand-new Mark 3 sleeping cars with a parcels van at each end, hauled by a Class 47/4 diesel-electric locomotive, approached the 50mph permanent speed limit for the severe curve through Morpeth station at between 85 and 90mph. Speed was not reduced and although the entire train left the rails, none of the passengers or crew was seriously injured. The driver was charged at Newcastle Crown Court with endangering the lives of 71 passengers through wilful omission or negligence.

The prosecution contended that the driver had either ignored the speed restriction or lost concentration through being under the influence of alcohol. He was said to have consumed some lager and whisky before taking charge of the locomotive at Edinburgh. However, the driver contended that he did not remember the crash and thought that he had 'blacked out' through hitting his head on the control desk during a coughing fit. The jury found him not guilty. The Inspecting Officer who held the public inquiry, Lt-Col A. G. Townsend-Rose, delayed the publication of his report until after the trial in order not to prejudice the proceedings, but concluded that 'approaching Morpeth he (the driver) may have fallen asleep, or become so drowsy that he completely forgot the approaching curve. I must say that I am strongly inclined to the possibility that he fell fully or nearly asleep as being the most likely.'

■ 10 June 1975 NUNEATON, West Coast main line. At 1.54am an electrically-hauled night sleeper from Euston to Glasgow, consisting of 12 sleeping cars, two parcels vans

and a buffet car, approached Nuneaton station at about 80mph. There was a temporary speed restriction of 20mph in force, but the driver failed to reduce speed. The lights of the lineside warning board were out but the driver knew of the existence of the speed restriction; he concluded that it had been withdrawn early. The entire train was derailed except for the last vehicle, and six people (four passengers and two sleeping car attendants) lost their lives. Ten people were seriously injured.

The driver appeared at Birmingham Crown Court on 9 June 1976 to answer six charges of manslaughter. After a three-day trial he was found not guilty and discharged. The Inspecting Officer who held the public inquiry, Major C. F. Rose, delayed the publication of his report until after the trial.

■ 4 December 1957 LEWISHAM ST JOHN'S, Southern Region. At 6.20pm the 4.56pm express passenger train from Cannon Street to Ramsgate passed a signal at danger and ran into the rear, at about 30mph, of the 5.18pm electric multiple-unit from Charing Cross to Hayes, which was at a stand. There was dense fog. The force of the collision dislodged a bridge pier, and part of the bridge collapsed onto the Ramsgate train. Ninety people were killed and 109 seriously injured were detained in hospital.

The driver of the Ramsgate train was tried for manslaughter at the Old Bailey on 21 April 1958. The jury disagreed, and at the second trial on 8 May he was acquitted, no evidence being offered by the Crown.

■ 13 October 1939 BLETCHLEY, West Coast main line. The 7.50pm express from Euston to Stranraer failed to reduce speed for the Bletchley stop, passed two signals at danger, and ran at 45 mph into the rear of the 7.37pm express from Euston to Inverness, which was standing at the platform. Three people were killed and six seriously injured. The driver was tried for manslaughter but the judge directed the jury to return a 'not guilty' verdict.

■ 10 December 1937 CASTLECARY, between Edinburgh and Glasgow, London & North Eastern Railway. An express passenger train from Edinburgh to Glasgow crashed at about 60mph into the rear of another passenger train from Dundee which was standing just beyond the station. There was some snow and there were disputes as to the position of the arm of the distant signal, the drivers of both trains maintaining that the arm was in the clear position, ie inclined downwards at approx 45°. On the other hand, the interlocking prevented the signalman from clearing the signal for the second train. The collision was exceptionally destructive and resulted in the highest casualty list in railway history in peacetime up to that date. No fewer than 22 passengers were killed in the Dundee train and 13 in the train from Edinburgh. 179 passengers were injured, many of them seriously.

The driver of the train from Edinburgh was charged with culpable homicide in the Edinburgh High Court on 30 March 1938 but the next day the Lord Advocate withdrew the charge and directed the jury to return a verdict of 'not guilty'. There have been other cases, but it has to be remembered that in many collisions and some derailments the driver loses his own

The Morpeth derailment, 24 June 1984, when the driver of the southbound 'Night Aberdonian' sleeping car express failed to reduce speed for the Morpeth curve. There was no AWS warning of the southbound curve. The locomotive turned onto its side, but the train went off at a tangent into adjacent gardens and struck the corner of a bungalow, the owners of which fortunately were on holiday in Spain. The repaired gable end and the severity of the curve can be seen in one of the photographs. *Ian Carr (above), S. Miller (2) (left/below left), Author (below)*

life. And the selection of accidents in which charges are brought appears to be almost quixotic, but none has ever succeeded in which a driver has pleaded not guilty. Whatever criticisms may be levelled at the British jury system, juries appear to have an instinctive recognition of the difficulties which drivers face in handling their trains day in and day out and are prepared to give drivers the benefit of the doubt, realising that they are only human and are unlikely to drive their trains recklessly or even carelessly when their own lives are clearly at high risk.

THE ROLE OF THE POLICE

The role of the police following an accident is somewhat complex and open to misunderstandings. They have their duties and responsibilities, but they are not experts in railway *Rules and Regulations* and must take guidance from those who are qualified to give it. They must not interfere with, or impede, staff engaged in their primary responsibility of protecting the line in order to prevent further danger arising.

This should not be a problem. The railways have always had their own police force, whose status is unique. In the early days of railways, when large armies of labourers and navvies were engaged in the construction of railway lines, Justices of the Peace found it necessary to appoint special constables to keep the Queen's peace, and in due course railway companies obtained powers under statute to appoint their own constables. Following the nationalisation of the railways in 1948 the police forces of the separate companies were combined in a new force, the British Transport Police (BTP), which is a properly constituted force the same as any other police force, and was at one time the second largest police force in the country after the Metropolitan Police.

There have traditionally been close working relationships between local BTP officers and local railway officials, and the responsibilities of the police might be summarised as follows:

◼ To safeguard railway property and goods in transit;

◼ To maintain order on stations and, where necessary, in trains;

◼ To prevent crime;

◼ To detect and apprehend wrongdoers and bring them before the justices.

However, problems can arise, and do so, when members of other police forces become involved. To put it in its simplest form, the railway system consists of long thin strips of property connecting main centres and it follows that BTP officers tend to be concentrated in those main centres. However, accidents have a habit of occurring somewhere along those thin strips of railway property and it is likely that the first police officers to arrive on the site come from the local, non-railway, force. It may be the first time that they have ever entered railway property on duty and it would not be surprising if occasionally an over-zealous constable put a foot wrong.

This is a fairly recent development, caused by changes in both railway and police organisations. Those with long memories can recall the village bobby calling in at the local station, and sometimes the local signalbox, for a cup of tea and a chat whilst on his rounds. He was a comforting presence and there were benefits on both sides. The bobby helped to keep the peace and he learned a bit about railway operation. That is history, and following some problems over 20 years ago when there was an instance of unfortunate interference by members of a local force following an accident, an Inspecting Officer of the Railway Inspectorate, Lt-Col Townsend-Rose, found it both necessary and useful to put forward some guidelines to help police officers when called to a railway accident. He suggested that when a local police force is called out it is mainly for the following reasons:

◼ To escort and help passengers to safety.

◼ To prevent theft and looting, and take charge of personal belongings left behind.

Morpeth 27 June 1994. Another derailment at Morpeth caused by excessive speed. The Class 47 diesel-electric locomotive, No 47783, of the northbound Mail train lies on its side; its driver had failed to react to the AWS warning for the curve, but escaped with minor injuries. *S. Miller*

■ To note the names and addresses of killed or injured passengers, so that next of kin may be informed.

■ To control crowds of onlookers who may interfere with rescue operations.

■ To provide radio communication.

■ To evacuate surrounding property if dangerous chemicals have been spilt, or if there are other hazards, eg fire or explosion.

■ To co-ordinate rescue and restoration activities being carried out by the emergency services and voluntary bodies.

■ To retrieve, identify and remove bodies on behalf of HM Coroner.

Lt-Col Townsend-Rose also gave some advice on what police officers should not do:

■ They should not delay traincrews in the protection of the lines.

■ They should not interfere with a signalman's duties.

■ They should not, without good reason, enter a signalbox unless accompanied by a railway official.

■ They should not interfere with any signalling equipment, either in the signalbox or on the ground.

These guidelines worked reasonably well until the Clapham disaster. The Court of Inquiry into that accident was held by a member of the legal profession, a Queen's Counsel, and it is not surprising that with his legal background he was concerned about the preservation of evidence. He therefore made an innocuous-sounding but in practice very cumbersome recommendation that what he referred to as fault-finding teams (actually, those looking for the cause) should be accompanied by a police officer and a photographer to provide for the proper recording and retention of evidence. This may be all very well for evidence that is unlikely to change, but braking equipment may do so quickly and heated surfaces will rapidly cool. A check of the position of signalling relays, point blades, etc, is essential as soon after the accident as possible. Accident investigators have enough to do without having to scour an area for a policeman.

Until Clapham, investigations into the causes of accidents were carried out by railway officers of the various departments, often working separately and simultaneously, who liaised with each other and came together with their various findings. Evidence was photographed and preserved where it was considered necessary to do so. The priorities after providing protection of trains (to prevent further mishap) were the removal of the dead and injured, the clearance of wreckage, and the restoration of the line, including signalling and other equipment, so that train running may restart as soon as possible. The tragedy of that part of the Clapham Report was that it not only provided a distraction from the railway officers' primary task of establishing the cause, but it also elevated the status of the police at the accident site, with the potential for greater interference in what ought to be regarded as primarily a railway

accident rather than the scene of a crime. The police had not previously had difficulty in establishing whether charges ought to be brought, and there was no justification for the change, nor is it likely that an experienced Inspecting Officer in charge of an inquiry would have felt it appropriate to make such a recommendation.

THE FATAL FLAW IN THE AUTOMATIC WARNING SYSTEM

It must be stressed that AWS has been of inestimable value to drivers and to the safe working of trains since it was first installed. It has relieved drivers of the awful and constant burden of having to drive trains day in and day out, in all weathers and under all conditions, and at all hours, without ever missing, or failing to respond to, a caution signal. It has enabled them to drive their trains at full speed in bad weather with complete confidence.

However, the application of AWS to four-aspect signalling has always been less than entirely satisfactory. The distance that is required between a signal displaying two yellows and a signal displaying a red aspect has to be based on the braking distance required for trains with the worst braking characteristics, eg heavily loaded freight trains. Electric multiple-units can brake much more quickly and hence in a much shorter distance. It follows that in many cases drivers do not need to apply the brake at a signal displaying two yellows but do need to do so at a signal displaying one yellow. The visual distinction from a distance between two yellows and one is not great. Worse, the AWS audible warning is the same. The system might almost have been designed to cause problems and it is significant that in most cases where a driver has passed a signal at danger and collided with another train, the signals concerned have been of the four-aspect type, each one capable of displaying a single yellow and a double yellow aspect. This was the system at Purley (and still is). It is the standard system on most main and suburban lines.

The Great Western Railway (GWR) recognised the need to provide clear differentiation in the audible warning given at a signal displaying two yellows from one displaying a single yellow, when it introduced such signalling on the approaches to Paddington in 1947. The GWR knew all about automatic warning systems — it had perfected one 40 years earlier. The Southern Region also had doubts about the wisdom of installing the standard BR system of AWS on its busy suburban lines for the same reason, but was overruled by the Railways Board. Finally, the Railway Inspectorate was becoming concerned in the 1980s about the unsatisfactory situation which was developing. Maj Rose, the Chief Inspecting Officer of Railways, voiced his unease in his Annual Report on the Safety Record of the Railways during 1986, when he wrote:

'Nevertheless, the time has come when the Board must face

*the questions and seek answers that will enable
it to establish a clear policy for the future. I have
made clear in previous reports the Inspectorate's
view that more needs to be done to assist the
driver in the cab.'*

THE PROSECUTION OF DRIVERS FOR PASSING SIGNALS AT DANGER

In view of what has been said earlier in this chapter, the policy which has existed for many years, even before the advent of AWS, of prosecuting drivers for causing a collision by wrongly passing a signal at danger surely needs to be reassessed. By no means does the policy apply in all cases; indeed, as previously stated, its application borders on the quixotic. And the author has been unable to trace any case in which a driver who pleaded not guilty has had the case against him proved. The most recent instance concerned a collision at Watford South Junction on 8 August 1996. Significantly, the train was an electric multiple-unit; the signalling was four-aspect colour-light. The driver was found not guilty. (This accident is described in detail in Chapter 12.) So why do the prosecution authorities continue to institute proceedings against drivers? Is it because they do not understand railway signalling? Or AWS? Or are they victims of the common failing of comparing the driving of trains (about which they know nothing) with the driving of cars (about which they would consider themselves experts)? If so, it is a common failing, and it might be advantageous to attempt to explain the fundamental differences.

A car driver is constantly receiving visual messages and he reacts accordingly, steering round corners, braking when he sees the need to do so, keeping to his side of the road, etc. The point is that he should always drive his car at such a speed as will enable him to slow down or stop safely when he sees a situation ahead which requires him to do so. In extreme cases, he might steer out of trouble. Driving a car can become so easy that it is possible to drive for several miles without the driver consciously considering his actions. The driver might be said to be on automatic pilot.

By contrast, a train driver does not constantly receive messages. He receives his instructions from lineside signals which are located at intervals alongside the track. They are often located without any reference to their surroundings. There is nothing to warn a driver that he may be approaching a signal except the signal's own light and eventually the AWS magnet. He is probably driving at high speed, at the maximum of the track or the train or both. He cannot steer out of trouble and he must

brake before he sees an obstruction or he is likely to hit it. Everything depends on his observance and correct reaction to a light in a lineside signal and an ambiguous audible warning. It is the intermittent nature of railway signalling that is the crux of the problem. The driver is subject to the cyclic nature of the demands upon his concentration, varying from an intense demand on the approach to a signal to a relaxed state between signals. That is what car drivers find difficult to comprehend.

Finally, one might invite the car driver to sit in the train driver's seat, at least in the imagination. Suddenly, on a journey that has so far been routine, something has gone wrong and the train is hurtling towards another one on the same line. A collision at fairly high speed is inevitable. Consider the thoughts that crowd in to the driver's mind. The sudden horror. What can I do? Will I die? Will I be seriously injured and possibly permanently disabled? There's not long for such speculation before the awful impact, the noise, the rending of metal, of being thrown around the cab for several seconds that seem like an eternity until the train finally stops.

If the driver survives and is conscious there will suddenly burst upon him the enormity of what has happened as he hauls himself from his cab and surveys the wreckage. If he feels that he might have been responsible, he will be overwhelmed by feelings of horror at the destruction and possible loss of life that he has caused, rapidly followed by emotional reactions of guilt and shame and disgrace. Fears of being hauled through the courts are secondary at this stage. He has let the side down and he will carry those feelings to his grave. This is the reality of the loophole in the Automatic Warning System, and it is little short of a scandal that nothing was done about it years ago. Everything has been done to make signalling ultra-safe; so little has been done for the driver. All that was needed was a greater distinction between a preliminary caution signal (two yellows) and a definite caution signal (one yellow), either in the signal aspect itself or in the response required by the driver. The proposed Train Protection and Warning System is a poor substitute in that respect.

And now the car driver may return to his car, somewhat chastened one hopes, but a little wiser.

POSTSCRIPT

Driver Morgan appealed against his sentence, and the Appeal Court reduced the custodial term to four months. He was released almost immediately. Lord Lane, the Lord Chief Justice, said that the jail term had been too long.

Hidden Dangers -
Single Lead Junctions

A Class 150 diesel multiple-unit passes over a ladder of single crossovers at Lenton South Junction, at the exact spot where the head-on collision referred to in Chapter 5 took place. *Author*

The term 'single lead junctions' is used in a special sense to describe those junctions where there is a short section of single line, connecting sections of double line, which is used by trains in both directions. Hence there is a danger of head-on collision if a driver should accidentally pass a signal at danger which gives access to that section of single line. Single lead junctions may be geographical (ie giving access to another route) or may connect one line with another on multi-track routes, but they are different in nature from ordinary single lines, which may be many miles in length and which form a complete length of railway, entire in itself.

In a traditional manually-signalled layout double junctions were the normal arrangement, and they gave some protection against the consequences of a driver running past a signal at danger. The interlocking between points and signals was so arranged that the facing points at a junction had to be set towards a branch line which diverged to the left before the points leading from that branch could be set for a movement from the branch. Thus, if a train had been signalled from the branch, a train proceeding towards the facing points would be diverted towards the branch out of harm's way if the driver ran past the junction signal at danger. This is known as 'flank protection'. It did not give protection against a driver running past a signal at danger from other directions, but additional signals were often provided as a precaution against that eventuality. Alternatively, a train would not be allowed to approach from the signalbox in rear if the junction signalman had given permission for another train to cross the junction.

The widespread extension of power signalling incorporating continuous track circuiting, colour-light signals and power-operated points enables single lead junctions to be signalled and operated to a high degree of safety. Although such layouts prevent trains from being run onto and off a branch line simultaneously, which is an operational handicap, they have substantial advantages for the civil engineer because they eliminate the need for a diamond crossing where one track crosses another, and they save both capital outlay and maintenance costs compared with a normal double junction. They

Left
An example of ordinary, traditional double junctions seen at Benton Quarry Junction, on the East Coast main line just north of Newcastle. Note the trailing trap points on the line curving round at the extreme left. They are open to the run-off position to protect the main line against any vehicles running back towards it. The neatness of the lineside cesses and the park-like quality of the landscaping in the 'V' of the line curving round to the left is astonishing by today's standards. This was 1946 — no sign here of wartime slippage in standards. The LNER was keen on having a neat and tidy permanent way, believing, rightly, that it encouraged the track workers' pride in their work and led to higher standards. *IAL*

the guard the 'train ready to start' signal. It may sound unlikely, but again bitter experience tells us that it is not.

Between 6 March 1989 and 21 July 1991 there was a remarkable series of no fewer than four head-on collisions in which single lead junctions were involved. Two of them resulted in loss of life, and passengers were injured in all four. The details are as follows:

DESCRIPTION OF THE FOUR ACCIDENTS
6 MARCH 1989 12.47PM BELLGROVE JUNCTION, GLASGOW
Bellgrove station lies on one of the Glasgow suburban lines, from Helensburgh to Airdrie, about a mile east of Glasgow Queen Street station. Immediately to the east of Bellgrove station there is a single lead junction with another suburban route leading to Springburn. Both lines are double track and are equipped with colour-light signals and continuous track circuiting. The junction is controlled from Bellgrove signalbox, situated opposite the junction.

Both trains were Class 303 three-car electric multiple-units. The eastbound train was the 12.20 from Milngavie to Springburn,

also remove a possible source of derailment if the crossing is not maintained to a sufficiently high standard.

However, single lead junctions place a high degree of responsibility upon the driver's unfailing obedience to signals, and the penalty of failure is high. If a signal giving access to a single lead junction is at danger it is most likely to be so because another train has already been signalled from the opposite direction, and any transgression creates a strong possibility of a head-on collision. Signal engineers would maintain that drivers should not pass signals at danger, and even operators have been heard to mutter that drivers are paid to obey signals, but that flies in the face of a century of bitter experience. The Automatic Warning System was therefore devised to help drivers in their obedience to signals, and it has been very successful in doing so, but there is a hidden danger when there is a single lead junction near the end of a station platform. In such situations the driver will already have passed over the warning equipment 200yd in rear of the signal when he stops in the platform and he may overlook its warning when he receives from

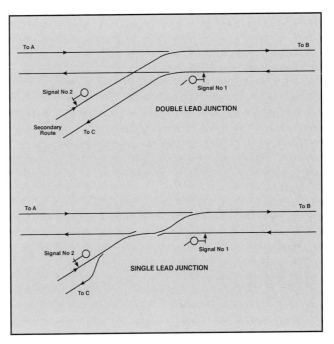

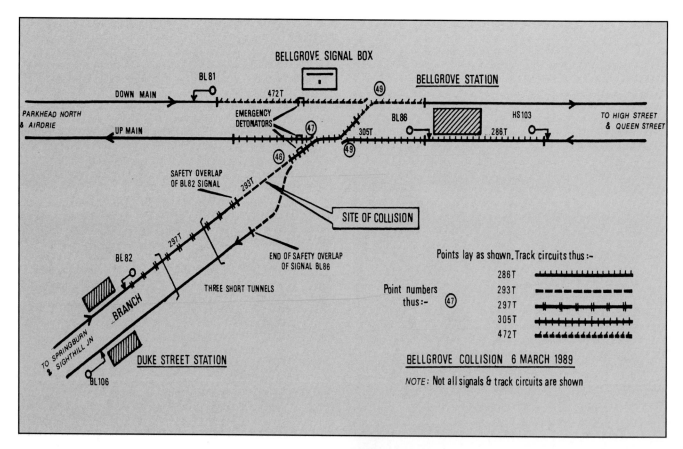

BELLGROVE SIGNAL BOX

BELLGROVE STATION

BL81

DOWN MAIN

472T

(49)

PARKHEAD NORTH
& AIRDRIE

UP MAIN

EMERGENCY
DETONATORS

(47)

305T

BL86

HS103

286T

TO HIGH STREET
& QUEEN STREET

(46)

(49)

SAFETY OVERLAP
OF BL82 SIGNAL

293T

SITE OF COLLISION

297T

BL82

END OF SAFETY OVERLAP
OF SIGNAL BL86

BRANCH

THREE SHORT TUNNELS

Points lay as shown. Track circuits thus :-

286T	+++++++++++++++
293T	- - - - - - - - -
297T	+-+-+-+-+-+
305T	++++++++++
472T	◄◄◄◄◄◄◄◄◄◄◄◄

Point numbers
thus :-   (47)

TO SPRINGBURN
& SIGHTHILL JN

DUKE STREET STATION

BL106

BELLGROVE COLLISION 6 MARCH 1989

NOTE: Not all signals & track circuits are shown

Right
**Looking east at Bellgrove. The single lead junction to the
Springburn branch can be seen on the left, the main line to
Airdrie in the centre and Bellgrove signalbox on the right.** *Author*

and as soon as it came to a stand in Bellgrove station with the
junction signal BL86 at danger, the signalman cleared the signal
for the other train, the 12.39 from Springburn to Milngavie, to
proceed from the branch over the single lead junction onto the
main line.

   As soon as station duties at Bellgrove were completed, the
guard of the train to Springburn gave the 'train ready to start'
bell signal to the driver, who promptly, and wrongly, set off past
signal BL86 at danger. The lie of the facing points ahead took
him into head-on collision with the other train a few moments
later, at a closing speed of about 30mph. Trailing points in a
route for which the signals have been cleared become facing
points for a train which has wrongly passed a signal at danger.
The driver and a passenger in the westbound train were killed and
five injured people were detained in hospital.

   The cause — the driver of the eastbound train maintained
that he saw the platform starting signal change to green, but the
report of the public inquiry concluded that he wrongly passed
that signal at danger. The guard of the eastbound train should
not have given the 'train ready to start' signal whilst signal BL86

was showing a red aspect. The accident would not have happened
with a normal double junction, as the eastbound train would
have been diverted out of harm's way. Signalling controls were
subsequently imposed to reduce the likelihood of the platform
starting signal being passed at danger.

   In the days before the junction was singled, trains to and
from the branch were timetabled to pass over the junction
simultaneously and they were not rescheduled when the junction
was singled, which meant that one train of the pair suffered a
signal delay on every occasion, which increased the risk.

Top Left
A Class 303 for the Springburn branch stands in Bellgrove station. The diagonal row of five white lights above the signal at the end of the platform denotes that the route ahead is set for the Springburn branch. *Author*

Below Left
A close-up view of signal BL86 at the end of the platform at Bellgrove station. Bellgrove signalbox can be seen to the left of the photograph. *M. H. Fowler*

1 AUGUST 1990 9.25AM READING STATION

The line from Waterloo to Reading of the former Southern Railway is double track and terminates at a dead-ended island platform 4A and 4B. Approaching Reading station, the line from Waterloo becomes single for 4yd before diverging again to run either side of the island platform. The line is equipped with colour-light signals and continuous track circuiting, and is controlled from Reading power signalbox.

The trains involved were the 09.23 from Reading to Waterloo, consisting of two four-car electric multiple-units (Class 423 and Class 411), which was standing in platform 4A, and the 07.01 from Tonbridge to Reading, a three-car Class 119 diesel multiple-unit, which was approaching the station. The signalman had set a route and cleared his signals for the Waterloo train to depart from platform 4A.

The collision at Glasgow Bellgrove on 6 March 1989. The front coach of the westbound Class 303 electric multiple-unit reared up, killing one of the drivers and a passenger. *Tom Noble*

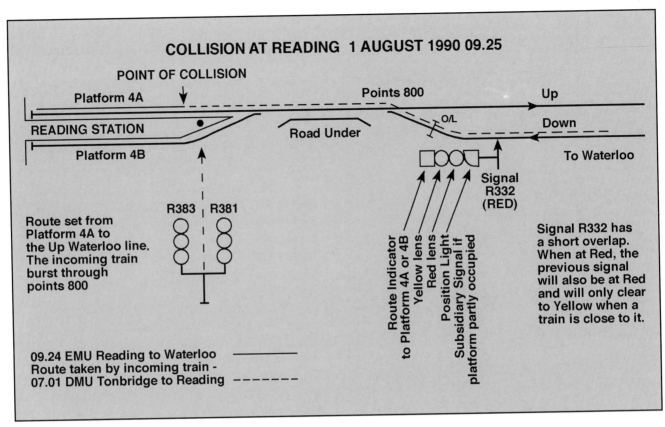

COLLISION AT READING 1 AUGUST 1990 09.25

POINT OF COLLISION

Platform 4A

Points 800

Up

READING STATION

Road Under

Down

Platform 4B

To Waterloo

Signal R332 (RED)

R383 R381

Route Indicator to Platform 4A or 4B
Yellow lens
Red lens
Position Light
Subsidiary Signal if platform partly occupied

Route set from Platform 4A to the Up Waterloo line. The incoming train burst through points 800

Signal R332 has a short overlap. When at Red, the previous signal will also be at Red and will only clear to Yellow when a train is close to it.

09.24 EMU Reading to Waterloo ——————
Route taken by incoming train -
07.01 DMU Tonbridge to Reading - - - - - -

The train to Waterloo had not started before the train from Tonbridge ran into the station and collided at about 15mph with the stationary train. The trailing points leading from platforms 4A and 4B had been set for the departing train, but they became facing for the train from Tonbridge. Twenty-eight people were taken to hospital for treatment but only one was detained overnight.

The cause — the driver of the train from Tonbridge maintained that the signal controlling access to the station platforms was showing yellow, but the public inquiry concluded that he wrongly passed that signal at danger. The guard was standing in the cab doorway and may have distracted the driver at the critical time. He should not have been there. The accident would not have happened if the line had been double throughout.

22 AUGUST 1990 9.50AM HYDE NORTH JUNCTION
Hyde North Junction lies on the line from Manchester Piccadilly through Guide Bridge to Glossop. There is a single lead connection with the line to Sheffield. Both lines are double track and are equipped with colour-light signals and continuous track

Above Left
Looking towards Waterloo from the end of island Platform 4A/4B at Reading. The inherent dangers of head-on collision on such a layout, if an incoming train should pass a signal at danger or if an outgoing train should pass the platform starting signal at danger, are readily apparent. *Author*

Left
A Class 411 electric multiple-unit, of the type involved in the Reading collision, leaves Tonbridge on an Ashford to Charing Cross service on 5 July 1977. *Les Bertram*

Above
A Class 119 diesel multiple-unit, of the type involved in the Reading collision, passes Acton main line en route for Paddington on 17 March 1977. *Brian Morrison*

Below
Hyde North station, looking towards Manchester Piccadilly. The signal which was passed at danger, GB365, is suspended from an overhead gantry at the ends of the platforms in order to give good sighting to a driver approaching it round the curve, but the sighting is not so good to the driver of a train standing in the station. Facing trap points have now been installed as a precaution against the effects of a driver passing this signal at danger and are located just before the two platform lines converge. *Author*

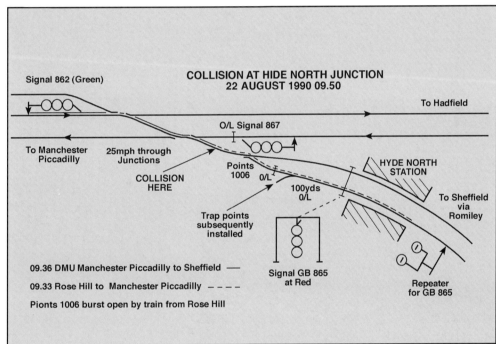

COLLISION AT HIDE NORTH JUNCTION
22 AUGUST 1990 09.50

Signal 862 (Green)

To Hadfield

O/L Signal 867

To Manchester Piccadilly

25mph through Junctions

COLLISION HERE

Points 1006   O/L

100yds O/L

HYDE NORTH STATION

To Sheffield via Romiley

Trap points subsequently installed

Signal GB 865 at Red

Repeater for GB 865

09.36 DMU Manchester Piccadilly to Sheffield ———
09.33 Rose Hill to Manchester Piccadilly – – – –
Pionts 1006 burst open by train from Rose Hill

Way out →

Above
A Class 101 Metro-Cammell diesel multiple-unit departs from the old Platform 12 at Manchester Victoria on 27 June 1988. The overall roof originally extended further along the platform, but was damaged during an air raid and subsequently cut short. This section of the old station was completely demolished during the reconstruction in 1992-4. *John Glover*

circuiting. The whole area is controlled from Guide Bridge signalbox, about two miles to the west. Hyde North station lies on the Sheffield line about 200yd from the junction.

The two trains involved were the 09.33 from Rose Hill to Manchester Piccadilly (a two-car Class 108 diesel multiple-unit) and the 09.36 from Manchester Piccadilly to Sheffield (a three-car train Class 101/108 diesel multiple-unit). The signalman had set the route and cleared his signals for the train to Sheffield when the train from Rose Hill came to a stand in Hyde North station. There is a signal, No 865, near the end of the station platform, and it was showing a red aspect.

As soon as station duties were completed, the guard of the train from Rose Hill gave a buzzer signal to the driver to indicate that the train was ready to start. The driver set off at once, passing signal 865 at danger, and collided head-on at low speed (5-10mph) with the Sheffield train on the short piece of single line. There were 42 passengers on the two trains, and whilst 28 required hospital treatment for minor injuries, only one was detained overnight.

The cause — the driver of the train from Rose Hill maintained that the platform starting signal changed to yellow, but the public inquiry concluded that he had wrongly passed that signal, and that the guard of that train had given the 'train ready to start' signal to the driver whilst the signal was at danger. The guard should not have done so, but there was no 'Off' indicator to help him. There should have been, and one was subsequently installed.

Above
The guard of a Manchester-bound diesel multiple-unit standing in Hyde North station on 21 January 1999 looks across to the 'Off' indicator to see whether it is in order for him to give the buzzer signal 'train ready to start' to the driver. The 'Off' indicator can be seen on the top of a tall post beneath the word 'Way' on the Way Out sign. *Author*

Trap points were also installed after the accident, to derail a train before it could reach the common piece of single line, should it pass the platform starting signal at danger. The accident would not have happened if there had been a normal double junction.

21 JULY 1991 9.56PM NEWTON STATION, NEAR GLASGOW
Newton station lies in a complex layout about six miles from Glasgow Central station on the West Coast main line towards Motherwell and Carlisle. It is also the junction of the suburban line from Kirkhill to Hamilton and there are connections between the two routes. Newton station platforms serve only the suburban

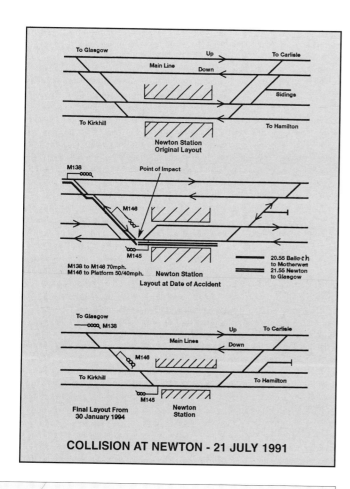

COLLISION AT NEWTON - 21 JULY 1991

This page
Newton: The westbound platform (top right) showing signal No M145, which was passed at danger, at the far end of the platform; Looking east towards the station (left), showing the common piece of single line adjacent to the '40' sign. The collision occurred on the bi-directional connecting line a few yards behind the place from which this photograph was taken. The lie of the points nearer to the camera diverted the westbound train into collision. Looking east (above). Up and down West Coast main lines on the left, bi-directional connecting line in the centre, up and down Kirkhill lines on the right. *All author*

Above
A Class 314 of the type used on the incoming train at Newton is seen arriving at Helensburgh Central on 24 July 1983.
Tom Heavyside

line. All the signals in the area are of the colour-light type and there is continuous track-circuiting. At the Glasgow end of the station there was a short piece of single line common to all train movements to and from both platforms, the West Coast main line and the Kirkhill line. Train movements in the area are controlled from Motherwell Signalling Centre.

The trains concerned in the accident were the 21.55 from Newton to Glasgow (a Class 303 three-car electric multiple-unit) and the 20.55 from Balloch to Motherwell (a Class 314 electric multiple-unit). The train from Balloch had been signalled into the station, which required it to pass over the common portion of single line, and whilst it was doing so it collided head-on with the other train which had just started from Newton station.

The latter train was worked without a guard under the single-manning agreement. It had been standing in the station for several minutes waiting for departure time, and when the driver decided that it was time to depart he closed the doors and set off, passing the signal at the end of the platform, known as the platform starting signal, at danger. The two trains met in violent collision on the common piece of single line at a closing speed which was estimated to be around 60mph. Both drivers, and two passengers, were killed and 22 passengers were injured, four being detained in hospital. It was fortunate that, being late Sunday evening and with one train just starting its journey and

the other nearing its end, there were few passengers in the two trains; indeed there was only one in the starting train.

The cause — it was concluded that the driver of the train from Newton to Glasgow wrongly passed the platform starting signal at danger, despite what amounted almost to a witch-hunt against the integrity of the signalling by various official bodies, legal representatives and the media, and regrettably by BR senior management, as though they could not comprehend that a driver might commit the simple human error of passing a signal at danger. It might be added that Scottish Region signal engineers identified the evidence of the platform starting signal being passed at danger within two hours of the accident.

New signalling had been commissioned at Newton only four weeks before the collision, and there had been repetitive and unusual faults, none of which was unsafe. However, it is sad to relate that these faults were used by parties with axes to grind to foment distrust in the integrity of the signalling, and months were to pass before common sense prevailed.

AN ANALYSIS OF COMMON FACTORS IN THESE ACCIDENTS

THE TYPE OF SIGNALLING

Multiple-aspect colour-light signalling was in use at all four accident sites, and the Automatic Warning System was in use. However, whilst colour-light signals are visually superior to semaphore signals in many circumstances, this may not be the case when a train is standing close to a signal in broad daylight. In such conditions the arm of a semaphore signal presents a visually arresting image, although it must be said that such signals have also been wrongly passed at danger.

LOCATION OF ACCIDENT

In all four cases the collision occurred in or very near a station platform.

TYPE OF TRAIN

Two of the trains concerned in passing a signal at danger were electric multiple-units. The other two were diesel multiple-units.

WEATHER CONDITIONS

Fine and broad daylight in three cases. Dusk was just falling at Newton.

TYPE OF TRAIN SERVICE

All four trains were working off-peak suburban stopping services.

THE EVIDENCE OF THE DRIVERS

All three drivers who survived the accidents contended that the signal concerned had been showing a proceed aspect, but the Inspecting Officers holding the inquiries concluded that the signals had been at red. After the traumatic experience of a collision, drivers may genuinely believe that the signal could not have been at red; in other cases the suggestion may be floated as a defence, and it has to be said that in the absence of event recorders in the signalbox or on the train (the 'black box') one can never be 100% sure. Event recorders can be the driver's friend as well as his accuser. It is significant that the drivers involved in the collisions at Reading and Hyde North were reluctant to speak openly at the public inquiry, and it is clear that they were influenced by the jailing of the driver involved in the Purley collision (see previous chapter).

In the Reading case the driver was advised by his legal counsel not to give evidence at the inquiry, although he did give a written statement and answered a few questions not directly relevant to the circumstances of the accident. In the Hyde North case the lawyer representing the driver read out the driver's statement, but the driver agreed to answer questions on his statement.

The reluctance of witnesses to answer questions fully and openly at public inquiries has been an increasing feature in recent years. Whilst such reluctance is understandable, it does not help in ascertaining the cause of an accident and although an Inspector is entitled to demand answers, he cannot require a witness to give evidence that might incriminate himself. The law, and the process of establishing the cause of an accident, are poor bedfellows, and whilst the law must have its due, it is surely important that there be no impediment to establishing the cause of an accident so that lessons can be learned and safety standards improved.

It is interesting to note that the driver at fault in the Bellgrove accident was not faced with criminal prosecution. The Scottish law office considered such prosecution inappropriate and said that the driver had suffered enough with the loss of a leg and the end of his career as a driver. One might have hoped that such sentiments existed south of the border.

AGE AND EXPERIENCE PROFILE OF THE DRIVERS

■ BELLGROVE — the driver was 23 years old with less than two years experience.

■ READING — a young driver with just over two years experience.

■ HYDE NORTH — a young driver of limited experience and inadequate training.

■ NEWTON — the driver was killed in the collision. He was 61 years old with a long experience, but the restructuring of the BR organisation in the 1980s meant that he was henceforth confined to tedious, repetitive inner-suburban workings, which had always been considered undesirable because it could lead to boredom and loss of concentration.

It is difficult to draw any firm conclusions from such a small sample, but there is known to be a boredom element in the constant operation of suburban stopping services which may affect young drivers to a greater extent than older drivers of greater experience and self-discipline. There is no obvious solution to this situation other than the provision of safeguards against human error, which will be discussed later in this chapter.

THE PHYSICAL LAYOUT OF THE JUNCTIONS

■ BELLGROVE — it would have been practicable to install a double junction which would have had operational advantages and no technical disadvantages. There was no justification for installing a single lead junction, and it resulted from civil engineering department preferences without regard to other factors.

■ READING — the provision of a normal double line layout would have required two additional points and the possible widening of a bridge, which would have been difficult to justify. Trap points beyond signal R332 would have provided some safeguard, but might have been considered not cost-effective.

■ HYDE NORTH — it would have been practicable to install a double junction.

■ NEWTON — the layout at Newton West Junction was absurd and was an engineering response to business demands for higher speeds on the West Coast main line. Given the history of platform starting signals being wrongly passed at danger, and particularly so in the Glasgow area, it was an accident waiting to happen. It should never have been authorised, and there was a simple alternative, which was adopted after the accident, that would have avoided the danger. The risks were high and the business benefit was negligible.

THE HISTORY OF PLATFORM STARTING SIGNALS BEING PASSED AT DANGER

There is no operational objection to single lead junctions other than a reduction in line capacity, and there may be engineering and speed advantages, but it is equally important to ensure as far as possible that drivers do not accidentally pass platform starting signals at danger.

This has been a problem of long standing, not restricted to single lead junctions, in which drivers inadvertently set off from stations against platform starting signals at danger after receiving the guard's 'rightaway' signal. There is a body of informed opinion which believes that the guard's signal can have

a considerable psychological effect on the driver, strange though that may seem. Incidents of this type, which often do not result in collision, are known in railway circles as 'ding-ding and away', and there have been several every year.

Following a particularly serious collision just outside Paisley station on Easter Monday 1979, in which seven people were killed, the rules were changed to require station staff and the guard not to give the 'all right' signal and 'train ready to start' signal respectively if the platform starting signal was at danger. It was recognised that curvature of the line and signal siting might make it impracticable for such staff to see the signal, and at those locations 'Off' indicators have been provided to enable the staff to comply with the rule. However, insufficient attention was given to the enforcement of this rule, and the situation was particularly bad in the Glasgow area, as demonstrated at Bellgrove, despite the awful example of the Paisley accident.

The Hyde North accident was another example of 'ding-ding and away', but despite the fact of the platform starting signal not

Below
Paisley. Signal No P31 at the end of the Glasgow-bound platform was passed at danger on Easter Monday 1979, and the train collided with one making the same conflicting movement as the Class 303 EMU in the right of the photograph. *Author*

being visible to the guard owing to its siting, no 'Off' indicator was provided until after the accident.

The Newton accident was unique in the sense that, even though there was no guard and the train was being operated only by the driver, the elements of 'ding-ding and away' could have been subconsciously in the driver's mind. His train was starting its journey at Newton, and he drove it into the station a few minutes before the booked departure time. The aspect being displayed at the time by the platform starting signal was irrelevant to him. He then opened the doors to allow passengers to join and concentrated his attention on the need to close the doors in time to achieve a punctual departure. About half a minute before departure time he would check that everything was in order for the doors to be closed and then close them, finally checking that no one was trapped in the doors. Everything was now ready for the train to depart, which is thought to have been the subconscious 'ding-ding' and the cause of the signal being passed at danger. There was some suggestion that the risk of the platform starting signal at Newton being wrongly passed at danger was lessened because the train was being worked without a guard, and therefore the risk of the guard's 'ding-ding' causing the driver inadvertently to set off past the signal at danger was removed. However, it could be argued that the risk was increased, because there was no guard to withhold the 'ding-ding' until the signal cleared.

The Automatic Warning System is of little use in these circumstances, because the train will have passed over the warning magnet before stopping in the station and its warning is likely to have receded from the driver's mind. Other measures need to be taken to achieve safety.

There remains the possibility that the signalman cleared the platform starting signal when the train ran into the platform from the turnback siding, then later restored it to danger before that train departed when he realised that the train from Balloch was closely approaching and should be given precedence over the single leads. In such circumstances the signalman should not have allowed the Balloch train to approach until he had ensured that the driver of the train standing in the platform knew about the change of aspect of the platform starting signal. There is evidence that the train from Balloch was checked by signals on the approach to Newton, which lends a measure of credence to this theory, but we shall never know.

THE ACHIEVEMENT OF SAFETY

The Automatic Train Protection system would be an effective safeguard against a driver setting off from a station and accidentally passing the starting signal at danger. The equipment would detect the event and immediately apply the brakes, bringing the train, which would be travelling at low speed, to a stand within a relatively few yards. The proposed Train Protection and Warning System will perform a similar function.

Following the sequence of four accidents described in this

Below
Paisley power signalbox. The collision occurred at No 221 switch diamonds on the second line down, above and slightly left of the signalman's index finger. *British Rail*

Bottom
'Off' indicator for Platform 1 at Skipton. As a safety precaution, the guard must not give the 'train ready to start' bell signal to the driver unless he can see either that the platform starting signal is exhibiting a 'Proceed' indication or that the 'Off' indicator is illuminated. *Author*

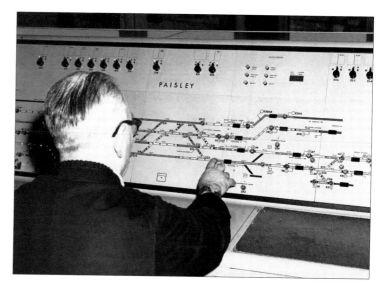

chapter, and especially after the disgraceful episode of Newton, British Rail finally took action specifically to deal with this problem. It carried out a study at all platform starting signals protecting pointwork which forms part of a running junction, to assess the degree of risk of collision in the event of the signal being passed at danger and the likely consequences of such collision. It was then decided that, depending on the degree of risk, special safeguards would be required, which may be:

◼ Automatic Train Protection or equivalent.

◼ Trap points ahead of the signal (may be undesirable if any derailment caused by them might block other lines).

◼ The interlocking must prevent any conflicting route being set up for another train when a route is set up to the platform starting signal or when a train is standing at that signal. However, this is inappropriate in busy areas, owing to the delays caused.

▨ Changing the track layout to avoid the problem.

▨ An additional AWS magnet immediately beyond the platform starting signal, active only when the signal is at red.

▨ An additional signal, known as a SPAD (signal passed at danger) indicator and normally unlit, located a few yards beyond the platform starting signal. The SPAD indicator flashes red if the signal is passed at danger.

Drivers have long been aware of the possibility of inadvertently starting away past platform starting signals at danger and have had their own methods of reminding themselves that the signal is at danger. This has now been regularised by the provision of a reminder appliance which the driver must place in the 'Waiting Signal' position when stopped at a platform starting signal at danger. When the appliance is in place, the application of tractive power is prevented.

CONCLUSIONS ON THE NEWTON ACCIDENT

At the Newton Inquiry and at the Sheriff's Fatal Accident Inquiry which followed, BR was criticised for installing single lead junctions, but it countered this criticism by explaining that such layouts are no different from the hundreds of miles of single line which exist on Britain's railways. This was a specious argument because they are different, but the argument was accepted by the various non-railway authorities because they knew no better and were not properly advised. They are different because the driver's mental attitude to single lines is different. The Newton layout should never have seen the light of day and is no credit to BR, nor, sadly, to the regulating authority. Even though the layout

conformed to all the standards laid down in the Signalling Principles, there should have been sufficient awareness of the hidden dangers in such a layout, given the recent examples at Bellgrove and elsewhere. Was it symptomatic of disarray within BR management circles caused by the change from a departmental-based organisation to one that was business-led, highly desirable as such a change was in other respects? And did it point to a lessening of the traditional expertise within the Railway Inspectorate?

It might be appropriate at this stage to say a few words about the role of HM Railway Inspectorate in the approval of signalling plans. The responsibility for setting track, signalling and operational safety standards is fairly and squarely placed upon the railway industry, as is the responsibility for day-to-day safety. It is not the responsibility of the Railway Inspectorate nor should it be. The Railway Inspectorate examines a signalling plan to see that it is generally in accordance with the industry's own standards. The Inspectorate is not a checking authority. However, if there were any aspects of a scheme which the Inspectorate felt uneasy about, they would normally discuss such matters with the industry. Single lead junctions were one such aspect and the principle was discussed at length, but the specific hidden danger at Newton was allowed to remain. Perhaps the extent of the danger was not appreciated, but it ought to have been.

The magnitude of the risk at Newton was dramatically highlighted subsequently when BR introduced a new safety measure to deal with platform starting signals. Such signals were assessed on the basis of the risk of collision if they were wrongly passed at danger, and a points system was devised taking into account the speed of trains, the frequency of conflicting movements, etc. The tolerable threshold figure is 4,000. Newton registered 11,664. That underlines the magnitude of the errors committed in the design of the Newton layout and its approval.

Right
SPAD indicator at Shipley, working in conjunction with signal L3971 on the Leeds line and protecting the trailing junction closely ahead with the Bradford line. If the signal is wrongly passed at danger, the SPAD indicator will flash red to alert the driver. *Author*

CHAPTER 8

Buffer Stop Collision at Cannon Street Station

Above
Cannon Street on 7 June 1976. A unit of Class 411/2, 4-CEP
No 7207, on the left forms the head end of the 17.16 to Hastings.
Brian Morrison

Do commuters on trains running into terminal stations ever have a moment's unease that the train might not stop at the platform but might actually run into the buffer stops, and prepare themselves for the impact? It seems most unlikely, judging by their behaviour in standing up and moving towards the doors, rather than remaining seated (if they have seats) or bracing themselves for the impact if standing, as the train runs into the platform. Did any of the 900 or so passengers on the 07.58 train from Sevenoaks to Cannon Street on Tuesday 8 January 1991 have any inkling of impending calamity?

It is most unlikely. Historically, the number of occasions in a year in which a passenger train has run into the buffer stops at a station has averaged about 25, which is a minute proportion of the millions of trains which run into terminal stations each year. There is every reason, therefore, for passengers to be confident that the train will stop safely short of the buffers. And no reason

for any doubts on that score. And yet, the unthinkable happened on that train.

The effect on the passengers of a train hitting the buffers at 5-10mph can be imagined. The coaches stop within a few feet, but those passengers who are not sitting with their backs to the engine continue forwards at undiminished speed until their progress is halted by an impact of 5-10mph either with a part of the train or with some other person. Rather like running into a brick wall. Standing passengers are likely to suffer a double impact; firstly when they crash into someone else, followed immediately by someone else crashing into them. Even passengers seated back to the engine are not immune; they are

likely to receive in their laps with quite a thud the persons sitting opposite, together with their briefcases catapulted from the rack above and aimed straight at their heads.

The shock of the impact is considerable, because it is instantaneous and unheralded, but physical damage is likely to be confined to cuts and bruises in most cases, with some broken bones in the more severe impacts. Deaths are uncommon; indeed they are rare. But two people lost their lives at Cannon Street on 8 January 1991.

THE ACCIDENT

The 07.58 passenger train from Sevenoaks to Cannon Street, one of London's main business district stations, consisted of three electric multiple-units with a total of 10 coaches. It picked up passengers at Dunton Green, Knockholt, Chelsfield, Orpington, Petts Wood and Grove Park, and was full when it arrived at London Bridge, where the usual interchange of passengers took place. On leaving London Bridge the front four coaches were very crowded, with well over 100 passengers standing, but there were almost 200 empty seats in the rear five coaches. Most of the standing passengers had joined at London Bridge or the inner suburbs and preferred to stand for the short journey in order to be able to make a quick exit from Cannon Street station.

Above
Cannon Street on 3 March 1984. Class 411/5 4-CEP No 411608 awaits departure. *David Brown*

Below
The destructive result of the low-speed collision with the buffer stops at Cannon Street on 8 January 1991, showing how the fifth coach reared up and partly telescoped the sixth. *The Times*

Above
Class 415/4 4-EPB No 5403 at Wandsworth Common on 26 March 1981. A sister unit, No 5484, formed vehicles five to eight of the train involved in the buffer stop collision. *Les Bertram*

Right
A unit of Class 416/2, 2-EPB No 6274, of the type which formed the last two vehicles of the train involved in the buffer stop collision, is seen at Staines on 13 October 1984. *David Brown*

According to reports, the train ran into platform 3 at Cannon Street at the normal speed and no one had any inkling of imminent disaster until the last moment, when the more perceptive passengers realised that the train was not braking and slowing down. They hardly had time to brace themselves before the awful thud of the impact with the buffers at a speed estimated to be in the region of 10mph. The time was 8.44am.

DESCRIPTION OF THE TRAIN
The train consisted of three electric multiple-units, marshalled as follows:

▪ Unit No 5618, Class 415/6
Driving motor brake second open No 61585
Trailer second open No 70444
Trailer second open No 70443
Driving motor brake second open No 61584
▪ Unit No 5484, Class 415/4
Driving motor brake second open No 14046
Trailer second open No 15308
Trailer second open No 15031
Driving motor brake second open No 14061
▪ Unit No 6227, Class 416/2
Driving trailer second open No 77526 (had some

individual compartments)
Driving motor brake second open No 65341

It might be helpful to describe these terms:

DRIVING	a coach with a driving cab
MOTOR	a powered coach
BRAKE	a coach with a guard's compartment
SECOND	all seats standard class
OPEN	all seats arranged in an open saloon/s with a centre aisle
TRAILER	an unpowered coach.

Unit No 5618 was built at Eastleigh in about 1960, to British Railways Mk 1 design. The outer coaches weighed 41 tons and had 84 seats. The inner coaches weighed 29½ tons and had 112 seats. They had received a facelift during their lifetime. They were fitted with the electro-pneumatic brake.

Unit No 5484 was older. Coach No 14046 emerged from Southern Region workshops to an SR design in 1953 but was built on an underframe dating from 1934. It received a facelift in 1986. It weighed 40 tons and had 82 seats. Coach No 15308 was built on an underframe dating from 1928 and was reintroduced into service with a new body to SR design in 1955. It weighed

27 tons and had 102 seats. Coach No 15031 was built by the Southern Region in 1948. It weighed 27 tons and had 102 seats. Coach No 14061 was built by the Southern Region in 1953 using an underframe dating from 1927. It weighed 40 tons and had 82 seats. All the coaches had been facelifted and were fitted with the electro-pneumatic brake.

Unit No 6227 was built in Southern Region workshops in 1954 to the BR Mk 1 design. The motor coach weighed 42 tons and had 84 seats. The trailer coach weighed 30½ tons and had 102 seats. Both coaches were fitted with the electro-pneumatic brake.

There were no gangway connections between individual vehicles and all doors were of the traditional hinged type, now known as slam doors, which were opened and closed by passengers themselves. The outer ends of each unit had the normal side buffers and an automatic coupling, but the internal couplings within each unit consisted of a centre buffer and chains.

THE BRAKING SYSTEM

There were two braking systems on the train, controlled by the same brake handle, which has five positions: (1) Release, (2) Full EPB application (variable between positions 1 and 2), (3) Lap — maintains current brake pressure, (4) Automatic Air Brake application, (5) Emergency — full application of both systems.

1 THE ELECTRO-PNEUMATIC BRAKE (EPB)
Each axle is individually braked by compressed air, and the application and release of the brake is controlled electrically from the driving cab. Although it is not fail-safe it is very reliable and responsive, and well liked by drivers.

2 THE AUTOMATIC AIR BRAKE
This is the normal air brake, operated through the air brake pipe which runs the length of the train. It is required to be used once on each journey and is fail-safe.

It should be stressed that there is no such thing as a separate emergency brake system, and the term 'emergency brake application' denotes a particular operation of the normal train braking system/s in which a full brake application is made almost instantaneously. When braking to stop at a station or signal, or at buffer stops, a partial brake application is made, known as a 'service brake application'.

DESCRIPTION OF DAMAGE TO THE TRAIN AND DISTRIBUTION OF CASUALTIES

The total weight of the train and its passengers was approximately 400 tons, and even at the low speed of 10mph at which the train is estimated to have hit the buffers there was a considerable amount of energy to be absorbed.

Energy can be absorbed in many ways, eg:
- Vehicles can deform laterally, ie crumple;
- Vehicles can override one another, ie telescope;
- Vehicles can concertina, but remain structurally mainly intact;
- Vehicles can be scattered randomly;
- The buffer stops will absorb some energy.

Low speed buffer stop collisions, up to 3-5mph, can usually be absorbed by the buffer stops without much damage to the train other than the displacement of internal fittings, but above those speeds some damage to the train is inevitable. It was estimated that the energy of the train in question was absorbed in the following approximate proportions:

By the buffer stops	40%
By the buffers and couplings between vehicles	10%
By the deformation of the first & second coaches	10%
By the overriding of the fifth and sixth coaches	40%

It is apparent that the shock of the impact was reduced step by step along the train, by about 15% in the third and fourth coaches, and by more than a half in the last four coaches (excluding the effect of almost half of the impact being absorbed by the buffer stops). This is naturally reflected in the proportion of passengers in each coach who were taken to hospital, which was approximately:

1st coach	50%	6th coach	35%
2nd coach	40%	7th coach	20%
3rd coach	35%	8th coach	nil
4th coach	35%	9th coach	nil
5th coach	50%	10th coach	nil

One passenger was killed in the second coach and one in the fifth.

The most serious damage was caused when the front of the sixth coach underrode the rear of the fifth to a distance of several feet. There is no specific reason why these two vehicles behaved in this manner, but it occurs when, at the moment of impact, a coach body is thrown forward slightly on its suspension, causing the front of the coach to drop slightly and the rear to lift, allowing the underframe at the dipped front of the following coach to force its way beneath the lifted underframe of the coach in front. This inevitably causes damage to both coach bodies, but particularly to the rear coach.

Telescoping has been an awful feature of many railway accidents, but strengthened coach ends and automatic couplings of a type that do not allow vertical uncoupling have done much to reduce the problem.

THE HISTORY OF BUFFER STOP COLLISIONS

During the fiscal year 1996/7 (presenting accident statistics in fiscal years is one of the more fanciful decisions of the Health & Safety Executive) there were only seven recorded cases of trains running into buffer stops or into other vehicles already standing at the buffer stops. For some unexplained reason this was far lower than any other year and may be due to under-reporting. In 1995/6 there were 20. In 1990 there were 41. There is no apparent explanation for this trend and none is forthcoming.

Top three pictures
Buffer stops come in all types, many of which date back to 'Big Four' or even pre-Grouping days. Here are three, seen at: King's Cross, 9 May 1977 (left). The old hydraulic buffers are being removed. Euston, 15 August 1931 (below left). An early design of friction buffer stop. Manchester Victoria, February 1978 (centre left). Hydraulic buffers, which are needed at the foot of the long, steep descent into the station from the east.
J. M. Capes/Modern Transport/Rodney Wildsmith

The great majority of buffer stop collisions occur at very low speed, due to the driver's misjudgement or handling of the brake, or of grease on the rails, but occasionally trains hit buffers at quite high speed, overriding and proceeding beyond them for some distance. However, fatalities are rare and serious injuries to passengers few. The previous occasion on which passengers were killed occurred in 1964 when the driver had a heart attack as the train was descending the steep gradient into Bradford Exchange station. Two passengers lost their lives.

BUFFER STOP DESIGN

Anyone travelling extensively around the railways of Britain cannot fail to be struck by the variety of buffer stops, many of which date back to pre-nationalisation days or even earlier. The older ones are mainly of two designs — fixed, rigid buffers which are mainly used to denote the end of the line and prevent accidental derailment, and hydraulic buffers, which are often provided where the station is approached on a falling gradient of some severity.

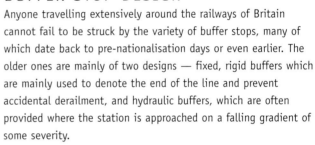

The buffers at Cannon Street were of hydro-pneumatic design, having two-stage pistons which resisted the impact of a train by oil pressure. The pistons were compressed by the accident to their full design stroke of 24in. They were rated to withstand the impact of a train up to 450 tons in weight at a speed of not more than 4mph.

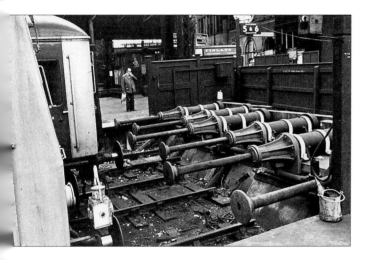

Subsequent recent design has concentrated on staggered impact absorption, where the buffer slides along the rails and has its movement checked by a series of arresters (clamps) which grip the rail. Momentum is steadily absorbed through friction as the buffer comes into contact with an increasing number of such arresters. This design allows the impact to be absorbed without subjecting passengers to severe shocks, provided that impact speed is not too high, up to 6mph.

Above Left
Modern buffer stops now installed at Cannon Street station.
Author

Left
Impact-absorbing buffer stops at Euston station. *Author*

REPLACEMENT OF OLD STOCK

The are several reasons for the replacement of old rolling stock:

■ It is too old and expensive to maintain,

■ Higher performance standards required,

■ Easier and cheaper maintenance,

■ Greater comfort and better facilities for passengers,

■ Economy in operation,

■ Higher safety standards desirable.

We are only concerned with the last one.

At the time of the accident there were thousands of similar electric multiple-unit coaches in daily use on the Southern Region. Some were of former Southern Railway design, but most conformed to the standard British Railways Mk 1 design introduced in the early 1950s. From a safety point of view, they were perfectly acceptable by the standards of the day, but by 1991 more recent designs had a higher standard of crashworthiness.

Above
The new generation of electric multiple-units on the Southern Region with power-operated sliding doors — brand new 'Networker' Class No 465001. *IAL*

Below
4-CEP units, Nos 1502 and 1610, of Class 411, pass Factory Junction (near Wandsworth Road) on 13 September 1991 with the 13.23 from Victoria to Dover. These units, now approaching 40 years old, still perform much of the work on the Kent Coast services. *Chris Wilson*

Facing Page
Cannon Street on 7 December 1998. A Class 423 4-VEP No 3560, stands in the new Platform 3 alongside a Class 466 'Networker', No 466029, in Platform 2. *Brian Morrison*

Plans were being developed in 1989/90 for a major programme of replacement EMUs, known as 'Networkers' (Class 465) for inner-suburban use, and Class 471 for outer-suburban services. Networkers began to enter service in 1991 and when the programme was completed in 1994, 150 four-car sets had been built, plus 43 two-car sets (Class 466). It had been hoped to build 800 coaches of Class 471, mainly for Kent Coast services, but owing to Treasury restrictions and the unfortunate hiatus in ordering new stock during the privatisation process only 41 four-car sets of the Networker Express type (now Class 365) have been built so far, all in 1994/5. Of these, only 16 are allocated to the South Eastern section.

Nevertheless, some progress is being made in replacing older stock, and all three classes involved in the Cannon Street accident have been completely withdrawn (Classes 415/4, 415/6 and 416/2). However, many units of Mk 1 design remain, the main ones being as follows (1998):

- Class 421/5 four-car sets   1970-2   South Western   22 sets
- Class 411/5 four-car sets   1958-63   South Eastern   80 sets
- Class 421/3 four-car sets   1964-70   South Central   44 sets
- Class 421/4 four-car sets   c1970   all sections   68 sets
- Class 423 four-car sets   1967-74   all sections   190 sets

The question which then has to be considered is whether there is the need to replace these sets (1,616 coaches) solely for safety reasons because they do not meet modern crashworthiness standards. On the HSE's own figures, there is estimated to be only one passenger fatality per year attributable to the poor crashworthiness of Mk 1 stock and that will be halved by the introduction of the Train Protection and Warning System. However, the fear of a major accident causing multiple casualties weighs heavily on the HSE's corporate mind. But on any reasonable and balanced assessment there is a very weak case to call for the premature replacement of Mk 1 stock, and the level of safety can be improved cheaply and easily by the fitting of a device to prevent overriding.

However, there is another consideration. Slam doors are regarded as undesirable because people fall out of them whilst the train is in motion, usually due to their own irresponsible actions. There are very good operational advantages in having central door locking even if slam doors are to be retained. Station working is more efficient and safer. Passengers can no longer try to board moving trains or jump out before the train stops. Train delays are reduced. Doors which are open whilst trains are moving can damage trains on the adjacent line and cause injuries to passengers. The Southern Region persisted with slam doors long after other Regions adopted sliding doors under the control of the guard because they believed it assisted the rapid movement of passengers joining and alighting. That may have been valid when every station platform was fully staffed but is not so today. The Health & Safety Executive is right to say that central door locking must be fitted to all slam door coaches that are to be allowed to remain in service beyond 1 January 2005, but the justification is

mainly operational. However, the whole subject of new trains and modifications to existing stock is bound up with the letting of franchises, an unholy mixture.

ABOUT THE DRIVER

The details in this section are based on the official report into the accident, by Mr A. Cooksey, HM Deputy Chief Inspecting Officer of Railways, and from evidence given at his public inquiry.

He states that the driver was experienced and should have had no difficulty in stopping safely in platform 3. He had been appointed a driver two and a half years earlier. Mr Cooksey could find no defect in the train's braking system which would have prevented the brakes from operating effectively and he concluded that the driver failed to make the proper brake application, thus being responsible for the accident.

The 24-year-old driver declined to give evidence at the public inquiry on the advice of his legal representatives because they were concerned that, if he were to do so, he could provide information which could subsequently be used against him in any prosecution. No immunity had been granted against any future possibility of a prosecution. They did however point out that the driver had co-operated with the BR private inquiry (the report of which would be available to the inspector). Mr Cooksey commented that the absence of direct evidence from the driver did make his assessment of the available evidence more difficult, and that regrettably it did appear to be becoming an almost automatic response of those representing some grades of railway employee to advise witnesses not to give evidence unless an immunity from prosecution was given. In the event, the Director of Public Prosecutions decided that there was not enough evidence to prosecute the driver.

However, there was a first-hand witness of events in the driving cab as the train ran into the station. A recently qualified driver travelled in the driving cab with the driver's consent and gave evidence at the inquiry, but it was unhelpful in arriving at the cause. He did however hear the driver exclaim that he had lost power in the electro-pneumatic brake and saw that the power controller was in the Off position. He also noticed that the driver had operated the driver's safety device (the well-known dead man's handle), which should result in a full application of the brakes, and he believed that he saw the brake lever in the emergency stop position.

The second driver should not have been in the driving cab because it is well known that there is a risk of distracting the driver at a critical moment. Whether there was any such distraction is not known.

During the inquiry, evidence was heard from the Southern Region's medical adviser, who examined the driver after the accident. As a result of that examination, he formed the opinion that the driver was unfit for driving duties. A urine analysis for drugs abuse had found traces of cannabinoid products. The medical adviser had sought advice on this aspect and this indicated that it would have been relevant at the time of the accident. However, Mr Cooksey, after considerable inquiry into the effects of cannabis use, was unable to reach any firm conclusion as to whether the driver's use of cannabis was the cause of his failure to make a proper brake application. It is, of course, against the British Railways Rules to report for duty under the influence of any drug which might impair the proper performance of duty. The Transport and Works Act 1992 now makes it an offence for an employee to allow the performance of safety-related duties to be impaired by drink or drugs.

One can only speculate, therefore, on the cause of the accident.

WOULD AUTOMATIC TRAIN PROTECTION (OR THE TRAIN PROTECTION AND WARNING SYSTEM) HAVE PREVENTED THE COLLISION?

There is no evidence as to whether ATP or TPWS would be sufficiently responsive to apply the brakes and avoid a collision with the buffers if the driver failed to do so when coasting along a platform line at about 10mph. The final brake application is made within a few yards of the buffers and the ATP system contains a 6mph margin outside the braking envelope before the brakes are automatically applied. Even if ATP/TPWS were effective, the cost-effectiveness of providing such equipment would have to be considered, and care would have to be taken not to allow an excessive reaction to an accident of rare severity. It is intended to provide TPWS equipment on the lines approaching about 700 buffer stops, but how can such expenditure be granted on either cost or safety grounds, and how could it have prevented the Cannon Street accident? Is it a practical application or merely a product of safety hysteria? It will certainly absorb a considerable amount of the available technical resources which could more effectively be employed elsewhere.

MARK 1 COACHES

On 20 July 1999, Deputy Prime Minister John Prescott announced that the Government had set a new deadline of 1 January 2005 for the withdrawal of all Mark 1 coaches. The previous deadline of 2007 had been recommended by the Health & Safety Executive. At the time of writing there are still almost 2,000 of these vehicles in regular service, almost all of them on former Southern Region trains. There is no justification for this change of date on the grounds of safety; it is entirely political.

CHAPTER 9

Terror in the Tunnel -
Two Trains Collide

Britain is regarded as a hilly country and it is therefore no surprise to learn that on the railway network there are many tunnels, ranging from the Severn Tunnel (over four miles long) at one extreme to a host of much shorter tunnels at the other. At one time there were more than 50 tunnels over a mile long, but the line closures of the 1950s and 1960s saw several fall into disuse.

It may be of interest to list the longer tunnels:

NAME	LOCATED BETWEEN	LENGTH
Severn	Bristol and Cardiff	4 miles 628yd
Totley	Sheffield and Chinley	3 miles 950yd
Standedge	Huddersfield and Stalybridge	3 miles 60yd
Woodhead	Penistone and Manchester	3 miles 13yd
Sodbury	Swindon and the Severn Tunnel	2 miles 924yd
(Woodhead Tunnel is now closed)		

A tunnel in its simplest terms is a fairly level hole bored through a hill (or occasionally under a river estuary) in order to avoid the line having to make a circuitous diversion around it. Other tunnels were built on the cut-and-cover principle, where a cutting was dug and then roofed over, but for railway operating purposes the two types of tunnel are regarded as one and it is highly unlikely that passengers make any differentiation.

Very few tunnels are lit and in steam days they were usually full of smoke; they came to be regarded by railway operators, and to some extent by the public, as places of special danger, rather like being in a thick, smelly fog on a pitch black night. It is difficult to visualise the utter blackness of the centre of a long tunnel for those who have not experienced it. They can be fearsome places, with the darkness in some way intensified by the complete silence, punctuated only by the drip, drip, drip of water seeping through the roof, accompanied by a dank, sooty smell. They are not places in which to be alone.

Not all tunnels are straight, which is perhaps a tribute to the skills of 19th century railway builders, but most of them are, and it was intriguing to find after steam working was abolished that it was possible to look all the way through some quite long ones.

This Page
Three views of Totley Tunnel, the second longest railway tunnel in Britain: A historic photograph (top right), showing the tunnel entrance in its Midland Railway days. The date of opening is inscribed as 1893 and the initials 'MR' can be seen on the keystone. A much later, but undated, photograph (above right). Flat-bottomed rails have replaced the earlier bullhead track. Note the enormous growth of trees. A fine shot of preserved 'Jubilee' class engine No 5596 *Bahamas* (right) emerging from Totley Tunnel on 17 June 1973. *IAL/H. Weston/M. S. Welch*

As might be expected, the *Operating Rules and Regulations* make specific reference to the working of trains through tunnels and for dealing with emergencies, and there have been remarkably few collisions in tunnels during the past century. The longest tunnel of all is the Severn Tunnel, 4 miles 628yd long under the Severn Estuary. It was built by the Great Western Railway and opened in 1886 after a very long and difficult period of construction lasting 13 years. It is double track. From the Bristol side the tunnel is on a down grade of 1 in 100 for about two miles; then, after a short level section, it climbs at 1 in 90 for roughly two miles to its exit on the Welsh side near Severn Tunnel Junction station. There is a gentle left-hand curve about three-quarters of the way through.

THE BACKGROUND TO THE ACCIDENT

Until Saturday 7 December 1991, the Severn Tunnel had an excellent safety record, with only two minor incidents in over a century of operation, during which time many millions of passengers had passed through safely. No doubt many of them had breathed a sigh of relief when they emerged safely into the daylight, but such fears were irrational, although understandable in the old smoky steam days. There is less perception in a modern high speed train of travelling through a long tunnel — no smoke, less noise, and a well-lit, comfortable train.

On that Saturday morning faults existed in the signalling equipment, which had the effect of holding signals at danger at the entrance to the tunnel. The train detection equipment in the

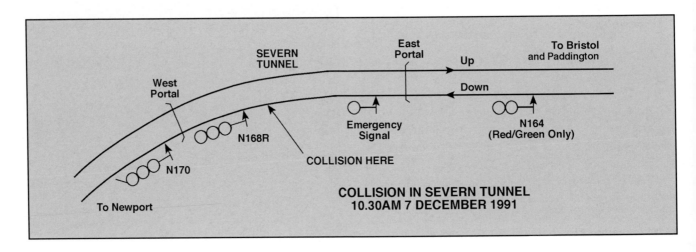

Above Left
The pumping station at Sudbrook 40 years ago. *R. M. Casserley*

Above
Class 31 diesel-electric locomotives Nos 31162 and 31138 coast downhill towards the Severn Tunnel with a mixed freight train on 29 August 1979.
Chris Perkins

Below Right
A Swansea-bound HST, No 253 003, passes through Severn Tunnel Junction station on 7 October 1976.
Les Bertram

tunnel was also out of use and the signalman in Newport power signalbox had no means of knowing whether a train had passed completely through the tunnel. An emergency system was therefore adopted, which consisted of the appointment of handsignalmen at each end of the tunnel, who worked to the signalman's instructions and informed him of the movement of trains.

The handsignalman at the entrance to the tunnel on the Bristol side was located at the signal (No N164) controlling the entrance to the tunnel. This was a two-aspect colour-light signal capable of displaying either a red or a green aspect. It was permanently at red during the failure. Trains therefore came to a stand at the signal and in normal circumstances the driver would have waited a couple of minutes and then climbed down from his cab to speak to the signalman, using the telephone at the signal. The handsignalman prevented that delay and conveyed instructions to the driver which he had received from the signalman. If the line was clear for the train to proceed, the

driver was informed of the circumstances and given permission to proceed past the red signal, obeying all other signals ahead. If the handsignalman had not been there, the driver would have received the same message directly from the signalman. There was no handsignalman present when the two trains involved in the collision passed the signal.

The signalman could not allow a train to enter the tunnel until he was satisfied that the previous train had left it and had passed clear of the first signal (number N170) outside the tunnel. He had therefore appointed another handsignalman to inform him when that happened.

Above
A two-car diesel multiple-unit, No 155304, restarts from Severn Tunnel Junction station on 7 October 1987, forming the 07.47 from Birmingham New Street to Cardiff Central.
A. A. J. Procter

DETAILS OF THE TRAINS CONCERNED

The first train was No 1B10, the 08.30 High Speed Train (HST) from London Paddington to Cardiff. It consisted of front and rear power cars and eight passenger coaches, weighing just over 400 tons. The train was quite lightly loaded with 123 passengers and there were three traincrew members.

The second train was No 1F08, the 07.00 from Portsmouth Harbour to Cardiff, a Class 155 'Super Sprinter' two-car diesel multiple-unit, weighing approx 77 tons. The train was full, and a number of the 168 passengers were standing. The seating capacity was 160. It was manned by a driver and a conductor/guard.

WHAT HAPPENED

The driver of the High Speed Train brought his train to a stand at signal N164 on the approach to the tunnel entrance because it was displaying a red aspect. There was no handsignalman present and he climbed down from his cab to telephone the signalman in accordance with normal practice. The signalman informed him that there were some problems with the signalling and instructed him to pass the signal at danger and obey all others. When a driver passes a signal at danger in such circumstances the Rules and Regulations tell him that he must proceed cautiously and at such a speed as will enable him to stop short of any obstruction. It should have been perfectly safe, because the signalman was satisfied that the previous train had cleared the tunnel and had passed signal N170. He was protected in the rear from the possibility of another train coming through the tunnel and

catching up with him whilst he was travelling cautiously at about 20mph, by signal N164, near the entrance to the tunnel.

The Super Sprinter slowed down as it approached signal N164, and may momentarily have stopped, before it picked up speed and entered the tunnel. There was no handsignalman present. Six minutes separated the two trains but the Super Sprinter, travelling much faster than the HST, rapidly caught it up and crashed into it at a closing speed estimated to be in the region of 30mph. The time was 10.30am. None of the passengers had any inkling of impending danger; so far as they were concerned it was a routine train journey, although those in the HST may have wondered why they were travelling so slowly, and may have wished that the train would get a move on and get out of the tunnel. There is always a slight feeling of unease when a train stops, or moves slowly, in the middle of a long tunnel. It's an irrational feeling, but it's real for some people.

At one moment people in the two trains were relaxing, reading, chatting, playing family games. All the things that people do in trains. The next moment there was an awful bang, which threw many of the passengers in the Super Sprinter from their seats. The Super Sprinter driver and five passengers were seriously injured.

Above
The operating room of Newport power signalbox on 20 January 1963, shortly after its commissioning. The control area was extended in 1968. *British Rail*

The HST was just coming up to the left-hand turn, and the driver was about to apply power for the rising gradient, when he felt an impact. He noticed that the brakes were being applied and he quickly brought the train to a stand. His first thought was that his train had become derailed, and he was satisfied that he had not run into an obstruction, because at 20mph the train's headlight would have picked it up. Nor did he think that another train had run into him. He climbed down from his cab, broke the emergency wire (described later) and walked forward about 100yd to a telephone. Within a couple of minutes he was in touch with the signalman.

He then walked back along his train and met his guard (the senior conductor), then together they walked further and found that the rear power car had become detached. This explained why the brakes had been applied; it had happened automatically when the brake pipes were torn apart. They then saw the Super Sprinter and telephoned for the emergency services.

THE EVIDENCE OF THE DRIVER OF THE SUPER SPRINTER

The driver of the Super Sprinter attended the public inquiry and had intended to take part, but on the advice of his lawyers he

declined to give evidence in public. However, the driver had given evidence at BR's internal inquiry, in which it is reported that he said that he saw signal N164 change from red to green as his train approached it at walking pace. This would indicate to him that the line ahead was clear through the tunnel and up to signal No N170. He therefore accelerated past the signal, as he would be fully entitled to do in such circumstances, and was travelling at 'not far short of line speed' (75mph) when he saw the twin tail lights of the HST ahead. He immediately placed his brake handle into the 'Emergency' position and released the driver's safety device by taking his feet off it (which would have the effect of causing an immediate brake application).

When passing through a tunnel the tail lights are reflected off the rail heads for quite some distance. There is no evidence as to how far they were visible to the driver of the Super Sprinter, but according to the HST driver the HST was just coming up to the left-hand turn, therefore both the HST and the Super Sprinter were on the straight section of line, and the HST's tail lights should have been visible for a considerable distance.

If the driver had driven exactly as he stated at BR's internal inquiry, there seems to be no valid reason why he could not have given the same evidence at the public inquiry. His lawyers could have stopped him at any time if he appeared to be in danger of incriminating himself, and a refusal to give evidence inevitably creates an impression of there being something to hide, no matter how unfair such an impression might be. And it might eventually lead to the bringing of prosecutions so that the driver can be questioned in open court. This is a difficult problem, but the driver's stance does his case no good. Had he stood up at the inquiry and given his evidence frankly and forthrightly he might well have been convincing, but his lawyers advised him not to do so.

THE SIGNALLING SYSTEM THROUGH THE SEVERN TUNNEL

The line is operated under the track circuit block system, with colour-light signals, and is controlled from Newport power signalbox. Track circuits, which are electrically-operated train detection devices operated through the running rails, were originally used to detect the presence of a train, but they were replaced with electronic axle counters in 1987. There had been difficulties in the operation of track circuits in the wet environment of the tunnel and there were frequent failures, which held signals at red and required trains to be sent through the tunnel under the emergency 'caution' procedure, leading to serious delays.

For many years axle counters had been viewed with disfavour, amounting almost to a vendetta, by the BR Board's signal engineers, despite their use worldwide, but eventually they were considered acceptable. Axle counters are attached to the running rails at each end of a section and, as their name implies, they count the number of axles passing over them. If the count at the exit from the section equals the count at the entrance the section is assumed to be clear. There is an axle counter at each end of the tunnel.

Emergency equipment was installed in the tunnel. A readily breakable wire ran along the down-side wall of the tunnel, and if it was broken it caused an emergency signal, a mile inside the tunnel from the Bristol end, to show a red light (the signal was normally unlit). It also gave a visual and audible warning in Newport power signalbox. Telephones connected to the same signalbox were provided every 200yd in tunnel-wall refuges.

An emergency train was stabled on the Welsh side of the tunnel, for use in the case of serious accidents. It consisted of a carriage with accommodation for stretcher cases, two wagons for emergency teams, a van containing fire and rescue equipment, and a 5,000gal water tank wagon. This is a unique arrangement — emergency trains are not provided at any other long tunnel, nor has there ever been a suggestion that they should. The distance in length between the Severn Tunnel and the Totley Tunnel is merely one of degree. Is there a concept of special danger regarding the Severn Tunnel because it has water above it? An emergency train would be of little use if the roof caved in!

THE FAILURE OF THE SIGNALLING EQUIPMENT

There were, in fact, two simultaneous failure conditions, which began with a failure of the electronic remote control equipment two days before the accident. In such a failure the signalman loses the ability to control the setting of routes and the clearance of signals in areas which are not in the immediate vicinity of the signalbox. A standby system is therefore provided, which sets routes in a pre-planned direction and clears the signals, which thereafter act in an automatic capacity, changing to red as soon as a train has passed, then to green as soon as the line ahead is sufficiently clear.

On the afternoon of the day before the accident a driver telephoned from signal N164 on the approach to the tunnel to report that the signal was displaying a red aspect. Although the signalman was unable to tell from his equipment what aspect the signal was displaying, owing to the failure, he knew that the previous train had cleared the tunnel and that signal N164 should have been showing green. He therefore arranged for handsignalmen to be appointed at the signals at each end of the tunnel, and that arrangement continued until 9.30am on the morning of the accident, when a handsignalman could no longer be found for signal N164. It was then necessary to revert to the form of working in which the driver himself has to telephone the signalman for instructions, and this explains why there was no handsignalman on duty when the Super Sprinter came along.

It should be emphasised that the standby system of through routes, and the arrangements for dealing with signals unaccountably at red, are both perfectly safe, provided, of course, that the Rules and Regulations applicable to the working of trains during a failure of the signalling equipment are fully adhered to.

The second failure of equipment concerned the working of the axle counters. With the axle counters out of use, trains were being worked from signal N164 on the approach to the tunnel, to the first signal beyond the tunnel (N170), using handsignalmen where available, which was a form of block working. Obviously, the failure had to be rectified before normal working could be resumed, and there was therefore a great deal of technical activity at the signalling equipment relay room at Severn Tunnel Junction, and elsewhere, in searching for the two faults.

THE PUBLIC INQUIRY

The public inquiry was held in Bristol from 27 to 31 July 1992, and at Cardiff from 26 to 28 October 1992. HM Chief Inspecting Officer of Railways was appointed by the Secretary of State for Transport under Sec 3 of the Regulation of Railways Act 1871 to hold an inquiry into the causes of the accident. He was assisted by two HM Inspecting Officers of Railways, and by other members of HM Railway Inspectorate, and had much specialist advice.

No man can be an expert in all fields of railway operating and engineering, and the evidence into the fault-finding and testing procedures concerning the signalling equipment was extremely complex and detailed. A large number of signal engineers and technicians gave evidence, but there was no indication that any of the activities of such staff had caused signal N164 to switch from red to green just as the second train approached it. It remains a possibility that some action of a member of staff caused such an event; the individual concerned may not even have realised it, or he may have done and kept quiet about it. Railway staff now often go into 'denial-mode' for fear of prosecution. There is no way in which technicians can prove their innocence — so many actions are unwitnessed and unrecorded.

Was there some other way in which signal N164 could switch from red to green? Nothing could be traced subsequently, despite quite exhaustive testing.

The third possibility is that the driver of the Super Sprinter passed signal N164 at danger without the signalman's authority, and that his statement to BR's private inquiry that the signal changed from red to green just as he approached it, and after he had passed over magnets of the Automatic Warning System apparatus in the track 200yd before the signal, is untrue. As is the case with the technicians, the driver has no way of proving his innocence. Even an event recorder (the 'black box') would have been of no help, because whilst it would have recorded that the driver received an AWS warning, which he admitted, it would not have recorded the aspect of the signal.

It may seem a remarkable coincidence that the change of the signal aspect should happen in the few seconds whilst the driver was between the AWS magnets and the signal, and that irregular aspects should not be seen by anyone else, but its possibility cannot be denied. It is also possible that the driver inadvertently passed the signal at danger, then after the trauma of the accident he convinced himself that the signal had changed to green. Such an occurrence is not unknown; it is the mind's defence against the overwhelming guilt of having caused a serious accident. But we shall never know. However, it is rare for a driver to 'miss' a red signal after being prepared to stop at it.

THE FAILURE OF THE INQUIRY

The Inspector in charge of an inquiry into a railway accident is in a very powerful position. He can call any witnesses he wants; call for any documents he wants; have any tests and trials, and technical investigations that he thinks would assist him in reaching a conclusion on the cause of an accident.

The Inquiry sat for many days. It interviewed many witnesses. It amassed a mountain of evidence. It had the assistance of many experts and could have called on the assistance of as many others as it wished. It was entrusted with finding the cause, but some might consider that it failed in that duty when it produced an unsatisfactory conclusion that the cause could be any of the three alternatives. Its duty was to reach a conclusion based on the evidence, and whilst it might have found itself unable to make a firm determination, it should at least have concluded that the weight of evidence pointed in certain directions and reached a qualified judgement.

It might be added that signal engineering staff all over the country were awaiting the Inquiry's report with a degree of apprehension because they, more than anyone, recognised the ever-present possibility of a potentially dangerous lapse by a technician in an equipment room, and they were particularly sensitive in that respect following the Clapham accident three years earlier. Industry insiders take the view that the weight of evidence tends to indicate that the cause of the collision was an accidental reset of the axle counter equipment rather than a signal being passed at danger.

THE AFTERMATH

In years gone by, public inquiries into accidents such as this would have been over in a day, or two at the most. The published report would have occupied less than half as many pages as this one, which has 51. It would have been succinct and positive. There would have been a conclusion as to the cause. There would have been fewer, but more pertinent, recommendations. That expertise seems to have gone.

The Severn Tunnel Inquiry, unable to perform its primary duty of establishing the cause, therefore concerned itself to a great extent with the aftermath, and was almost profligate in its criticisms of BR's preparedness to deal with such an accident. It is easy after an accident to produce a shopping list of precautions, or systems, or equipment or other measures which would have prevented the accident, or dealt more speedily with the aftermath. After an accident, it would be a brave man who would quarrel with such a shopping list, when faced with grieving relatives and the injured. But if such measures are justified after a foreseeable accident, they are surely justified to an even greater degree before the accident, in order to prevent it. However, in the cold light of day, with no accident to influence judgement, all such measures would be carefully examined for practicality and worth. The risks would be assessed, based on expert judgement and experience, and the cost of precautionary measures would be balanced against their value. It has always been so. And the same objective degree of judgement should be exercised when making recommendations after an accident. It is too easy to dream up a shopping list after an accident, especially when you don't know what caused it.

After all, the Western Region had already taken several exceptional measures to deal with emergencies in the tunnel to an extent which did not apply in any other tunnel on Britain's railways. The Region had installed an emergency wire throughout the tunnel; it had provided telephones every 200yd; and it had an emergency train on permanent standby. This did not appear to be sufficient to satisfy the emergency services; they deal in absolutes because they have no bottom line and therefore can afford to do so. The railways, by contrast, cannot afford to deal in absolutes because they must live within their means, and that requires that all expenditure be justified, a philosophy which some organisations appear to find difficult to understand.

CHAPTER 10

Hidden Dangers -
Single Lines

The obvious danger that attends single lines is the ever-present possibility of a collision between two trains travelling over the one line in opposite directions — the head-on crash. Thousands of miles of Britain's railways were built with single track, and much ingenuity was applied in the 19th century to ensuring as far as possible that a train was not allowed to enter a single line from one end after permission had been given to another train to enter the line from the other end.

This was achieved on the more important lines by the use of a token which was issued to the driver by the signalman before the driver was allowed to enter the single line. The tokens were kept in instruments at each end of the single line and the instruments were electrically linked with each other in such a manner that only one token for the section could be available for issue to drivers at any one time. Drivers were instructed that they

Below
One of the traditional token instruments. Tokens can be seen at the bottom of the two inner slots. They are removed through an aperture just beneath the top dial. *Author*

must not enter the single line without a token, which was an added safeguard in addition to the normal lineside signals. Eventually, the signals were interlocked with the token instruments, so that a clear signal could not be given unless a token had been withdrawn from the instrument at that end of the section.

It was (and still is) a very safe system, and served the railways well for many years with only the very occasional lapse, but the extensive use of track circuits allowed different methods to be introduced which did not require the use of tokens. In areas which were not controlled from power signalling centres, a system known as 'Tokenless Block' was introduced after World War 2. Track circuits registered that a train had entered a single line section, and electrical locking on the signals prevented them from being cleared to allow any other train to enter that section in either direction until the first one had occupied and cleared track circuits at the further end of the section. The safety of the system depended heavily upon obedience to the signals by drivers, without the added security of a token, but the safety record of such sections of line is good, aided in some cases by the provision of the Automatic Warning System.

In large areas controlled from a central power signalbox, single lines are worked under the track circuit block system. Single line sections are track-circuited throughout and have colour-light signals at intervals. A signal can only be cleared if a previous train in the same direction has passed beyond the overlap of the next signal, and if no train is approaching in the opposite direction. This system also depends heavily upon obedience to signals by drivers, but has a good safety record. There is a school of thought which suggests that drivers are subconsciously 'programmed' to take extra care when approaching single line sections.

During the rundown of the railway network in the 1960s, there was a fashion for singling long stretches of former double track main line, and this was particularly marked on the former Western Region, which gleefully singled the former Southern Railway West of England main line between Salisbury and Exeter,

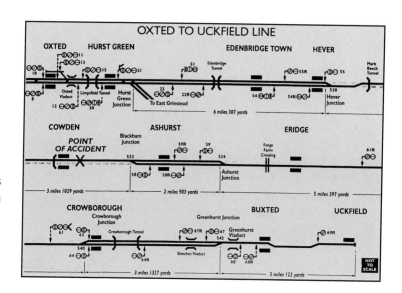

an erstwhile competitor. Railway rivalries die hard, but there was no reason at that time to believe that the decline in railway traffic would not continue unabated, and that the decision to single might not later be regretted. Railway crystal balls are notoriously inaccurate. However, the economics of singling were always dubious, and it was really done to placate politicians who believed that BR had too many miles of track. Cynics would say that engineers can always produce costings to suit any preference. This could only happen on the nationalised railway where no actual money changes hands. The picture on a privatised railway is quite different, an advantage of the latter.

THE SINGLING OF THE LINE FROM OXTED TO UCKFIELD

One line which fell victim to singling runs through the leafy glades of Southern England's commuter territory for 26 miles between Oxted and Uckfield. This former double track line ran through to Lewes at one time, but was cut short at Uckfield in 1969. The track layout on the branch was altered in 1989/90 to include three stretches of single line, and was resignalled with

Facing Page
Views of the South Western Salisbury to Exeter main line: Before singling (top left). 'King Arthur' class 4-6-0 No 30453 *King Arthur* **climbs towards Semley with the 'Atlantic Coast Express' from Bude on 9 August 1958. Before singling (centre left). An undated photograph showing a rebuilt 'Merchant Navy' Pacific awaiting the 'rightaway' from Templecombe with a down West of England express, as an up express enters the station behind unrebuilt 'West Country' Pacific No 34106** *Lydford.* **These were the glory days of the South Western main line. Its unjustified singling by its new owners, the Western Region, destroyed an excellent service and left whole swathes of Dorset and much of the West of England without a decent train service, or without any train service at all. After singling (left). The 16.15 from Waterloo to Yeovil Junction runs into Templecombe behind diesel-electric No 47702 on 7 May 1991.** *Ivo Peters/Paul Riley/Melville T. Holley*

Right
DEMU No 1108 passes Oxted signalbox on 9 September 1982 with the 17.10 from Uckfield to London Bridge. Oxted signalbox controls the signalling on the Uckfield line. *A. O. Wynn*

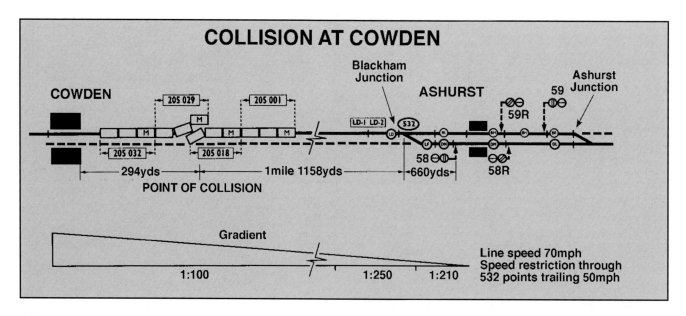

COLLISION AT COWDEN

Line speed 70mph
Speed restriction through
532 points trailing 50mph

Below
Cowden station in the days of the London, Brighton & South Coast Railway. *IAL*

Bottom
A Class 207 diesel-electric multiple-unit (DEMU), No 1309, leaves Cowden station with the 15.10 from Uckfield to London Bridge on 5 June 1982. *Les Bertram*

Below and Bottom
Class 205 diesel-electric multiple-unit No 1114 stands in the old Uckfield station with the 12.10 to London Bridge on 5 June 1982. It is later seen leaving Mark Beech Tunnel with the 14.13 from London Bridge to Uckfield the same day. The heavily-wooded nature of this line is very evident. *Les Bertram*

Above
The new Uckfield 'station', having been moved northwards to clear the level crossing. DEMU No 205025 has arrived with the 14.04 from Oxted. *Brian Morrison*

colour-light signals controlled from Oxted signalbox. AWS was provided at all signals. The line is track-circuited throughout.

This singling scheme was developed in 1986 owing to the condition of the line, and a business case was made for singling parts of it. There are three single line sections (1) from Hever Junction to Blackham Junction, 3 miles 1,029yd, (2) Ashurst Junction to Crowborough Junction, 5 miles 397yd, and (3) Greenhurst Junction to the terminus at Uckfield, 3 miles 122yd. The single line sections are separated by two double line sections: (1) from Blackham Junction to Ashurst Junction, 2 miles 903yd, and (2) from Crowborough Junction to Greenhurst Junction, 3 miles 1,327yd. The timetable is so arranged that trains on the branch travelling in opposite directions can pass each other at normal speed on the quite long stretches of double line. The length of these double line sections also provides some flexibility if trains are a few minutes late, and the points at each end of a double line section are engineered for the moderately high speeds of 40/50mph.

The signals are, with one exception, of the two-aspect red/green type, preceded by a repeater signal capable of displaying either yellow or green. AWS is provided at all signals. The line is sparsely signalled, with approximately five miles between each stop signal, and there are no junction signals at either end of the Ashurst double line section for trains travelling from the single line section onto the double line section.

The economics of this singling scheme must have been finely balanced, when one considers the cost of five sets of expensive points and their associated signalling controls, and illustrates BR's

almost desperate struggle to meet the government's increasingly stringent financial demands in the late 1980s.

THE ACCIDENT

Saturday 15 October 1994 was a typical autumn morning with drifting mist, but colour-light signals and AWS have made the driver's job so much easier and safer in those weather conditions. Trains customarily run at the same speeds as in clear weather.

A head-on collision on a single line is an awful concept, yet it is so rare an event that the possibility of its happening hardly ever enters the passenger's mind. One has to go back to 1921 (at Abermule, on the Cambrian Railways) to find such an accident in which passengers were killed.

The 08.00 from Uckfield to Oxted ran into Ashurst station, passing signal OD58R which was showing a yellow aspect because the stop signal, No OD58, which was beyond the station, was at red. The driver should also have received, and acknowledged, the AWS warning at signal OD58R. After station duties had been completed, the train set off from Ashurst station and should have stopped at signal OD58, half a mile further along, which was still at red, but it failed to do so and continued forward at normal speed and went through the trailing points leading from the double line to the single line at Blackham Junction, 660yd away,

damaging the points as it did so. The permitted speed through these points was 50mph.

Running in the opposite direction was the 08.04 from Oxted to Uckfield. Signal OD58 at Ashurst, mentioned above, was at danger because the signalman at Oxted had decided to give the train to Uckfield priority over the single line section from Hever Junction to Blackham Junction and had cleared signal OD55 at Hever station to allow the train to run over the 3 mile 1,029yd single line section and onto the double-line section into Ashurst station. The scene had inexorably been set for disaster and no power on earth could now stop it.

Up to that point, it had been a normal Saturday morning in Oxted signalbox. The signalman no longer had to worry about the special fogsignalling regulations; they were no longer needed thanks to colour-light signalling. However, he was suddenly alerted by an audible warning that there was something wrong with the points at Blackham Junction, and when he looked at his control panel he was appalled to see that the train to Oxted had burst through the points (which were set in the other direction for the train to Uckfield) and was now running on the single line. Another glance at the panel confirmed his fears — the train to Uckfield had already left Hever station and had passed the last signal, OD55, at which he could have stopped it. The trains were now about two miles apart and were racing towards each other in the mist. There was nothing the signalman could do to prevent a collision, so he telephoned the Control Office to warn them that one was imminent and to ask them to call out the emergency services. The time was 8.28am.

Neither driver had much warning of imminent disaster; the driver of the train to Uckfield had just left Cowden station on the single line and his train was picking up speed. So far as he was concerned it was just another routine Saturday morning. Then he saw the other train, probably not more than 50yd away, hurtling towards him at a closing speed in the region of 60mph. One can hardly imagine what went through his mind at that point, but he

Above Left
Ashurst station in 1962, with new DEMU No 1303 on trial.

Above
Unit No 205028 enters the dilapidated Ashurst station on 13 March 1999 en route for Uckfield. Despite a recent lick of paint, Ashurst station urgently needs the attention of Railtrack's Station Regeneration Programmers. *Author*

Facing Page
Looking towards Cowden from Ashurst station. The line is straight for ½ mile, which provides excellent sighting of signal OD58 in clear weather, but is of little use in fog. *Author*

can barely have had time to realise the full horror of what was about to overtake him. He was killed in the collision less than two seconds later. Also killed were the driver and guard and two passengers in the other train. The passengers were travelling in the first class accommodation at the front of the train.

The casualty list might have been higher if both trains had been travelling at full speed, but the train to Oxted was slowing down for the Cowden stop and was travelling at about 40mph at the moment of impact. The other train was accelerating away from Cowden, but had travelled only 300yd and had hardly reached 20mph.

THE TRAINS

Both trains were lightly loaded, it being Saturday morning, and there were only 15 passengers in total. None of the survivors was seriously injured. Each train was composed of two three-car sets of Class 205 diesel-electric multiple-units. Set Nos 205029 (leading) and 205032 formed the train to Uckfield. They were of Mk 1 design and were built in the period 1960-2. The train to Oxted was similarly formed with sets 205018 (leading) and 205001. They dated from the period 1956-9. The trains would normally have been limited to one three-car set each, but had been strengthened to provide better adhesion during the leaf-fall season, which is a particular problem on the heavily wooded sections of this line.

The collision was very destructive, as might be expected, but of the 12 vehicles in the two trains no fewer than nine remained on the rails. The force of the collision was almost entirely absorbed by the leading vehicle, a driving trailer composite, of the train to Oxted, whose body was completely demolished by being overridden by the leading vehicle of the other train, a driving motor brake standard open. The driving cab of that vehicle was destroyed.

Inevitably, there was criticism of what is considered to be an inadequate degree of crashworthiness of the vehicles concerned, and which resulted in the complete destruction of the body of one coach. If that coach had been full of commuters the death toll would have been very high. However, if a coach body had not absorbed most of the energy of the collision, it would have been absorbed by the other coaches to a greater degree than was actually the case, and it is impossible to say how the coaches of a more recently built train would have behaved, nor what casualties would have occurred. The amount of energy that has to be dissipated remains the same.

THE ACTIONS OF THE TRAINCREW OF THE 08.00 FROM UCKFIELD TO OXTED

The driver was stationed at Norwood Junction and was 31 years old. He had passed out as a driver in September 1993, but did not sign for the Oxted-Uckfield route until May 1994. The public inquiry was told that he was a loner and had a police record concerning drink and assaulting the police 12 months earlier, for which he was fined £200. The guard was stationed at Selhurst depot, and had 10 years' service as a guard. He was 36 years old and had wanted to be a driver but had failed to qualify.

It was perhaps the guard's desire to be a driver that had caused him to ride in the driving cab with the driver on a number of occasions. This is a practice which is forbidden except in two specified circumstances, because there is an increasing belief that the presence of another person in the driving cab can distract the driver at a critical moment. It is, of course, not possible to prove this but circumstantial evidence points in that direction. The guard was riding with the driver on the day of the accident, and it cost him his life. He had already been cautioned twice when

Above
**Signal OD58 (the signal which was wrongly passed at danger) at the
end of the ½-mile straight and just before the line curves left under
Willetts Bridge. The signal is situated in an open area with no
adjacent physical features which might help drivers to locate it in
fog. Since the accident additional safety equipment has been
installed: an AWS warning magnet just a few yards beyond the signal
to alert the driver if he were to pass the signal at danger (although
of no use if the AWS equipment on the train were isolated, ie out of
use); and a SPAD indicator about 100yd further along, identified by
the blue plate surrounding the indicator's aspects. The indicator
flashes red when the signal is passed at danger.** *Author*

caught riding with the driver and had received a final warning
but it had evidently not deterred him. Whether distraction caused
the driver to ignore AWS warnings and pass a signal at danger is
unknown, but it remains a possibility.

There was also the possibility that the guard was actually
driving the train when it passed signal OD58 at danger, and that
both he and the proper driver were so engaged in manipulating the
driving controls that they overlooked the signal, but to do that
they would have had to ignore the AWS warning 200yd before the
signal, assuming that the AWS equipment was working normally.

The next question, therefore, concerns the possible isolation
of the AWS. There are some circumstances in which the AWS has to
be isolated, ie taken out of use, if it malfunctions. The train then
has to be driven without the protection of the system and, in fog,
at not more than 40mph. It was not possible, due to damage, to
determine whether the AWS had been isolated or not, but it is very
unusual for a driver to pass a red signal when he has been alerted
to its presence by an AWS warning. In the case of a two-aspect
red/green signal, such as signal OD58, an AWS warning is a
positive message that the signal is displaying a red aspect. Most of
the serious cases of signals being passed at danger occur when the
driver fails to react to a single yellow aspect; it is rare for a driver
to fail to react to a red aspect, and that lends weight to the
possibility of the AWS being isolated. It may be significant in that
respect that the AWS equipment in the leading cab of the train
from Uckfield had a very bad failure record.

Two final questions — why didn't the driver or guard notice
that the trailing points at the end of the double-line section at
Blackham Junction were set in the wrong position for their train?
And didn't they feel a jolt as the point blades were forced over
when their train ran through them?

THE SEQUENCE OF EVENTS IN THE DRIVING CAB ON APPROACHING AND LEAVING ASHURST

1 ASSUMING THAT THE AWS WAS OPERATIVE

■ An AWS warning would be received when approaching
signal OD58R, which was showing yellow and would
indicate that signal OD58 beyond Ashurst station was then
at red.

■ The driver would acknowledge the AWS warning by
pressing the AWS button on his driving console. (If he did
not do so, the brakes would have been applied automatically
and the train would have been brought to a stand.)

■ The AWS 'Sunflower' in the driving cab would change
from all-black to black and yellow segments as a reminder
to the driver that he had acknowledged an AWS warning
and had taken control of the brakes himself.

■ 200yd further along, the train would pass signal OD58R,
which was showing yellow. The driver would have been
alerted to the imminence of the signal by the AWS warning
even if the signal was not visible when he received that
warning owing to the fog.

■ The train called at Ashurst station, and restarted. This
event could cause the driver momentarily to overlook the
warning he had received at signal OD58R, although the
AWS 'Sunflower' would act as a reminder.

■ Trains are timetabled to pass at Ashurst. It is not
known whether the traincrew realised that they had not
seen the down train and that they might therefore be
stopped at signal OD58 because that train was proceeding
towards them over the single line ahead.

■ Approximately 600yd beyond Ashurst the driver would
receive an AWS warning 200yd before reaching signal OD58,

which is assumed to have been at red. He may not have been able to see the signal at this point owing to the fog.

■ The driver would acknowledge the AWS warning. If he failed to do so the brakes would be applied automatically, but in any case he should have been braking to stop at signal OD58.

■ 200yd further along the train would pass signal OD58. No matter how thick the fog was, the AWS warning would alert the driver to the imminence of the signal.

■ About 200yd beyond the signal the train would pass under Willetts Bridge. If the driver was uncertain of his precise whereabouts in the fog, the bridge would have helped him to locate his position, even in the fog. The driver should also have appreciated at that stage that he had not seen signal OD58, and he should have stopped at once.

■ The train approached and passed through points 532 onto the single line. The train crew did not notice that the points were set in the wrong position for their train, nor did they feel any lurch as the train burst open the points.

2 ASSUMING THAT THE AWS WAS ISOLATED

■ The train would approach and pass signal OD58R, which was showing yellow. The degree of visibility in the fog is not known.

■ The train called at Ashurst station. If the driver had failed to see signal OD58R in the fog he would have realised it by this time, and was required by rule to have assumed that it was showing yellow.

■ Both up and down trains are timetabled to pass at Ashurst. It is not known whether the traincrew realised that they had not seen the down train and that they might be stopped at signal OD58 because that train was proceeding over the single line ahead towards them.

■ Approximately ¹/₂ mile beyond Ashurst station, the train would approach and pass signal OD58, which is assumed to have been at red. Without AWS, and in fog, there would have been nothing to assist the driver to locate the signal. Before the advent of AWS, drivers were skilled in pinpointing their signals in fog, but having had the assistance of AWS for many years that innate, sharply-honed skill may have become a little blunted.

■ About 200yd beyond signal OD58 the train would pass under Willetts Bridge. This would have helped the driver to locate his position if he had been uncertain of his precise whereabouts in the fog, and he should have realised at once that he had not seen signal OD58 and should have stopped his train immediately. There was probably still time to stop safely before reaching the single line about ¹/₄ mile ahead if the driver had made an emergency application of the brake, as the Rules require a maximum speed of 40mph in fog with AWS isolated.

■ The train approached and passed through trailing points 532 onto the single line. The traincrew did not notice that the points were set in the wrong position for their train, nor did they feel any lurch as the train burst open the points. By this time the driver should certainly have appreciated that he had not yet seen signal OD58, although it would have been too late to have avoided a collision.

3 CONCLUSION

It is difficult to understand how the driver could have missed, or failed to react to, the signals and the other significant events described above, even without the help of AWS. With the help of AWS it is inexplicable, and lends some weight to the theory that the AWS had been isolated.

THE USE OF RADIO EQUIPMENT

There are two radio systems in use on BR/Railtrack: the National Radio Network, known as NRN, and Cab Secure Radio (CSR).

The National Radio Network was introduced in 1973 to provide radio communication between the radio control office and men out on the line, and to allow more efficient management of engineer's possessions of the line during maintenance and repairs. The system took a long time to reach its full potential due to the unreliability of the software, insufficient signal strength and inadequate radio coverage. It provides communication between one radio set and another and gives access by radio to the railway ETD telephone system.

The advantages of having radio communication are obvious, particularly in the day-to-day operation of the railway, but the high cost of cab secure radio, and the technical difficulties of installing it nationwide, meant that thoughts turned to the use or adaptation of NRN for this purpose, which was done. A driver can use his radio to communicate with the radio control centre or to obtain access to the BR telephone network, but it is not possible for a signalman to initiate a call to a driver. Whilst, therefore, a driver can give immediate information of a dangerous situation (and he is usually the person who is in the best position to do so), a signalman cannot call to a driver because he does not know the radio call number of the particular multiple-unit or locomotive being used on a particular train, but he can broadcast an Emergency Stop message to all trains in a specific area. NRN was not in use on the Uckfield line.

Cab secure radio is a much more expensive system and its main justification is the ability it gives to operate trains without guards, known as Driver-Only Operation (DOO). It can only be installed in conjunction with a signalling system, the train description system of which is computer-controlled, because the train radio call number is linked with the train identity number shown on the signalbox control and indications panel. Calls between signalmen and drivers cannot be heard by anyone else and signalmen can be assured that they are speaking to the correct driver. It is an excellent system, but excessively costly.

The installation of Cab Secure Radio has been proceeding throughout the London suburban area since the 1980s as quickly as funds can be found for the purpose, but such allocation has to take its turn amongst all the other demands for investment funds. CSR had been planned for the Uckfield line for installation in October 1992, but reductions in the Government's financial support for the railways resulted in the project being deferred. Had it been in operation on the day of the accident, the signalman could have spoken to both drivers and instructed them to make an emergency stop. There was time for this to be effective and prevent the collision. So who is to blame for the delay in installing CSR on the Uckfield line? It must be remembered that CSR was only one of many safety initiatives clamouring for funds. There have never been sufficient funds for all desirable safety initiatives. And there never can be, so it is necessary to be realistic about this and not point the finger of blame in any direction for the lack of CSR on the Uckfield line on 15 October 1994.

THE CONCLUSION

The official report concluded that the driver of the train from Uckfield to Oxted wrongly passed signal OD58 at danger and was therefore responsible for the accident. He paid for his error with his life. Drivers carry a heavy responsibility, and not just for the lives of their passengers. However, as in all collisions where drivers are killed, we shall never know exactly what was happening in the driving cab at the time, but train data recorders will provide some clues. The train concerned in the accident was not equipped with one.

The report also concludes that the line was adequately and safely signalled. But if that was so, how did the accident happen? The line was only safely signalled provided that drivers never, ever, made a mistake, and one must assume, therefore, that drivers are superhuman, because normal human beings are subject to normal human frailties, among which fallibility is one. Signal engineers and operators have never properly come to grips with the need to bridge the gap between the aspect of a signal and the driver's response to it, and it is little short of scandalous that at the end of the 20th century the lives of passengers are at the mercy of human frailties on a line such as the Uckfield branch, where the penalty of the driver's inadvertent passing of a signal at danger is likely to result in his meeting another train head-on.

Irrespective of whether the AWS on the train was isolated or not, the provision in the Rules allowing a train to commence a journey with the AWS isolated should have been withdrawn several years before this accident so far as lines equipped with AWS are concerned. This relaxation is still in force, and even though there is a maximum speed limit of 40mph in fog, it was ineffective in this case.

It is intriguing to note that BR was sufficiently uneasy about the safety of operation of trains under the singling scheme that it went beyond the requirements for the provision of AWS track equipment at signals as set out in its own Standard Signalling Principles, and provided AWS additionally at the two-aspect red/green signals. AWS equipment was also provided a few yards beyond signal OD55 at Hever station (as was done at signal OD58 after the accident) because signal OD55 acts in the nature of a platform starting signal, and there was the obvious danger that, if a driver were wrongly to set off from Hever station on receipt of the guard's 'train ready to start' buzzer or bell signal, the train would enter the single line without authority. No such problem existed at Ashurst with signal OD58, but its location created a different problem in fog if the AWS on the train were isolated. A risk analysis would have identified signal OD58 as a high risk because Ashurst station was situated between that signal and its associated distant signal OD58R — a known risk. In such circumstances the stopping of the train at the station and its restarting creates a risk of the driver's overlooking the warning he has had from the distant signal. Furthermore, signal OD58 is located anonymously without regard to any physical features. It would have been safer to have provided an additional distant signal at the Oxted end of the platform to act as a reminder. Signal OD58R would then have acted as an outer distant and exhibited two yellows. It is evident that the hidden dangers of working trains over this line in fog had not been sufficiently examined, and it is noteworthy that after the accident an additional AWS magnet was provided a few feet beyond signal OD58, plus a SPAD indicator.

There is a modern trend for accident reports to contain long lists of recommendations and this one is no exception, as it contains no fewer than 22. This practice is undesirable on several counts: all recommendations are given the same weight, both the nit-picking and the vital; the distinction between the two categories is blurred; and the railway authorities are given the opportunity to pick and choose which recommendations to follow. There should have been only one recommendation following this accident — *DO SOMETHING TO STOP DRIVERS PASSING SIGNALS AT DANGER*. The new railway companies should stop wasting time in trying to discover why drivers occasionally ignore signals at danger and accept that occasionally they do so. Then do something about it.

At the Coroner's Inquest the jury returned unanimous verdicts of accidental death on the driver and guard of the train from Uckfield to Oxted, and open verdicts on the other three deaths by a majority of 10 to 1. Would it be unkind to suggest that the jury might not have fully understood the evidence presented to them, with its technical complexity and use of railwaymen's jargon?

CHAPTER 11

More Hidden Dangers -
Disaster in the Northern Pennines

HISTORY

There is a line, engineered for high speeds, which
runs for 72½ miles through the fells and valleys of
the northern Pennines, frequently plunging into
long, dismal tunnels and just as frequently striding
across deep ravines on lofty viaducts. For much of
its length it is hardly within sight or sound of any
human life, excepting the remote farmsteads which
are still sparsely scattered in this bleak and
intimidating landscape. Only the hardy sheep see
the trains go by. It is one of the most magnificently
scenic lines in the country and has become one of
the most famous. People travel over it just for the
sheer pleasure of doing so. It is a line that is now
known as the Settle-Carlisle line.

This is the line that some say should never
have been built, but they are wrong. It was built to
give the Midland Railway its own access to Carlisle
and make it independent of its detested rival, the
London & North Western. By the cruel whims of
fate, it lost some of its glory under the rule of the
LMS. It lost still more under nationalisation, when it
became an island within the London Midland
Region, but dependent for its lifeblood on the
uncaring Eastern and North Eastern Regions. For
many years its main role was as a carrier of freight
and when that traffic withered away its future was
in doubt.

The planners then considered what to do with
the line. It had hardly any freight trains, only a
couple of passenger trains, only two stations, and
was fiendishly expensive to maintain. But it had a
hidden role in life — to act as a diversionary route
when the nearby West Coast main line was blocked
by accident or by engineering work. There is no
other suitable alternative, although there were
idiotic suggestions that trains could be diverted via
the Cumbrian coast route, which is far longer, far
slower, and encumbered with loading gauge restrictions. However,
planners were not to be diverted from their objective of closure
by such mundane considerations and they discovered an ally in
the shape of the Serpell committee.

That committee had been established by the Conservative
government in the early 1980s to consider the size of the railway
network. Its report gave three options, ranging from (1) do

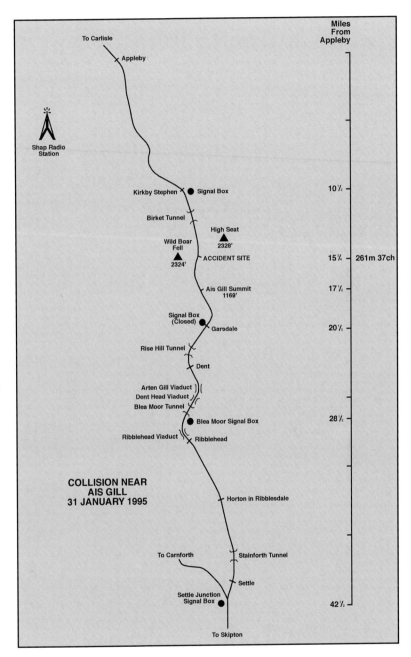

nothing, to (2) slash the mileage by two-thirds, with a midpoint
(3). It was given a scornful reception, but the British Railways
Board felt that it had to make a gesture and it offered three
routes as sacrificial lambs, including the Settle-Carlisle line.
There was a certain amount of tongue-in-cheek about the latter
because the line runs through typical Conservative rural
constituencies and there was bound to be an uproar about the

proposals, but no one could have expected the extent of that uproar. The line suddenly became popular and passenger traffic blossomed assisted, most oddly, by very attractive cheap fare offers. If BR had wanted to close the line it proceeded in a very strange manner by encouraging its passenger business with cheap fares, but then not everyone on BR was in favour of closure.

In the end, the government decided that the line should remain open, since when many local stations have been reopened, an improved passenger service has been provided and, since BR's freight business was purchased by an American entrepreneur, several freight trains run every day. The future of the line seems assured for the first time in almost 40 years.

Top Left
Train 1S68, the northbound 'Thames-Clyde' express, coasts down the remote Mallerstang Valley on 21 October 1972, headed by a 'Peak' class diesel-electric. *D. E. Canning*

Below Left
A Class 47 diesel-electric heads an up express over Arten Gill viaduct, at the head of Dentdale. *Author*

Top Right
'Austerity' class 2-8-0 No 90012 climbs towards Ais Gill summit with a heavy southbound unfitted (unbraked) freight train on 13 May 1961. This photograph brings out well the nature of the terrain, with the lower slopes of Wild Boar Fell on the left. The landslip occurred on the left-hand cutting slope just before the line curves out of sight. *G. W. Morrison*

Centre Right
A fine photograph of a Midland Division 'Anglo-Scottish' express passing Marley Junction, near Keighley, in LMS days, headed by rebuilt 'Royal Scot' No 6103 *Royal Scots Fusilier*. Judging by the stock, this is the 10.30am from Leeds to Glasgow. *E. Treacy*

Below Right
The same engine in early BR days heads a southbound Glasgow to Sheffield service towards Ais Gill summit. The bleak slopes of Wild Boar Fell fill the background. *E. Treacy*

Early in the 1960s, under pressure to cut costs, BR developed plans to close the central, most expensive, section of the line and divert all through trains to the West Coast route, but this was deferred firstly to handle trains diverted from the West Coast main line during its electrification and then to provide a route for loose-coupled freight trains until all such trains were fully fitted with the automatic brake. This had to be done because loose-coupled freight trains could not be allowed to run over the modernised West Coast main line, on which all runaway catch points had been removed. These were spring-loaded points set in the throw-off position, and were provided at intervals on rising gradients steeper than 1 in 260 to derail the rear section of a loose-coupled goods train which had broken in two during the climb and was running away down the gradient towards oncoming trains.

THE PHYSICAL NATURE OF THE LINE

The line diverges from the Leeds-Morecambe line at Settle Junction, near the 235 milepost (measured from St Pancras), at a height above sea level of approximately 400ft. Northbound trains are then immediately faced with an unremitting climb of 1 in 100 for the next 15 miles before plunging into Blea Moor tunnel, the longest on the line. The next 10 miles of the line hug the upper

Top Right
A trainload of gypsum from Drax power station to the British Gypsum works at Kirkby Thore neatly fills the length of Ribblehead viaduct on 3 August 1995. *Author*

Right
Ais Gill summit, at the 259¾ milepost. The derailment occurred just south of the 261½ milepost. *J. Scrace*

Bottom
Arten Gill viaduct stands high above the diminutive beck. *Author*

slopes of Dentdale and Garsdale on fairly easy, undulating gradients, until the summit of the line is reached at Ais Gill, 1,169ft above sea level. There is then a correspondingly long descent along the upper slopes of the lonely Mallerstang valley, under the brooding escarpment of Wild Boar Fell (2,324 ft), mainly at 1 in 100 for the next 15 miles almost to Appleby, after which the gradient eases all the way to Carlisle.

The line runs above the 1,000ft contour line for 17 miles from near Ribblehead to just south of Kirkby Stephen, and for almost all of that distance the trackbed is cut into the slopes of the fellsides. Frequent spells of bad weather are to be expected; rainfall is heavy and snow plentiful. Surface strata are unstable and often waterlogged, and landslips are not uncommon. The major engineering works on the line are mainly in this upland area, with Blea Moor tunnel (2,629yd long); Rise Hill tunnel (1,213yd long), between Dent and Garsdale; and Birkett tunnel (424yd long), between Garsdale and Kirkby Stephen. There are lengthy, high viaducts at Ribblehead, Dent Head and Arten Gill.

TRACK, SIGNALLING AND STATIONS SOUTH OF APPLEBY

The line is double track throughout except for a short section of

Top Left
Kirkby Stephen station and signalbox, looking south, on 25 October 1987. A tunnel inspection train is in the sidings. The station has recently been 'regenerated' by Railtrack at a cost reputed to be £1/2 million. *David Bousfield*

Top Right
A diverted West Coast express passes northbound through a deserted Garsdale station on 29 March 1986. *Author*

Above Left
A wintry scene at Blea Moor signalbox. *Author*

Above Right
A Class 47 diesel-electric passes Settle Junction with a southbound diverted West Coast express, the 11.00 Glasgow to Euston, on 2 May 1987. *Author*

single track over Ribblehead viaduct, and there are signalboxes at Kirkby Stephen; Garsdale (normally closed), 9³⁄₄ miles away; Blea Moor, 18 miles from Kirkby Stephen; and Settle Junction, 14 miles from Blea Moor. The Absolute Block System of signalling is in use. During the line's heyday there were no fewer than five intermediate signalboxes between Kirkby Stephen and Blea Moor.

There are unstaffed passenger stations at Kirkby Stephen, Garsdale, Dent, Ribblehead and Horton-in-Ribblesdale. Settle station is manned on one shift.

The maximum permitted speed on the line is 60mph.

THE RADIO SYSTEM
(AT THE TIME OF THE ACCIDENT)

The National Radio Network provides coverage of the line through radio base stations located at intervals. These base stations were provided to give coverage of the nearby West Coast main line and calls from trains are therefore transmitted to the Railtrack Control Office at Crewe, even though control of the line is exercised from York Railtrack Control Office.

A separate radio unit is installed in the driving cab of each train, and every radio unit has its unique radio call number. Calls are normally initiated from trains; they cannot be initiated to trains from other places unless the caller is aware of the unique radio call number of the radio unit located in the cab occupied by the driver, and the area code of the radio reception area where the train is.

In addition, there is an emergency facility which the driver can activate by pressing an 'Emergency' button. This puts him in immediate contact with the Radio Control Office and the controller can then broadcast an emergency message which is relayed through loudspeakers in the driving cabs of all trains within the coverage of the particular radio base station being used.

The Shap radio base station covers the area in which the accident occurred, but coverage extends northwards only as far as the southerly end of Birkett tunnel, about two miles to the south of Kirkby Stephen.

All calls to the Radio Control Centre are recorded.

WEATHER CONDITIONS

The weather during January 1995 was a mixture of frost and snow followed by rain and thaw punctuated by sunny intervals. During the week preceding the accident, which happened on 31 January 1995, there was a moderate snowfall on the 25th, a slow thaw on the 26th, a severe overnight frost on the 27th followed by a blizzard which quickly turned to rain. A thaw set in on the 28th, accompanied by rain. The 29th was reasonably fine, but heavy

Above Left
Dent station signalbox on a winter's day, 11 February 1983. The low buildings beyond were for shelter for men engaged in snow clearance. *G. Scott-Lowe*

Above Right
A southbound fitted freight, headed by Class 5 4-6-0 No 44671 working hard, passes Ais Gill signalbox in August 1963. *P. Hocquard*

rain started late on the 30th and continued unabated until late on the 31st. A local weather station recorded 2½in of rain in those 24hr.

The snow and thaw of the week before the accident had caused the ground to become waterlogged and it could not absorb the downpour. Water cascaded down the fellsides with a ferocity rarely observed. Normally dry gullies became rivers, and streams became torrents. Roads were flooded and impassable and Stainforth tunnel, just to the north of Settle, was blocked by floodwater. The sodden ground became unstable and landslips are not unknown on this line.

On the morning of the accident, the trackwalker had patrolled the line, but no sign of a landslip was evident.

EVENTS LEADING UP TO THE COLLISION

The trains involved in the collision were the 16.26 and 17.45 stopping passenger trains from Carlisle to Leeds. They were each formed by a single two-coach Class 156 diesel multiple-unit.

The 16.26 train left Carlisle on time, but at about 17.00 the line was closed through Stainforth tunnel owing to flooding. The train was held at Kirkby Stephen from 17.23 to 17.51 pending a decision to run the train as far as Ribblehead, conveying passengers for the intermediate stations. It was then the intention to reverse the train there and cross it to the northbound line so that it could return to Carlisle. The operations at Ribblehead were under the control of Blea Moor signalbox, which was the next signalbox open from Kirkby Stephen.

Left
A Class 156 'Super Sprinter' stands in Carlisle station awaiting departure for Leeds via the Settle line on 31 October 1990. *Ian S. Carr*

Centre Left & Below Left
The landslip, the derailment. *Author's collection*

Bottom Left
A Class 156 'Super Sprinter' stands in Ribblehead station on a Carlisle to Leeds service on 4 October 1990, with Whernside (2,416ft) in the background. The northbound platform has since been reinstated and the station buildings are being restored. *Tom Clift*

The 16.26 returned from Blea Moor at 18.34 en route to Carlisle and ran nonstop. It passed Ais Gill summit (at 259 miles 60 chains from St Pancras) and started the long 1 in 100 descent. The weather was atrocious with heavy, driving rain, and it was pitch dark in the upper Mallerstang Valley, which lies between Wild Boar Fell on the west and the almost equally high escarpment of the Pennine moors to the east. It would be difficult to imagine a more desolate spot on such a night.

The train was running at about 60mph (the driver had no reason to do otherwise) in the inky darkness, with the windscreen wiper making little impression against the force of the rain. The driver could see nothing and would have little idea as to his precise location but Birkett tunnel, a few miles further along, would help him to locate his position. He never reached it. Less than two miles from Ais Gill the train ran into a landslip which had covered the northbound line (the down line) with several feet of mud from the fellside slope on the left. The front coach veered away to the right and came to rest with the front of the coach blocking the other, southbound, line. The landslip occurred at 261 miles 31 chains at a location known as Ash Bank, grid reference 776985, altitude just over 1,100ft. The time was probably 18.47 or 18.48, the latter being the time that an emergency radio call was recorded as being received in the Railtrack Control Office at Crewe.

Meanwhile, events were building up to a climax. The 17.45 from Carlisle left 11min late, and although the traincrew had not been informed that the line to Leeds was blocked, the signalmen assumed that the train would be dealt with in the same manner as the 16.26. The train arrived at Kirkby Stephen at 18.47, and when the normal station duties had been completed the train set off once more for the south. Nothing was said to the driver about the line ahead being blocked in Stainforth tunnel, and certainly nothing was said about the derailed train now blocking his route only five miles away. The two events — the derailment, and the 17.45 departing from Kirkby Stephen — were almost simultaneous.

Rising gradients of 1 in 100 hold no terrors for Class 156 units and speed built up to almost 60mph. Drivers on the Settle-Carlisle line are used to dirty weather and no doubt find conditions much more comfortable in the cab of a DMU than on the windswept footplate of a steam engine as in former years. It may have been a dirty night but otherwise it was a normal

journey and the driver was sitting relaxed at the controls waiting for the road bridge at Ais Gill and the lights of the cottages to give him a landmark. He never reached Ais Gill. Suddenly he saw two faint red lights less than ¼-mile ahead and made an emergency application of the brake, reducing speed to about 35 mph when the collision with the derailed DMU occurred with a sickening thud, cab to cab almost head-on. The time was 18.55, 7-8min after the derailment.

RESCUE OPERATIONS

Both trains were fairly lightly loaded; there were no passengers in the rear coach of the 17.45 and only about six in the front coach of the 16.26 on its northward journey.

A more remote and difficult-to-reach location could hardly be imagined. The nearest towns from which help might come were Penrith, almost 30 miles away, and Carlisle, nearer 50. The only road access was the narrow B6259 down in the valley, which might well be flooded and impassable. However, help did arrive, but the only way for the emergency services to reach the train was to struggle up a very muddy, slippery slope through a field. It would have been impossible to transfer injured passengers down that slope, therefore a rescue train was sent from Carlisle, which then took both injured and uninjured passengers to Carlisle. Twenty-six people were treated in Carlisle hospital, six of whom were detained, including both drivers. There were five serious injuries.

THE DUTIES OF THE TRAINCREWS — SAFETY OF THE LINE

The term 'Safety of the Line' is one of those revered phrases stamped in the minds of all railway operators. It implies that when the line is blocked by accident, or in any other way measures must immediately be taken to prevent any train from running into the blockage. Such measures are known as 'Protection of the Line' and are set out in the Rule Book. They have always been part of the railwayman's safety culture and his reaction following a mishap has traditionally been almost instinctive — that the line must be protected at all costs. Examples abound of injured railwaymen struggling down the line to raise the alarm.

The London, Midland & Scottish Railway Regulations Book, quaintly titled the General Appendix, in operation until 1960, set it out clearly and succinctly:

> *The FIRST duty of drivers and guards is to see that proper protection is afforded to their train; their SECOND duty is to take steps to prevent fire; and their THIRD duty is to render assistance to passengers. Though they will be most anxious to do the latter, it must be clearly understood that the other two points which require attention to prevent further disaster have prior claim over anything else, and in the order named.*

The detailed arrangements at the time of the accident were set out in Section M of the Rule Book, and the relevant parts are as follows:

■ If the train is stopped by accident, obstruction, etc, the driver and guard must immediately ascertain whether any other line is obstructed.

■ If it is immediately apparent that another line is obstructed, the driver and guard must take a hand danger signal (ie a handlamp at night) and detonators (small explosive devices which fasten to the rail head and are detonated by the wheels of a train) and proceed to carry out protection.

■ The driver must protect any line used by trains in the opposite direction, and the guard any used by trains in the same direction.

■ If only one person is available he must carry out protection on the line from which trains approach (ie the opposite line).

■ The person concerned must exhibit a hand danger signal (ie a red light) and place detonators on the line at specified distances up to 1¼ miles from the obstruction, but if a train approaches before that distance has been reached, detonators must be put down as far from the obstruction as possible.

■ The signalman must be informed and, if he gives an assurance that adequate signal protection is being given, it is not necessary to proceed more than 300yd from the obstruction.

The Rule Book instructions make no reference to the use of radio for protection purposes. There is, however, a reference to emergencies and protection in the instruction booklet for the use of the National Radio Network, some of the relevant parts being:

■ The driver has the ability to make an emergency call by pressing a single red button, which cuts off normal calls and connects immediately to a Radio Control Centre (at Crewe in this case).

■ Radio Control Centres can broadcast a priority call to all drivers in a particular base radio station area. This will be heard over the loudspeaker in driving compartments.

■ Communication by radio with the signalman does not reduce the urgency of any protection required by the rules. *However, the instructions are silent on the question of communication by radio with Radio Control, so far as protection is concerned; it should also have been stressed that such communication similarly does not reduce the urgency of protection.*

THE ACTIONS OF THE TRAINCREW OF THE 16.26 FROM CARLISLE

The driver of the 16.26 became trapped in his cab with a broken ankle when the derailment occurred, but he pressed the emergency button on his radio, giving him immediate contact with the Railtrack Control Office at Crewe. The driver reported that his train was derailed after hitting a landslide and was fouling both lines between Kirkby Stephen and Blea Moor. He also confirmed that the emergency services were needed and asked for both lines to be protected, which the controller agreed to do. The actual words were:

Driver: 'Blea Moor to Carlisle, derailed blocking both roads. Can you stop the job between Kirkby Stephen and Blea Moor.'

Control: 'We'll arrange all that, driver. Over and Out.'

Note: In railway jargon, 'stopping the job' means stopping all train movement.

The white lights at the front of the train were changed to red by either the driver or the guard, it is not known which.

It is understood that the guard (conductor) of the 16.26 was informed by the driver that the controller was arranging for the job to be stopped, although the precise words used are not known as the driver cannot remember them. Passengers gave evidence that the guard escorted passengers from the leading coach, on which the lights were out, to the rear coach, on which they were still lit. He was near the gangway between the two coaches when the collision occurred and he was thrown out of the train by the impact, suffering fatal injuries. Several passengers also were injured.

COULD THE COLLISION HAVE BEEN AVERTED?

The 16.26 was derailed at about 18.47 or 18.48. The collision occurred at 18.55. If the guard had carried out protection immediately he might have been able to proceed northwards far enough to be able to give timely warning to the driver of the 17.45, even taking into account the awful weather conditions; and even though he might have been too late to prevent the collision, it might have occurred at a lower speed. In any case, the guard would have avoided losing his life. The 17.45 was booked to leave Kirkby Stephen at 18.41 and had it done so it would have arrived at the accident site virtually as the derailment was taking place at 18.47/8. Whether either driver or guard of the derailed train appreciated, in the abnormal conditions, the imminence of the 17.45 and the urgency of protection, is not recorded.

The driver of the 17.45 did not have a distant view of the red lights on the 16.26 because the latter was standing round a curve, hidden from a distant view, but the guard would not have had to proceed very far before reaching the straight section of line, in which case he could have given earlier warning. That assumes that the driver of the 17.45 would have been able to see the red light from a handlamp at a reasonable distance in the prevailing weather conditions, which was not necessarily the case. So there is no certainty that, even had the guard set off at once to protect his train, he would have been successful in alerting the driver of the 17.45 any earlier.

One can only speculate as to why the guard did not immediately carry out protection, but the assurance which he had from the driver that Control would arrange for the job to be stopped must have played a part, even though such assurance did not override the requirement to carry out protection. It is also possible that the change of emphasis in the guard's duties in recent years from being in charge of the train and responsible for safety to a more business emphasis on fare collection and general customer care had some effect.

The actions of Crewe Control were critical. They received the emergency call from the driver of the 16.26 at 18.48, at about the same time as the 17.45 was leaving Kirkby Stephen. Even had the radio telephone number of Kirkby Stephen signalbox been readily to hand, it is doubtful whether a call could have been made to the signalman in time for him to throw his starting signal back to danger before it was passed by the 17.45. However, there was time for a call to be made by the Control directly to the driver of the 17.45 by responding to the emergency call with a general emergency alarm to all drivers within the Shap base radio station area. Unfortunately, the driver of the 17.45 might not have received it, because he could have been north of Birkett tunnel, or even in the tunnel, at the critical moment, and he may then have been outside the range of the Shap radio station.

It must also be borne in mind that the Crewe Controller had no knowledge of train movements on the Settle-Carlisle line, and could not be expected to know how urgent the situation was. He could not be expected to divine that if he had repeated an emergency warning a couple of minutes later to all trains in the Shap radio reception area, there was every chance that it would have been heard by the driver of the 17.45 and the collision averted.

Both York Railtrack Control and York Regional Railways Control were helpless because, whilst they might have had some idea that there was a southbound train within a few minutes running time of the derailed DMU, they could not immediately warn the driver. It seems common sense that train control, line control and radio control should be in the same office, but it was not so. It was a casualty of railway reorganisation, but following the accident Railtrack proposed to transfer both radio control and operational control to Manchester.

THE HIDDEN DANGERS

Had this derailment occurred in the days before radio and when guards were guards and not conductors, it can fairly confidently be expected that the guard would have carried out protection without delay and the collision might then have been prevented. That is how it had always been.

However, this accident reveals two hidden dangers which illustrate the hazards of introducing new concepts without sufficient appreciation of their effect upon established patterns of behaviour in a disciplined operation:

■ The introduction of radio as a means of giving early warning of an emergency.

■ Giving the guard responsibilities for ticket inspection, fare collection and customer care.

Both concepts in themselves are admirable.

The introduction of radio involved Controllers for the first time in protection of the line responsibilities, through the use of the Emergency button by the driver. Controllers are not trained and qualified in the Operating Rules and Regulations (although they generally acquire some knowledge) because it has not been necessary. Protection has been the responsibility solely of drivers, guards and signalmen. If Controllers are to be involved in emergency life-and-death situations they need to be trained in how to react instantly and correctly. A properly trained Controller would not have given an assurance that he would arrange for 'the job to be stopped' unless he was in a position to do so. He would also have reminded the driver of the need to carry out protection duties.

One has a great deal of sympathy for the guard. He had received some sort of assurance from the driver that Control were arranging for the job to be stopped. He had also received a lot of training in the complexities of ticket issuing and inspection and his responsibilities for his 'customers' were repeatedly, and rightly, emphasised. These were part and parcel of his daily life; protection of the line was not, but merely a remote possibility that may never occur. Management's enthusiasm to make the guards an integral part of the commercial, business-led railway had led inevitably to a shift of emphasis away from the requirements of the Rule Book. The priorities which were set out in the old LMS General Appendix are still applicable today. Protection of the line must come first.

It is interesting to note that the Rule Book edition issued in 1999 recognises the changes in the role of the guard and the reducing need to protect the rear of the train. Henceforth, protection of the train will be carried out exclusively by the driver, leaving the guard free to look after the passengers, with the very important proviso that the guard must satisfy himself that the driver is able to carry out protection. If the driver is unable to do so for whatever reason, the guard must undertake the driver's protection duties, which incidentally is exactly the situation which arose in the Mallerstang accident.

POSTSCRIPT

Mrs Irene Rawnsley was a passenger on the 16.26 from Carlisle and has kindly allowed the author (a neighbour) to quote from some notes she made the same evening whilst in the Cumbria Hotel at Carlisle after being taken there by BR.

'I had been watching the rain all day and felt uneasy, so I phoned BR and was assured that trains were running normally. When I got to the station I bought a local paper and was taken aback somewhat by a headline "Carlisle will be cut off by floods at 6pm". I boarded the train and we left safely. I sat opposite a girl with a tiny baby in her arms. The conductor was a friendly man who came to talk to us and he

explained that there were floods outside Settle and he was waiting to see if we could get through.

'After leaving Garsdale station we were told that the train would be turning back at Ribblehead and returning to Carlisle. The rain was still spilling over the windows on the return journey and it was pitch dark outside.

'Sometime before seven we crashed; there was a heavy thump, the train slewed sideways and I clutched the table. All the lights went out. Our conductor came to explain that we had hit a landslide and that the driver was trapped in his cab and probably hurt. The last coach still had the lights on and he ushered us through. We were not to see him alive again.

'My friend with the baby was holding a hanky to her nose, which was dripping blood. She asked me to take the small bundle to allow her to mop it up.

'Suddenly there was another impact, bigger this time, as the southbound train hit the front of ours which was blocking the line. The baby set up a loud yell but mercifully she wasn't hurt. The lights went off again and we were really frightened.

'We were at the highest point of the line where there is nothing but hills all round and a long way from the road. The rain was still noisy on the windows and there was a smell of mud. There was nothing to do but wait.

'After what seemed ages we saw lights outside and the yellow helmets of firemen, followed by the paramedics, and the mountain rescue with hot coffee and muddy blankets. They had come over the fells below Wild Boar Fell, where it had been impossible to stay upright, one said.

'Before midnight a train came down from Carlisle to take us to hospital. Seeing the wreckage from outside, lit up by floodlights, I began to sob, realising what I had been through.

'At the inquest into the death of the conductor I talked to a former BR officer and confessed to him my nervousness about trusting myself to a train since the accident. "You've no cause to worry," he said. "It's not likely to happen to you again. Most people live a lifetime without being in a rail accident. You were in two within 20 minutes."

'There's a plaque on Leeds City station, a memorial to Stuart Wilson, our kind conductor. I leave flowers there whenever I pass through.'

AN ASTONISHING COINCIDENCE

Almost four years to the day, on Friday 15 January 1999, there was another derailment and collision caused by a landslide less than 10 miles away, near Crosby Garrett tunnel. Weather

conditions had been remarkably similar, with snow, frost, thaw and several inches of rain, which caused quite a small landslip on the downside cutting slope only about 50yd before the southern portal of the tunnel. None the less, there was sufficient mud to derail a northbound train, the 17.47 from Leeds to Carlisle, a two-coach Class 156 diesel multiple-unit (a 'Super Sprinter'), which came to a stand at 19.40 with about half of the front coach outside the northern end of the 181yd-long tunnel, and partly obstructing the other line. It was pitch dark.

The conductor guard of the Sprinter had noticed that Kirkby Stephen's up distant signal was in the clear position when he passed it a few minutes earlier, and he knew that there was already a train in the section on the opposite line. After the derailment, driver and conductor guard rapidly conferred and the driver, John Metcalfe (a former mayor of Carlisle), made an initial radio contact with Northern Spirit's control centre. Knowing that he must also carry out detonator protection as required by the Rules, he went forward on foot to place detonators on the southbound line. He had not had time to reach the full distance of 1¼ miles when he heard the throb of a diesel locomotive working hard, a Class 60 with 32 loaded coal hopper wagons, but he managed to put one detonator on the line about 300yd from his train and waved his red lamp vigorously.

He had several anxious minutes as the freight train went by him with brakes squealing. He wondered whether he had gone far enough to prevent a collision, but then he heard what he described as 'an almighty clatter'. However, by his prompt action in raising the alarm he succeeded in warning the driver of the coal train, who almost managed to stop his heavy train before hitting the Sprinter corner to corner, pushing it back into the tunnel. The speed at the time of impact was no more than 3mph. The freight train had in fact stopped a short time previously because the driver had noticed that the engine was overheating, and it is possible that his train had not yet regained normal speed when the detonators were exploded.

Right
Looking northwards towards Crosby Garrett tunnel on the morning after the accident. The landslip occurred on the left-hand cutting slope about 50yd before the tunnel, and had already been partially cleared when this photograph was taken. *Author*

Right
Looking into the gloomy rock cutting at the north end of Crosby Garrett tunnel. The kink in the up line, denoting where the collision occurred, can be seen just beyond the man nearest the camera. The diesel locomotive is at the head of the breakdown train working in the tunnel. *Author*

Below
A dramatic view of the derailed and damaged Super Sprinter in the tunnel, after it was pushed back by the force of the collision. Damage to the diesel locomotive was slight. *Photograph courtesy of Cumberland News, Carlisle.*

The radio report to Northern Spirit's control centre concerning the derailment had resulted in a broadcast message being sent to the driver of the freight train, instructing him to stop, but by that time the driver had already applied his brakes.

There were more than 20 passengers in the Sprinter, but all escaped serious injury and they were taken to Crosby Garrett village hall about half a mile away, where a pie and pea supper, followed by a slide show, had been in progress. A member of the audience was alerted by his pager and several of the audience, including a doctor and local farmer, went to give assistance.

By great good fortune, and thanks to the prompt action of Driver Metcalfe, the consequences of this accident were not so severe as the accident four years earlier, but they could easily have been much worse. If the coal train had been a little nearer, and travelling faster at the point of impact, its 1,400-ton gross weight would have made mincemeat of the lightweight Sprinter in the confines of the tunnel, a scenario too awful to contemplate. But accidents are full of 'ifs'.

The Settle-Carlisle line has always been prone to landslips due to the nature of the terrain through which it passes and the foul weather which is not uncommon in the area. Railtrack has now taken steps to identify, if possible, the more vulnerable parts of the line, so that remedial action can be taken to improve the drainage and stabilise the cutting slopes. If remedial action is not practicable on the scale required, consideration should be given to imposing a speed limit when weather conditions dictate caution. Such action is needed to reassure both passengers and traincrews, as no one can predict with any degree of accuracy the timing and precise location of landslips. The HSE has issued improvement notices requiring Railtrack to take action to reduce the possibility of a similar accident in the future.

CHAPTER 12

Watford South Junction -
Thursday 8 August 1996

One of the previous accidents at Watford. On 23 January 1975 the electric locomotive and first vehicle of the 22.15 sleeping car express from Euston to Glasow plunged down an embankment after striking a glancing blow to a derailed train, the 19.10 express from Manchester to Euston, coming the other way. The Manchester train had become derailed after it ran into some steel stillages which had fallen from a freight train. The latter had been attacked by thieves in the North London area who had left the van doors unsecured. *M. C. Barker*

The West Coast main line through Watford is a very busy place, and it is not surprising to find that over the years before 8 August 1996 there had been several serious accidents in the area. The causes were a miscellany of faulty loading, mechanical defects, vandalism and faulty permanent way, but none of the accidents resulted in passenger fatalities, although two drivers were killed. It is also noteworthy that drivers were not responsible for any of them, which is remarkable in view of the number of trains passing through that area, often at full speed.

Thursday 8 August 1996 was a perfectly normal, routine day. The 17.04 from Euston to Milton Keynes, a North London Railways service, called at Harrow & Wealdstone and was approaching its next stop at Watford Junction, running on the down slow line. There were about 200 passengers in the four-car Class 321 electric multiple-unit and many of them were preparing to alight.

The down slow line signal at Watford South Junction, No WJ759, was at red because the signalman had decided to divert an empty stock train (ie a train of empty coaches) from the up slow line to the up fast line across its path. He was entitled to do this as a routine train regulating decision because its path across the down slow line was protected by a red signal, and the signalman was equally entitled to believe that the driver of the 17.04 from Euston would stop at that signal. That is the whole basis of signalling — that drivers stop at signals when required to do so.

However, this was not to be a routine day. The driver of the 17.04 from Euston did not stop at the signal but passed it at over 40mph and finally came to a stand with the front of the train 167yd beyond the signal and foul of the points between the down slow line and the up fast line. The time was 17.24.

At that precise moment the empty stock train, travelling at about 50mph, entered the series of crossovers to take it from the up slow line to the up fast line, and partway through that movement it struck the stationary passenger train at a slightly oblique angle, resulting in the crushing of the driver's side of both cabs. The slightly angled impact caused the leading coach of each train to be thrown sideways and upwards, with the passenger train coach coming to rest on its side partially overhanging an embankment. One passenger was killed, being thrown by the force of the impact through the rearmost right-hand window of the first coach, and of the 69 injured passengers who were taken to hospital, 15 were detained. The drivers and guards of both trains were also taken to hospital with injuries and detained.

All accidents are surrounded by 'what ifs' and 'if onlys'. If the driver of the passenger train had applied his brake a split-second sooner, his train would have stopped a few yards clear of the empty stock train, and there would have been only a near-miss, heart stopping for both drivers, but unnoticed by most of the passengers. If it had travelled a few yards further the two trains would have met head-on, because the lie of the points ahead, which had been set for the empty stock train to travel southbound from the up slow line to the down slow line and thence to the up fast line, would have diverted the passenger train across and on to the up slow line. It is a matter of speculation as to the manner in which the kinetic energy of the empty stock train would then have been dissipated.

DESCRIPTION OF THE TRACK AND SIGNALLING

This section of the West Coast main line has four tracks, running roughly north and south. Reading from west to east, the tracks are down fast, up fast, down slow, up slow. Watford South Junction is about 700yd south of Watford Junction station, and consists of two ladders of crossovers, from down fast to down slow, and from up slow to up fast.

The maximum permitted speed of trains is 110mph on the fast lines and 90mph on the slow lines, with a restriction to 75mph on the slow lines through the platforms at Watford

Junction station. Train movements from one running line to another through the crossovers at Watford South Junction are restricted to 50mph.

Both fast and slow lines are electrified at 25kV ac on the overhead line system.

The area is signalled with four-aspect colour-light signals, controlled from Watford power signalbox, and is track-circuited throughout. The Automatic Warning System (AWS) is in use.

DESCRIPTION OF THE TRAINS

Both trains were composed of Class 321 four-car electric multiple-units, built by British Rail Engineering Ltd at Derby between 1988 and 1990. They have a maximum speed of 100mph. The passenger train had one four-car set; the empty stock train had two.

Below
A Class 310 electric multiple-unit, No 310093, arrives at Watford Junction with the 12.35 from Euston to Milton Keynes on 5 February 1983. *R. S. Freeman*

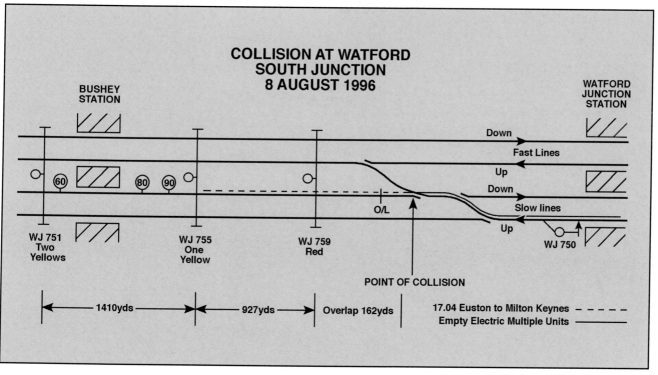

COLLISION AT WATFORD SOUTH JUNCTION 8 AUGUST 1996

BUSHEY STATION

WATFORD JUNCTION STATION

Down

Fast Lines

Up

Down

Slow lines

Up

60   80   90

O/L

WJ 751 Two Yellows

WJ 755 One Yellow

WJ 759 Red

WJ 750

POINT OF COLLISION

1410yds   927yds   Overlap 162yds

17.04 Euston to Milton Keynes – – – – –
Empty Electric Multiple Units ————

DETAILED DESCRIPTION OF THE RUNNING OF THE 17.04 FROM EUSTON

The sequence of signals approaching Watford South Junction on the down slow line, and the aspects which were being displayed for this train, were as follows:

- Signal WJ167   Green
- Signal WJ751   Two yellows (preliminary caution)

Bushey station

- Signal WJ755   One yellow (caution - next signal showing red)
- Signal WJ759   Red - stop.
- Signal WJ751 is 1,410yd from signal WJ755, which is 927yd from signal WJ759. The sighting distance from the driving cab of signal WJ755 is 470yd, and for signal WJ759, 402yd.

There are permanent speed restrictions of 60mph for 487yd through the area of Bushey station, and of 80mph for 387yd immediately following.

This page
A Class 321 electric multiple-unit of the type used on both trains involved in the collision at Watford South Junction on 8 August 1996: Unit 321320 (top) approaches Kenton on the up slow line heading for Euston on 28 February. Another Class 321 (above left) approaches Bletchley on 26 February 1989. The neat layout of controls in the driving cab of a Class 321 unit (left), photographed in 1989. The AWS acknowledgement button is located in the centre of a white disc on the desk.
Brian Morrison/Barry Smith/Brian Morrison

Above
Electric locomotive No 86219 passes Bushey with the 07.00 from Manchester to Euston on 29 April 1978, running on the up fast line. *Brian Morrison*

THE ON-BOARD TRAIN DATA RECORDER

These recorders are fitted to all North London Railways Class 321 units, in each driving cab. They record a whole range of activities, including speed, acceleration, brake application and AWS activity. The recorder in the leading cab of the 17.04 from Euston had stopped some hours before the accident, but most detail was recorded on the recorder in the rear cab, except for AWS activity. The information stored in the recorder was found to be very slightly inaccurate, reading 4min slow and about 2mph on the low side. The following details have been adjusted accordingly.

The on-board data recorder provided valuable information of the running of the train. After the Harrow stop, speed reached 82mph on the approach to Bushey station (at which the train is not booked to stop) before the driver braked to 60mph for the permanent speed restriction. At this point he had already passed signal WJ751 showing two yellows and had acknowledged the AWS warning.

At the end of the 60mph restriction the driver accelerated on full power past signal WJ755, which was showing one yellow. At this point the train was travelling at 65mph and continued to accelerate for a further ¼ mile, reaching 68mph, when power was shut off and a full brake application initiated 455yd before signal WJ759, which was passed at about 45mph.

The AWS equipment was in proper working order, therefore the driver would receive warnings 200yd before reaching signals WJ755 and WJ759. He must have acknowledged the warning at WJ755 or the brakes would have been applied. The warning approaching WJ759 was irrelevant, as the driver had already made a full brake application when the signal came into view and he saw that it was at red.

WHY WASN'T THE AUTOMATIC WARNING SYSTEM EFFECTIVE?

There have been many cases in which drivers have failed to respond to AWS warnings and have run on into collision or derailment. In four-aspect signalling, drivers receive two warnings when approaching a red signal, the first one 200yd before the signal displaying two yellows, and a second one 200yd before the signal displaying one yellow (there is also the same warning 200yd before the red signal, but by then it is too late). Each warning has to be acknowledged by the driver pressing a button on his control desk, and if he fails to do so within a couple of seconds the brakes are immediately applied.

It seems inconceivable that a driver can acknowledge receiving two warnings and yet take no action to apply the brake to stop the train at the red signal, yet it happens. Distinguished psychiatrists and behavioural psychologists have spent many fruitless hours, and earned large consultancy fees, in trying to discover why this happens, but without success. An experienced railwayman might retort, without any fee, that it happens because drivers are human beings and human beings make mistakes, therefore it would be more productive to apply scientific methods to counteract such errors.

Automatic warning systems are over a century old and the BR Automatic Warning System was devised almost half a century ago. Unfortunately, in the understandable haste to devise a system on the postwar nationalised railway, a fundamental risk was built into it — the use of the same warning sound in the driving cab to denote a colour-light signal showing two yellows and one showing one yellow. In either case, only the same common response was required from the driver (the pressing of the acknowledgement button), which did nothing to bring to his attention the vital distinction between the two signals. Fifty years ago this was not quite so important as it has become in the intervening years. Braking systems were not as efficient as they are today and there were many more freight trains, which required long braking distances. The double yellow signal was of much greater importance then.

It still is in the case of HSTs and other trains running at high speed, but not so far as electric multiple-units are concerned. The driver of a Class 321 unit approaching Watford would not need to take any action to brake when passing signal WJ751 showing two yellows, because he would have ample braking distance between signals WJ755 and WJ759 — 927yd — and he would see signal WJ755 ¼-mile away. Even if had he failed to act then, he should have been alerted by the AWS warning 200yd before the signal, giving 1,127yd distance in which to brake safely before reaching signal WJ759.

On the day in question the driver braked from 67mph to zero in about 600yd. This surely underlines very clearly the superfluity of the warning at the double-yellow signal for trains with highly effective braking systems, and the vital need for a quite distinguishable warning at a single yellow signal. However, British Rail and its successors have chosen to go down different paths.

THE SPEED RESTRICTIONS AT BUSHEY — THE HIDDEN DANGERS

Were there any other factors that might have had a bearing on the driver's passing signal WJ759 at red, that might have misled him, or even led him into a trap? Consider the series of external influences on the driver's actions when approaching signal WJ759 at red. He passes signal WJ751 showing two yellows when he is already braking for the 60mph permanent speed restriction approaching Bushey station. Just beyond the station there is a sign inviting him to accelerate to 80mph, followed fairly quickly by another one enticing him to accelerate still further to 90mph. The 90mph sign is 3yd beyond AWS warning magnets in the track, and just short of 200yd to signal WJ755, which is showing one yellow, the vital signal. Is it possible that the proximity of the acceleration signs and the yellow signal might occasionally cause some confusion in the driver's subconscious?

There is an intriguing reason for the speed restrictions at Bushey, which has nothing to do with that station nor with the condition of the track there, but has everything to do with signal WJ759.

When the resignalling at Watford South Junction was commissioned in 1993 it had the effect of reducing the overlap beyond signal WJ759 (the signal which protects the junction) from 200yd to 162yd. It might not have been considered particularly significant at the time — a reduction of only 38yd — but it was

critical on 8 August 1996. If the standard overlap of 200yd had been in existence then, the collision would not have occurred, but perhaps that might be considered fortuitous. An overlap is provided as a safety margin in case a driver should misjudge his brake application; it is not there as a protection against a driver's failure to react to a yellow aspect at signal WJ755 and not apply the brakes until he sees signal WJ759 at red.

The correct solution would have been to move signal WJ759 38yd further from the fouling point at the junction, but that would have introduced other problems, because in its new position it would have been directly underneath some electricity company power lines, which was felt to be undesirable. An alternative solution was therefore considered.

It was initially decided to impose a 60mph permanent speed restriction for ¼-mile on the approach side of signal WJ759, which would probably just have been effective in this case. The commencement point of the speed restriction would have been 602yd from the end of the overlap beyond signal WJ759. The train concerned braked from just over 60mph to zero in about 500yd on the day of the accident. However, that was rightly thought to be cutting things too fine, and it was therefore decided to impose the speed restriction at Bushey station, on the basis that if a train left the speed restriction at the required 60mph, and if the driver correctly acted upon a single yellow at WJ755, safety would be assured. It did not, and was not intended to, provide for a driver who failed to react to a single yellow at WJ755. The signalling system is not meant to provide safeguards against a driver who fails to respond correctly to the signal aspects displayed; that is the role of automatic warning systems.

WAS THERE ANY PARTICULAR HAZARD AT SIGNAL WJ759?

Records are maintained of all cases in which drivers pass signals at danger without authority. They are known as SPADs (signals passed at danger). It transpired that the SPAD record of signal WJ759 (the signal protecting the junction) was abnormally bad, and four SPADs had occurred there in the previous three years. There are 36,000 signals capable of showing red on Railtrack's lines, and WJ759 holds the equal worst record in Railtrack's Midland Zone.

The previous SPADs all appear to have been mismanagement of the brake by the driver, and resulted in overruns of 48yd, 20yd, 41yd and 54yd. If at any signal there are two SPADs in 12 months, or three in three years, the signal must be the subject of an inquiry, but no such inquiry was held.

WOULD THE TRAIN PROTECTION AND WARNING SYSTEM (TPWS) HAVE BEEN EFFECTIVE?

There is little doubt that an Automatic Train Protection system (ATP) of the type which has had extensive trials on the Great

Western line and the Chiltern line would have prevented this accident, but it has been decided that such a system is too expensive for general adoption. In the meantime the West Coast main line, and indeed much of the railway system, is no better protected now against a driver's error than it has been for the past 30 years. In the next few years it is intended to install on the West Coast main line a highly technical system of train control which does not rely upon the driver's observation of lineside signals but conveys instructions to him in the driving cab and incorporates ATP. To fill the gap, Railtrack intend to install a Train Protection and Warning System (TPWS).

To assess whether TPWS would have been effective in preventing the Watford South Junction collision it is necessary to consider the relevant principles of TPWS. At locations such as Watford South Junction, where failure to stop at the junction protecting signal is likely to cause a collision, a speed trap will be installed on the approach to that signal (WJ759 in this case). The equipment will measure the speed of the train, and if it exceeds a predetermined level the brakes will be applied automatically.

The location of the speed trap is critical. It must not be too far from the signal to inhibit train speeds unnecessarily, but it must be sufficiently far away to bring safely to a stand within the overlap any train caught in the trap. It will only be effective in doing so for trains travelling at less than line speed. Other trains are almost certain to stray beyond the safety overlap, but that is inherent in the scheme. It might just have been effective in the current case if the speed trap had been installed at the maximum distance of 500yd, because it would have initiated an immediate full application of the brakes a couple of seconds before the driver did so, and the train might then have stopped a few yards clear of the fouling point of the crossovers, instead of a few yards beyond it.

RAILTRACK'S ACTIONS AFTER THE ACCIDENT

In order to reduce the risk of signal WJ759 being passed at danger, the 60mph permanent speed restriction at Bushey was extended all the way to that signal, which had two benefits:

■ The possibility of a driver being misled by the 80 and 90mph lineside signs just past Bushey station and in the immediate proximity of signal WJ755, so that he overlooked the message being displayed by the signal, was removed.

■ If a driver failed to respond to a yellow aspect at signal WJ755 and did not apply the brake until the junction signal WJ759 came into view, it is probable that he would be able to stop his train just within the overlap.

There was, however, a disadvantage. Trains which did not stop at Watford Junction would then have had to keep within the 60mph limit for an additional ¾-mile before accelerating.

After the trial (see below), special controls were imposed

on the aspects displayed by signal WJ755. When signal WJ759 is at red, signal WJ755 will also remain at red until a train is close to it, after which it will change to yellow. Whilst this will not ensure that the speed of the train is reduced if the driver should fail to react to the signal aspect (the AWS warning at a red signal is the same as it is at a yellow signal), experience shows that a red signal has more impact on a driver's mind than a yellow signal, as indeed happened in this case. The 60mph permanent speed restriction was then withdrawn. Those special signalling controls should have been imposed in the first place when the junction was remodelled, instead of a speed restriction, in which case it is unlikely that the accident would have happened. Why wasn't it done? Was it because business management had replaced functional management without the appropriate safeguards?

THE TRIAL

The driver of the 17.04 train from Euston to Milton Keynes was charged with manslaughter, in that on 8 August 1996 he unlawfully killed a passenger. The trial took place at Luton Crown Court between 26 February and 11 March 1998. The judge, the Hon Mr Justice Wright, gave not only an admirable summing up of the case but also a very good definition of the term 'manslaughter'. He said that it means causing the death of another person by gross negligence, by a reckless disregard of the lives and safety of other people.

The prosecution alleged that the driver had failed to brake after passing signal WJ755 at yellow because he anticipated that the next signal, the junction signal WJ759, would have changed from red to one of the proceed aspects by the time it came into his view and that there would be no need for him to reduce speed.

The defence admitted that the driver had wrongly passed signal WJ759 at danger, but put forward two factors which we have already explored — the potential for misleading the driver in the close proximity of speed restriction signs, AWS magnets and a signal near Bushey, and the substandard overlap of signal WJ759. The defence also suggested that there were more effective and therefore safer ways of dealing with the problem of the short overlap.

The role of the jury is to be judges of fact, but whether its members fully comprehend all the technical detail put before them in a complicated case such as this must be a matter for conjecture. However, the driver chose to give evidence and thereby subjected himself to cross-examination by the prosecution; it also gave the jury the opportunity to study the driver's mien. One never knows what happens in a jury room, but it is quite possible that the jury considered whether the man they had seen in the witness box was capable of reckless disregard not only of the lives of his passengers but also of his own life — he is more vulnerable in his driving cab at the very front of the train than are his passengers. That, surely, is one of the virtues of the jury system. In this case they found the driver not guilty after a very short retirement.

So far as can be ascertained, no driver has ever been found guilty of manslaughter, or of endangering the lives of his passengers, in cases to which he has pleaded 'not guilty'. In this case, the driver had to wait, on tenterhooks, for 18 months before he knew his fate. That seems unreasonable and unjust. If justice is to be done, it should surely be done more speedily.

The effect of such an accident on a driver is considerable. In his subconscious mind he is travelling on green signals when suddenly, and without warning, he is confronted by a red. He brakes at once and is concerned that the signalman may have replaced the signal to red owing to a sudden emergency. The nature of that emergency is almost immediately revealed to him when he sees another train heading straight towards him and he realises in a flash that a very heavy head-on collision is imminent and inevitable. It has probably not entered his mind at this stage that he himself may have made an error. His mind is fixed on whether he will survive. In the event he is badly injured.

The mental processes that drivers commonly go through in such circumstances start with asking what went wrong. Who is to blame? There is a feeling of anger, followed by denial. The driver in this case initially believed that he had green signals, but then there may have come a dawning realisation that he himself might have been to blame. This can lead to an overwhelming feeling of guilt, at having possibly caused deaths and injuries to his passengers, as well as millions of pounds worth of damage. In such circumstances it could be almost too much to bear and be followed by a period of rationalisation, during which the driver attempts to come to terms with reality. Following the trauma of a serious accident and severe personal injuries, it is not surprising that a driver's recollection of events may not always be wholly accurate.

Drivers carry a heavy responsibility; they are not given the status the job deserves, nor the pay. And every minute they face the possibility of a human error that might land them in court. Fortunately, juries are more perceptive than they are sometimes given credit for.

In his summimg up, the judge said that the prosecution's case was that the driver deliberately took a chance, when he passed signal WJ755 at a single yellow aspect, that signal WJ759 would have cleared at least to a single yellow by the time it came into view, even though he must have known that if it was still at red he could not possibly pull up in time. Was that ever a credible and realistic allegation?

DETAIL TAKEN FROM THE ON-BOARD DATA RECORDER

TIME (min/sec)	SPEED (mph)	LOCATION	POWER/BRAKE	REMARKS
18.39	72	WJ751		Double yellow 571yd to PSR board
			Step 3 braking	
		AWS for PSR	Coasting	
	58	60mph PSR		
19.08	58	Bushey stn		
19.21	60	AWS for WJ755	Notch 4 Power	90mph line speed starts in 3yds
19.26	63	WJ755	Notch 4 Power	Single yellow
19.41	67		Notch 4, then Notch 3,	
			Notch 1, then coasting	
19.44	67		Brake handle to full application	
19.48		384yd from WJ759	Braking	Brakes fully applied
19.58	41.86	WJ759	Braking	Red
20.14	3.14	167yd beyond WJ759	Braking	Point of collision

NOTES
PSR — permanent speed restriction
AWS — Automatic Warning System
Notch 4 — full power
Times in minutes and seconds
Actual clock time 4min later than shown on recorder
Actual speed 2mph faster than shown on recorder

CHAPTER 13

Southall – 19 September 1997:
Just Another Step on the Long Road to Safety

Southall lies about nine miles from Paddington station, London, on the main line of the former Great Western Railway to the West of England and South Wales. There are four lines at this location, reading from south to north: down main, up main, down relief and up relief. Each line is bi-directional, ie signalled for train movements in the up direction (towards Paddington) and in the down direction (towards Reading).

In addition, there are a number of crossovers between adjacent lines and there are connections to sidings on both sides of the line. The line speed at Southall on the main lines is 125mph. There was a temporary speed restriction of 100mph in force about six miles away between Reading and Slough but it is likely that full line speed would have been attained by Southall.

Above Left
Southall, a few days after the accident, looking towards Paddington. The ladder crossing has been removed and replaced with plain line. A Class 165/1 'Thames Turbo' heads towards Paddington on the up main line, whilst Class 60 No 60044 hauls a train of empty 'Yeoman' wagons from Acton Yard to Merehead. *Brian Morrison*

Above
Looking towards Paddington from the footbridge at the end of Southall station on 2 February 1999. From left to right the lines are: up relief, down relief, up main (on which the HST involved in the accident was travelling), and down main. The ladder of crossovers has been restored and are in the distance opposite the diesel unit on the up relief line. *Author*

Four-aspect colour-light signalling is installed and all four lines are continuously track-circuited. The standard British Railways Automatic Warning System (AWS) is installed both on

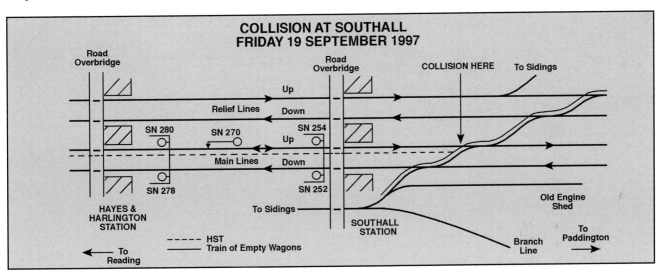

COLLISION AT SOUTHALL
FRIDAY 19 SEPTEMBER 1997

Road Overbridge · Road Overbridge · COLLISION HERE · To Sidings

Up · Relief Lines · Down

SN 280 · SN 270 · SN 254 · Up

Main Lines · Down

SN 278 · SN 252

HAYES & HARLINGTON STATION · To Sidings · SOUTHALL STATION · Old Engine Shed · To Paddington · Branch Line

- - - - - HST
————— Train of Empty Wagons

← To Reading

Above
A massive gantry erected to carry signals SN252 and SN254 on the approach to Southall station. The gantry was constructed to such a height to clear the overhead electric wires and to provide for the safety of technical staff attending to the signals. These signals protect the ladder of crossovers beyond the other end of the station. *Author*

Below
A view of the wreckage of the collision at Southall on 19 September 1997, looking towards Paddington. *Ken Brunt*

the track and on trains. Automatic Train Protection equipment is laid in between the rails.

The sequence of signals approaching Southall on the up main line is as follows:

■ Hayes & Harlington station, 10¾-miles from Paddington. Just beyond the Southall end of the platform. A gantry straddling both main lines and carrying signal SN280 for the up main line and signal SN278 for up direction movements over the down main line. Long-range sighting of signal SN280 is restricted by an overbridge at the station and the gentle left-hand curve of the line, but its location is well defined by the overbridge and the station.

■ Signal SN270 on an unusually tall, straight post, with the red aspect 16ft 2½in above rail level and grossly misaligned - focussed into the ground approx 90yds from the signal instead of at driver's eye level 220yds away.

■ A gantry straddling both main lines and carrying signal SN254 for the up main line and signal SN252 for up direction movements over the down main line. The gantry is located immediately before a road overbridge, immediately beyond which is Southall station, nine miles from Paddington.

■ When the crossovers at Southall are set for a movement to cross the up main line, signal SN254 will show a red aspect, signal SN270 one yellow, and signal SN280 two yellows.

DESCRIPTION OF THE ACCIDENT

The 10.32 High Speed Train from Swansea was approaching Southall on the last leg of its journey to Paddington, and running at almost 125mph. It was a fine day and passengers would be on the point of collecting all their belongings together and thinking about their forward journey from the terminus. Should they take a tube, or perhaps a taxi if there wasn't too long a queue? Or even the mundane, but often very convenient, bus? They probably did not know that the section of line between Slough and Paddington had seen more than its share of accidents in recent years, but even if they had been aware of that fact it was unlikely to have worried them unduly; railways are very safe.

They were also not to know that at that very moment, the signalman was setting a route at Southall for a train of empty hopper wagons to cross from the relief lines to some sidings on the south side of the line, a move which would require the goods train to cross the line on which their own train was approaching at well over 100mph. Even if they had known, they would

Below
Class 59 diesel-electric locomotive *Yeoman Challenger* stands at Old Oak Common on 15 February 1987. A locomotive of this type was in use on the freight train involved in the accident.
M. J. Collins

probably have trusted in the signalling system to ensure that their train did not miss the signals and crash pell-mell into the empty wagons. It should have been an entirely safe and proper action by the signalman, because the movement of the goods train was protected on both sides by colour light signals at red, preceded by another signal at yellow and, further back still, another signal displaying two yellows. The protecting red signal on the up main line, No SN254, was approximately 600yd from the crossovers.

At 1.14pm the unthinkable happened. What had been to the passengers a normal, routine journey, suddenly became a nightmare. They were not to know that the AWS was not working and that the ATP System was out of use. The HST did not stop at the protecting red signal. It did not even stop before the crossovers, but continued forward and smashed into the empty wagons across its path. It was travelling at an estimated speed of 100mph. The leading power car of the HST caught the wagons of the stone train a glancing blow but remained upright and came to a stand in about 100yd. The first coach, a first-class vehicle, followed it, then overturned but was not badly damaged. Much of the force of the impact was absorbed by the second coach, also a first-class vehicle, which was almost bent double. The remainder of the train received significantly less damage, especially those vehicles towards the rear.

Seven passengers lost their lives, and 13 were seriously injured. The fatalities all appear to have occurred in the badly damaged second coach. A massive electrification mast which had unwittingly been erected near the junction between the main and relief lines may have contributed towards the extent of the damage to that coach, because it impeded the free movement of the vehicles of the HST across the full width of the formation whilst the train's momentum was expended. However, that was a misfortune, and no one's fault.

TRAIN FORMATIONS

The High Speed Train, No 1A47, the 10.32 Great Western Trains service from Swansea to London, was marshalled as follows: power car, two first-class coaches, a trailer restaurant first buffet, four standard-class coaches, power car.

The freight train was No 6V17, the 09.58 from Allington to Southall. It conveyed 20 empty bogie hopper wagons used for carrying stone and was hauled by a Mendip Rail Class 59 diesel-electric locomotive, No 59101.

THE DEVELOPMENT OF THE GREAT WESTERN RAILWAY'S AUTOMATIC TRAIN CONTROL (ATC) SYSTEM

Towards the end of the 19th century many railway companies were experimenting with equipment to warn a driver when he was approaching a distant signal which was in the 'caution' position, both as a means of reinforcing his visual observation of the

signal and as a safeguard if he should fail to do so.

The incentive to devise such a system for the Great Western was provided by a serious accident at Slough, 10 miles from Southall, on 16 June 1900. The 1.5pm passenger train from Paddington was standing in Slough station when the signalman at Slough East signalbox was asked by the signalman at Dolphin signalbox, a mile along the line towards Paddington, if he could allow a Paddington to Falmouth express to approach Slough station. As the line through the station was occupied by the 1.5pm from Paddington, the signalman at Slough East responded that the Falmouth express could only be allowed to approach if the driver of that train was informed of the situation and warned to approach cautiously.

The signalman at Dolphin signalbox therefore maintained all his signals at danger in order to stop the Falmouth express and inform the driver accordingly, but the driver ignored all the signals and ran past at over 50mph. Disaster might still have been avoided if the driver had then responded urgently to the distant signal on the approach to Slough East signalbox, but he failed to do so and ran into the rear of the train standing in the station at 25-30mph, killing five passengers and seriously injuring 35 more.

This was a great blow to the Great Western's pride, and the company's staff set about devising a suitable Automatic Warning System. In January 1906 experimental apparatus was installed on the branch line to Henley from Twyford. Briefly, it consisted of a ramp laid lengthwise between the rails, which made contact with a spring-loaded shoe fixed underneath the engine. When the distant signal was in the 'clear' position the ramp was electrified, and the current passing through the shoe rang a bell in the engine cab. If the signal was at 'caution', no current passed through the ramp, and the raising of the shoe broke a circuit on the engine and caused a steam whistle to blow.

Later that year there was a more extended trial on the branch to Fairford, which starts a few miles north of Oxford. These trials were so successful that in November 1908 ramps were laid at all distant signals between Reading and Slough, then in 1910 between Slough and Paddington. The system was refined to apply the brake if the driver failed to acknowledge the warning. The line between Paddington and Reading thus became one of the safest sections of line in the country, at least during Great Western days. Since nationalisation there have been several serious accidents on it, although mainly from causes other than drivers wrongly passing signals at danger.

THE BR AUTOMATIC WARNING SYSTEM (AWS)

The Great Western was the only one of the four main line companies to install ATC on a wide scale between the wars, but after nationalisation BR developed its own system — AWS — which was similar in some ways to the Great Western's system, but used a non-contact system, the ramp being replaced by permanent and electro-magnets. Over the years, the ATC equipment was replaced by AWS equipment in the interests of standardisation, allowing universal working of all traction units.

Although Great Western and BR Western Region drivers had had the benefit of ATC/AWS since almost the beginning of the century, BR's AWS was regarded only as an aid to drivers and it was still their duty to observe and obey signals. Instructions regarding the working of AWS, issued in 1960, emphasised in heavy print that 'the system is merely an aid to a Driver and does not relieve him of his responsibility for observing all signals'. This is understandable, because most lines and some traction units had not yet been equipped with AWS, but it is also the case that AWS was a vital safeguard in case the driver should fail to obey a signal.

Similarly, if the equipment failed to operate correctly and had to be isolated, the driver was required to work his train without its assurance, which at that time was reasonable because a driver might be working with AWS one day and not the next. However, the position became less and less satisfactory as the years went by and drivers everywhere grew used to having the 'aid' of AWS. If the AWS failed, the driver had to isolate it before he could continue, but he was not required to take any further action except to report the defect at the first locomotive depot or stabling point at which they arrived.

The 1972 instructions are similar, except that the driver was required to report a failure to the signalman at the first convenient signalbox, whose signalman was then required to inform the Traffic Control Office. The latter had to arrange for the locomotive or train to be taken out of service as quickly as practicable, no other guidance being given.

Even as recently as 1984, the emphasis on the system being merely an aid to drivers was still included in the instructions for its use. However, there was a new instruction that a locomotive or multiple-unit fitted with AWS apparatus must not leave a depot or stabling point/siding to enter service with the AWS isolated (ie out of use) in any part of the train. There was also some guidance for the Traffic Control Office — the taking out of service of a locomotive or unit had to be done at the earliest opportunity commensurate with the avoidance of unnecessary cancellation or delay, but no guidance was given on the interpretation of 'unnecessary'. Did it allow a passenger train to work from a point of isolation for several hundred miles without AWS?

By 1990 the reference to leaving a depot or stabling point/siding had disappeared, and the instructions merely stated 'must not enter service'. The instruction that AWS was an aid to a driver was no longer emphasised nor was it in heavy print, but its retention indicates the official view that AWS was still merely an aid and not an essential safeguard. The word 'unnecessary' referred to in the previous paragraph had disappeared from the instructions, which now simply read 'The train must be taken out

of service at the first suitable location, without causing delay or cancellation.' This would certainly allow a passenger train to run for several hundred miles without AWS if a replacement train set were not available to which the passengers could be transferred without delay. Under privatisation, and indeed during the later years of BR, replacement trains were not thick on the ground. During fog or falling snow speed is not allowed to exceed 40mph, if the AWS is isolated.

Revised instructions issued in October 1993 merely restate the instruction that the train must be taken out of service at the first suitable location, without causing delay or cancellation, whilst the most recent instructions, dated February 1998 (six months after the accident), state that 'the driver must take the train out of service at the first suitable location, without causing delay or cancellation'. No guidance is given to the driver as to how he is to achieve this; it is in fact a matter for Operations Control.

Does this give carte blanche for an HST to shuttle back and forth all day long between Paddington and Bristol or South Wales, with the AWS isolated in one or even both power cars, if a replacement set were not available? This would not only be quite unsatisfactory but also potentially dangerous, and the time has surely come for AWS to be regarded as an essential safeguard and not just an aid. No train should be allowed to begin a journey with the AWS isolated; a driver would be unlikely to work a train if the horn were defective or if the windscreen wipers didn't work, and AWS might be considered even more vital. If the AWS were to become faulty during a journey and had to be isolated to allow the train to proceed, there should be a limit on both distance and speed — not more than 50 miles at not more than 50mph.

The catalogue of subtle changes in the precise wording of the isolation instructions in periodic reissues of the Appendix is an example of the hidden danger in not examining, and updating where necessary, instructions in line with changed circumstances. When HSTs were introduced, and for several years afterwards, two drivers were required to be on duty in the driving cab if speeds were to exceed 100mph, but subsequently the requirement to have an additional driver was dispensed with under a productivity agreement. It had proved to be unnecessary, but only with the AWS operative. This was the moment when consideration should have been given to the critical situation that would arise if the AWS were isolated on a train required to run at more than 100mph, and the instructions should have been amended. It was not done.

Fortunately, some of the Train Operating Companies have recognised the inadequacy of the 1993 instructions, and have taken the initiative to limit the distance by making arrangements for defective trains to be replaced at specific locations or, in the case of trains capable of being driven from either end, for the units to be turned on a triangular layout.

After the accident, the Railway Inspectorate wrote to all Train Operating Companies, giving more precise guidance on the interpretation of 'a journey', meaning a single journey in one direction, but far more firmness was needed to clarify the confusion which appears to have arisen in the interpretation of 'enter service' and 'journey'. 'Enter service' means exactly that; the engines are started up and the train is put into running order after being out of use. It is all very well for the Railway Inspectorate to write to the Train Operating Companies and to quote Railtrack's Group Standards, but men at the workface who have to deal with these matters follow the instructions in the Rules and Regulations. Those are their bible, not the Group Standards, and it is the Rules and Regulations that are defective and need amending to lay down clearly and unambiguously what is required.

THE USE OF THE AUTOMATIC TRAIN PROTECTION SYSTEM

This system is described in detail in Chapter 5. The Great Western line was one of the two which were chosen for trials, and contracts for the installation of the equipment were awarded to ACEC Transport in 1990. The trials began in 1991 with High Speed Trains but have been prolonged and the system is still not regarded as being sufficiently satisfactory for it to be taken into service as an integral part of train operation. It is not considered to be an essential part of the train's safety equipment, therefore it is perfectly in order for trains to enter service and remain in service indefinitely without the use of ATP, even though the train may be equipped with ATP.

This is a very unsatisfactory situation. Millions of pounds have been spent and it should be possible by now to have ATP operating day in and day out on High Speed Trains working between Paddington and Bristol, and vice versa. Failure to do so robs the railways of the additional security which ATP can bring. It is a bitter irony that the the ATP equipment was serviceable on the journey from Swansea, but the driver who manned the train from Swansea was no longer qualified to use it, his qualification having expired. It was therefore not switched in. He was relieved at Cardiff by a driver who was passed out in its use, but the Rules do not allow it to be switched in during a journey. The train therefore went forward without the benefit of ATP, which would have prevented the accident.

INVESTIGATIONS INTO THE CAUSE

The crash investigators need to satisfy themselves on a number of points. Was the signalling system working correctly and were all point and signalling changes recorded in the signalbox event data recorder? Was there conclusive evidence of the aspect being displayed by the protecting signal on the up main line, No SN254? Was the AWS track equipment working correctly?

So far as train equipment was concerned, was the train's braking system in order? Was the AWS working correctly (we know now that it was not), and if not, when and where had it been isolated? Was the ATP in use, and was it working correctly (we

know now that it was not)? There was no requirement for it to be in use for the train to be worked normally. Was the train equipped with data recorders (ie 'black boxes')? Were they working and what did they reveal? (They were not working, because they only work when the ATP is switched on.)

It is suggested that the driver's view of some of the signals approaching Southall on the up main line had been worsened , consequent upon changes to the location of those signals caused by overhead line electrification masts erected for the new Paddington-Heathrow service. Some signals are now erected on gantries 18ft above rail level, whereas they were previously at eye level. Railway Group Standard No 37 requires a red aspect on a straight post to be 11ft above rail level; on the critical signal SN280 (the double-yellow signal) it was 17ft 10½in. According to evidence, the driver failed to see the double-yellow aspect of signal SN280 at Hayes and Harlington station, which would be in his view for only a few seconds at full speed owing to the overbridge at the station and the gentle lefthand curve. He also failed to observe the next signal, SN270, (the single-yellow signal) but owing to its faulty focussing he would have been in its beam for less than one second at the speed at which he was travelling. He saw the red aspect of signal SN254 at long range, approx 1400 yds, but, travelling at almost full speed, he could only manage to reduce speed to about 60 mph before the collision.

It is interesting to note that the driver had been accompanied in the driving cab between Swindon and Reading by a railway manager who wished to observe lineside features. Whether he appreciated the significance of both AWS and ATP being inoperative remains to be seen. An Operations Manager would surely have arranged for the train to be terminated at Reading (from which point there are plenty of alternative services into Paddington) or would have remained in the cab to Paddington to provide a second pair of eyes. But it is easy to be wise after the event. After the train left Reading, it is said that the driver had to negotiate no fewer that three separate temporary speed restrictions between there and Slough in a distance of less than 18 miles.

THE INQUIRY

It was customary in the case of serious accidents causing fatalities for a public inquiry to be held within two or three weeks of the accident. This had been the procedure for many years even when a criminal prosecution was being considered, but it appears now to be felt that if staff are questioned at a public inquiry, any evidence that they might give may prejudice them in any subsequent prosecution. This difficulty has been overcome in the past by holding back the publication of the report of the public inquiry until after the trial, whilst the prosecuting authorities did not use evidence given at the inquiry; but for reasons yet to be disclosed this procedure appears to be no longer available.

There is therefore a clash between the desire of the prosecuting authorities to take action, and the desire of the Railway Inspectorate to hold a public inquiry to establish the cause. It is a very unsatisfactory situation.

One of the main concerns of the Inquiry was to establish the history of events concerning the AWS in the 24 hours before the accident, because it is very convoluted; indeed it may never be possible to establish exactly what happened owing to conflicts of evidence. It appears that the AWS failed the previous day at Oxford and caused the train to stop just as it was entering the platform. There were various conversations between the driver and the station supervisor, and between the latter and the signalman, but there is a suggestion that the signalman was not informed that the AWS was isolated, and therefore Control was not informed of the event.

The train ran from Oxford to Paddington with the AWS isolated, and then went to Old Oak Common Depot. it is alleged that the fitters there discovered an entry in the repair book in the driving cab, which mentioned the defective AWS, just before the train was due to leave the next morning, but there was insufficient time to carry out repairs. However, whilst the AWS may have passed the static test, the AWS isolating handle was restored to the positive position, but was not sealed. the Rules state that a train must not enter service without such a seal.

The AWS had to be isolated before the train left Paddington en route for Swansea, although it was operative in the front cab. There is a conflict of evidence as to whether the fault was reported to Swansea Control.

THE LEGAL PROCEEDINGS

Four separate charges arose from this accident:-

1 Great Western Trains faced seven separate charges of corporate manslaughter.

2 Great Western Trains also faced prosecution by the Health & Safety Executive for failing to ensure 'that the public were not exposed to risks to their health and safety'.

3 The driver of the HST was charged with manslaughter.

4 The driver of the HST also faced prosecution by the Health & Safety Executive for failing to take 'reasonable care' of his passengers.

This is a situation without parallel in the history of railways.

THE TRIAL

All four of the charges mentioned above were taken together in the trial at the Old Bailey, London which concluded on Friday 2 July 1999. The Judge, Mr Justice Scott Baker, ordered that Great Western Trains be acquitted of manslaughter. He is reported to have said that a corporation could be found guilty of manslaughter only if the prosecution could prove that a particular senior executive was grossly negligent. The prosecution did not produce such evidence.

Following this judgement, the prosecution said that it would offer no evidence against the driver of the HST 'for parity'. It also said that psychiatric reports indicated that the driver had been psychologically damaged by the accident. As has been discussed elsewhere in these pages, that is quite understandable. Furthermore, his condition cannot have been helped by his having to wait so long (approaching two years) for this action to have reached a conclusion. That is an injustice. However, it maintains an unbroken record stretching back for over a century that no driver who pleaded not guilty has ever been found guilty of manslaughter for inadvertently passing a signal at danger.

Great Western Trains pleaded guilty to the charge under Health & Safety legislation and was fined 1½m at a later hearing on 27 July 1999.

The Health & Safety charge against the driver was dropped at the judge's direction, as no evidence had been presented by the prosecution.

WHAT WENT WRONG? WHO ERRED?

The driver erred in passing a signal at danger. There can be no doubt of that, but there were less apparent features which contributed to that failure. Signals exist to convey vital messages to drivers, but they need to be positioned to give the longest and clearest possible view to approaching drivers. The signals concerned in this accident were inadequate in that respect. Railtrack is the authority concerned with signals.

The driver was required to drive without the benefit of either AWS or ATP, which is an astonishing situation bearing in mind that automatic protection systems have been installed on this section of line for almost a hundred years because experience teaches those who are prepared to learn, that drivers are human beings and an infallible human being has not yet been born. Driving a train at 125mph without AWS should not have been allowed. This was a failure of the system, and the controlling authorities are Railtrack and Great Western trains.

There were other participants in this tragedy, minor players perhaps, but possibly significant. The accident would not have happened if some had acted differently. The full story of events at Oxford on the day prior to the accident, and at Old Oak, Paddington and Swansea on the morning of the accident (and in the Control Offices concerned, assuming that they had any knowledge of the AWS failure) will emerge at the Public Inquiry, when it finally takes place. It will be of great interest.

POSTSCRIPT

Just before this book went to press, there was yet another case of a collision caused by a train reported to have passed a red signal. This occurred at 8.52am on Wednesday, 23 June 1999, 400yd north of Winsford Junction, a few miles north of Crewe, on the main line to Glasgow. Between Crewe and Winsford Junction there are two fast lines and two slow lines, with the fast lines in the middle, but the slow lines merge into the fast lines at Winsford Junction.

An empty four-coach 'Pacer' (2x2-cars) is reported to have passed a red signal on the slow line at the end of the four-track section and proceeded on to the two track section just as a Virgin Express, the 06.30 from Euston to Glasgow, was closely approaching at 110 mph on the fast line. The driver of the express saw the Pacer on the main line ahead of him and made an immediate brake application, reducing speed to about 40 mph before his electric locomotive, No 87027 *Wolf of Badenoch*, slammed into the stationery Pacer, ripping open its rear coach. The impact tore the bodies of both coaches of the rear unit from

their underframes and forced them forward several feet. Several coaches of the express were derailed, but remained upright, and there appear to have been no serious injuries.

This could be another case of failure of the AWS to ensure that the Pacer stopped at the red signal protecting the junction, but until the inquiry has reported it is not possible to say. It is likely that the Train Protection and Warning System would have prevented the accident.

The extent of the damage to the Pacer seems to indicate an alarming and long-suspected lack of crash-worthiness. Pacers are essentially bus bodies on a freight wagon chassis. They are cheap and nasty vehicles that were introduced in the early 1980s during the nadir in the British Railways Board's fortunes when the Board was desperately seeking a way to introduce replacement diesel multiple-units at a price that the government would accept.

Pacers were the unfortunate result of these economies. Many are still in use, and indeed they are currently being refurbished, but it is quite clear that they can no longer be allowed to share tracks with heavier trains running above a certain speed. This is a considerable problem - replacement will be expensive and take years, but it is a far more important issue than the premature replacement of Mk 1 coaches of the former Southern Region. HM Railway Inspectorate will need to take a firm hand.

Below
The flimsiness of Pacer bodies is sharply demonstrated at Winsford on 23 June 1999. The electric locomotive *Wolf of Badenoch* is hardly damaged, apart from loosing its front bogie.
Alan Sherratt

CHAPTER 14

The Development of Government Regulation of Railway Safety

THE ORIGINS

Governments, through Parliament, became involved in railway affairs from the very beginning because the promoters of a new railway company had to obtain powers for the purchase of land, but the safety of passengers did not become an issue for another 20 years or so.

Following the success of the Liverpool & Manchester Railway, opened on 15 September 1830, businessmen and promoters all over the country began to develop their own schemes, and plans already in development received a great boost. In the 1830s, the number of Acts passed for new railways was as follows:

1831	15	1834	5	1837	15
1832	4	1835	8	1838	2
1833	12	1836	29	1839	1

It is not surprising that the rapidly developing railway system soon attracted parliamentary attention, and it was felt that some form of control over the railways may be necessary in the public interest. A Parliamentary Select Committee was therefore appointed in 1839 to consider the subject and its recommendations led to the Regulation of Railways Act of 1840, which commenced:

'Whereas it is expedient for the Safety of the Public to provide for the due supervision of the railways...'

It contained the following main provisions:

■ No railway may be opened for the public conveyance of goods or passengers without a month's notice being given.

■ Returns of traffic, charges and of accidents causing personal injury are to be made by the railway companies.

■ The Board of Trade may appoint persons to inspect railways.

Thus was the Railway Inspectorate born. Civil engineers with the necessary knowledge were already fully engaged on new construction and it was not considered appropriate to appoint them as inspectors, therefore the Board of Trade turned to the Corps of Royal Engineers, starting a tradition which lasted for the next 150 years. Three inspectors were appointed.

NINETEENTH CENTURY DEVELOPMENT

The Inspectorate had no powers other than to inspect railways, and it could do nothing to prevent a new railway from opening even if it were found on inspection to be unfit for the carriage of passengers safely. The Inspectors had no power to insist on changes, nor did they have any powers to inquire into accidents, but nevertheless they made inquiries without any authority, and

their reports bring out clearly the primitive operating methods of the day. In 1841 the Inspector General reported on the measures he thought were necessary to enable him to supervise the railways effectively, stating that whilst the government should not attempt to regulate matters of detail and take the management of the railways out of the hands of the directors and their officers, it was necessary that the government should have the power of enforcing the observance of all precautions and regulations which were approved by experience and were obviously conducive to the public safety.

A new Act was therefore passed in 1842 — 'An Act for the Better Regulation of the Railways and for the Conveyance of Troops' — which gave the Board of Trade power to postpone the opening of a new line if an Inspector reported that the opening 'would be attended with danger to the public using the same'. No powers were given regarding the holding of inquiries into accidents, but the Inspectors continued to do so. Similarly, the Act contained no provisions for the recommendations of Inspectors, following inquiries into accidents, to be enforced. The government felt that such powers would take the responsibility for managing railways out of the hands of the directors and place it fairly and squarely upon the Board of Trade, a very undesirable development (such views are still relevant today).

The threefold responsibilities of the Inspectorate began to take shape:

■ To advise the Board of Trade on railway affairs;

■ To inspect new lines and new works;

■ To inquire into accidents.

The limited powers of the Inspectorate sometimes hindered the holding of inquiries into accidents, and Parliament was persuaded that additional powers were justified and necessary. These powers were given in the Regulation of Railways Act 1871 — 'to make an inquiry into the cause of a railway accident', including powers to enter and inspect any railway, to summon railway officers or staff as witnesses, to require answers or returns, and to require the production of books, papers and documents. These powers were sufficient for the next 120 years without change.

During the second half of the 19th century, the Inspectorate had campaigned for the railway companies to adopt, in the interests of passenger safety, what was known as 'Lock, Block and Brake', ie the interlocking of points and signals, the use of the Absolute Block System of train signalling, and the adoption of the continuous automatic brake on passenger trains. Some railway companies found the necessary funds difficult to obtain; others could well afford the necessary expenditure but were reluctant to embark upon it. However, most companies were gradually adopting Lock, Block and Brake, but progress was slow and the Inspectorate became exasperated with the delay. A serious accident to a special train conveying a Sunday School outing on the Great Northern Railway of Ireland on 12 June 1889, resulting in the deaths of 78 passengers, including 22 children, was the last straw so far as the Inspectorate was concerned. Public opinion, too, was inflamed and Parliament passed the only Act in railway history that dealt with the detail of railway operation, until recent days. It made Lock, Block and Brake compulsory.

THE 20TH CENTURY, TO 1950

By 1900 the railway companies had become mature and responsible and safety levels were high, judged by the standards of the time. Indeed in 1901 no passenger was killed in a train accident, the first year without such fatalities in railway history. This was an incredible achievement when one takes into account the volume of traffic being handled and the lack of many safeguards which are taken almost for granted today. What is more, the achievement was to be repeated in 1908 and much of the credit must be due to a disciplined and loyal workforce, most of whom were fiercely proud of their own company.

The duties of the Railway Inspectorate, consisting of a Chief Inspector and three or four Inspecting Officers (as it had been throughout its history), continued unchanged, although the inspection of new lines occupied less time, being replaced by more frequent inspections of new works resulting from the application of new technologies.

There followed a period of very considerable stability in the ways by which railway operations were conducted, lasting at least until the 1950s, being little changed by the two world wars, by the Grouping in 1923, and by nationalisation in 1948. There was considerable co-operation between the railway companies and the Inspectorate, each respecting the other's professional expertise and both working together in the common aim of a safer railway at an affordable cost. Safety was never spoken of in financial terms, because it was felt to be provocative, but the cost implications of any proposed changes were always borne in mind and the Inspectorate never pressed the railways with unreasonable demands. The railway's overall safety record was considered to be very high and it was not necessary to do so, and although the Inspectorate had no powers to enforce the adoption of its recommendations, the lack of such powers was never a problem. The persuasive power of the Inspectorate was sufficient when it had a good case.

When the railways were nationalised it might have been thought that the Inspectorate could be disbanded, because the railways were now almost an organ of the state and profit was no longer the first concern. But the Inspectorate continued to play a valuable role as public auditor and touchstone, providing the railway with a defence against unreasonable attack from either the media or the government.

The challenge of major technical changes which faced the Inspectorate: Continuously-welded rails (top left and right). The Victoria Signalling Centre (bottom left). The Dartford power signalbox (bottom right). *IAL (2)/The Marconi Company/ AEI-General Signal Ltd*

FROM 1950 ONWARDS

The challenges of the major technical changes

▓ in traction with diesels and overhead electrification at 25kV, and speeds up to 125 mph,

▓ with continuously-welded rails on concrete sleepers,

▓ with signalling modernisation, route-relay interlocking, large scale power signalling installations, solid state interlocking, automated level crossings

were all met and dealt with effectively by the Inspectorate, although there were anxious times in the late 1960s with buckled track and derailments of four-wheeled goods vehicles. Working together, railway engineers and the Inspectorate gradually found solutions to all the problems that emerged, and by the mid-1970s a situation of relative stability was reached, but so far as the Inspectorate was concerned it was not to last.

From 1840 to the 1980s Inspecting Officers had always been drawn from the among the officers of the Corps of Royal Engineers with railway operating and engineering experience, but that source was drying up. It was inevitable that the next generation of Inspecting Officers would have to be drawn from other spheres, but mainly from within the railway industry itself. This process was hastened by the formation of a new body — the Health & Safety Commission (HSC) — following the passing of the Health & Safety at Work, etc, Act 1974. Initially the Act had little impact upon either the railway industry, apart from a massive increase in administration and paperwork, or the Inspectorate, which continued to perform its traditional responsibilities in respect of the safety of passengers, and continued to concern itself with the safety of railway staff as agent for the HSC.

THE SAFETY OF RAILWAY STAFF

It is now appropriate to consider the question of staff safety. The Inspectorate had no responsibilities in this direction until 1900, nor indeed did anyone else other than the railway companies themselves, who might be considered to have taken a somewhat robust, almost cavalier attitude to the safety of their staff. This was, of course, a commonplace attitude among industry at the time.

Staff fatalities in the 1890s approached, and sometimes exceeded, 500 per year, mainly in the grades of guards, shunters and workers on the track. In 1900, 24 railwaymen were killed in train accidents and no fewer than 559 from other causes. In that year, the Railway Employment (Prevention of Accidents) Act was passed, and a body of Railway Employment Inspectors was established, as part of the Railway Inspectorate. They were recruited mainly from the ranks of railwaymen, who were the only people with the necessary practical experience.

Various measures were taken to remove the more obvious and frequently met hazards, with some success. In 1921 the number of deaths was 231, less than half the prewar figures, and with an increased workforce, but the annual total remained stubbornly around the 200 mark up to 1939. After 1945 more attention was given to the subject and the annual totals fell from 187 in 1950 to 129 in 1960, 67 in 1970, 32 in 1980 and 22 in 1990. This partly reflects a considerable reduction in the numbers of railway staff exposed to risk, but is still very creditable. There were only three deaths in 1997. The reduction has been continuous since World War 2 and it could be said that the Health & Safety at Work Act was almost an irrelevancy so far as the railway industry was concerned. It had had its own HSW Act since 1900 (The Railway Employment [Prevention of Accidents] Act), following which a number of Railway Employment Inspectors were appointed, reporting to the Inspectorate. The main effect of the 1974 Act was a massive increase in bureaucratic procedures and paperwork, backed by threats of condign punishment for failure to conform — quite unnecessary, so long as the railways continued to be in public ownership.

THE HEALTH & SAFETY EXECUTIVE

The Railway Inspectorate had always been an independent and tightly-knit body, initially reporting to the Board of Trade, and later to the Minister of Transport. It had direct access to the Minister. However, the government decided that a body responsible for overseeing safety on the railways (the Inspectorate) ought not to be part of a government department responsible for transport, in case there were conflicts of interest, although there had never been any suspicion of such dealings. It therefore decided to transfer the Inspectorate to the Health & Safety Commission, despite the fact that the HSE was primarily concerned with the health and safety of the workforce, whilst the Inspectorate was mainly concerned with the safety of the operation of the railways, including the workforce. The transfer took place in December 1990, ironically the 150th anniversary of the founding of the Inspectorate.

What were the reasons for the change? It stemmed from the growing inability to recruit Inspecting Officers from among officers of the Corps of Royal Engineers with the necessary knowledge and experience, although there were plenty of railway officers who would have been perfectly suitable and could have been appointed. However, the authorities may have considered that the latter might look too kindly upon their former employer, although in a later expansion of the Inspectorate there was little alternative to the filling of the new posts by railwaymen in mid-career.

The second reason arose from the fire at King's Cross Underground station on 18 November 1987, when 31 people lost their lives. There was a feeling that the Inspectorate had failed in some way to protect the public against such a disaster. The King's Cross fire was not a railway disaster; it was an escalator problem which happened to occur on London Underground premises.

The third reason was a feeling that the achievement of improvements in safety on the railways, in particular the safety of staff, was being handicapped by what was seen as a too cosy relationship between the Inspectorate and the British Railways Board. This was a misunderstanding of the nature of the relationship, which was one of cooperation in the improvement of safety standards, whilst the ethos of the HSE was a stand-off relationship backed by the punitive force of the Health & Safety Act.

When Major C. F. Rose retired in 1988 as Chief Inspecting Officer, he was replaced, to widespread astonishment, by someone from within the Health & Safety Organisation, Mr Robin Seymour, who had been working since 1984 as Her Majesty's Deputy Chief Inspector of Factories in the Hazardous Substances Division. His previous career had been within the Factory Inspectorate and the HSE. He had no experience of railways, which was a considerable snub to generations of dedicated Inspecting Officers. It would seem that the preparation of the Railway Inspectorate for its transfer to the HSE, and changing its whole culture, was the first priority so far as the Health & Safety Commission was concerned.

After the transfer, the HSE decided that the Inspectorate should be more proactive, by examining and inspecting current railway operations, using the powers of the 1974 Act. This was unnecessary so long as BR remained in existence — safety standards had never been higher. It required a very large increase in the size of the Inspectorate, and a recruitment campaign was launched, mainly aimed at serving railwaymen, who were the only practical source and who formed the great bulk of the new intake. Staff numbers and salaries within the Inspectorate had always been tightly controlled, but in order to tempt sufficient serving railwaymen to apply for the new posts it was necessary to offer higher salaries than had been the practice within the Inspectorate.

THE IMPACT OF PRIVATISATION

The imminence of the privatisation of the railways changed the picture radically and placed new demands upon the Inspectorate, which fortuitously had recently been expanded. The government's declared method of privatisation had very serious implications for safety. BR's finely structured organisation for achieving high safety standards, with continuous improvement, was to be shattered and it was not easy to see how those standards were to be maintained and safeguarded in a highly fragmented and profit-driven railway industry. The task of solving this problem was handed to the Inspectorate.

The scale of the problem was enormous. The monolithic BR was to be fragmented and sold off in a large number of separate organisations, the main ones being:

- A new public company, to be called Railtrack, which would own the infrastructure (ie track, signalling, stations, electrification systems, etc).
- Maintenance and renewals would be dealt with by contractors.
- The operation of the train services would be by franchise, of which there would be 26.
- Rolling stock would be allocated to three Train Leasing Companies.
- The freight business would be sold off in four companies (eventually two).

The preservation of safety on the new railway was a daunting task for the Inspectorate, which came up with a solution that was remarkable for its ingenuity and was based on the arrangements in the oil industry. It proposed that all companies should prepare a safety case, setting out in great detail how they proposed to

The new railway. (above) A pair of 'Connex'-liveried Class 319s passes Coulsden at speed on 29 October 1997 with the 10.50 express from Victoria to Brighton, and (below) an EWS-liveried Class 73/1 propels a train of military equipment into the sidings in south London on 12 May 1998. *Brian Morrison (2)*

ensure that their activities would be carried out safely. The report, dated January 1993, nevertheless took 156 pages to set out the detail. The Inspectorate sensibly recognised that it did not have the resources to supervise the safety of all railway activities, nor was it appropriate that it should do so. It went further and proposed that the approval of all safety cases should be the responsibility of Railtrack, and that only Railtrack's own safety case should require approval by the Inspectorate. The Secretary of State for Transport gratefully accepted the proposals; privatisation could not have gone ahead without them.

Privatisation has had a marked effect on the workload of the Inspectorate in several directions. Railtrack, with its guaranteed income from the Train Operating Companies, has embarked upon a programme of new works and enhancements to an almost unprecedented degree. The detail of these plans has to be approved beforehand by the Inspectorate, and the work has to be inspected when complete, or at particular stages. An increased workload comes also from another unexpected source. The spread of what might be called 'Heritage Railways' (ie preserved railways, usually run partly or wholly by enthusiasts) is nothing short of astonishing, but their activities have to be monitored by the Inspectorate and their plans approved and finished work inspected. Finally, the Inspectorate now has responsibility for approving rolling stock, and many new designs are being built. These three items alone will require another increase in the size of the Inspectorate if it is to function efficiently.

THE OUTCOME

It is one thing to draw up safety cases; it is another to perform them unfailingly and without external supervision. It was feared that commercial pressures on companies to maintain their profitability might cause them to cut corners on safety on such matters as staffing levels, training, examinations and supervision, and the maintenance of equipment. These are easy options when cost reductions are sought, as BR long ago discovered, and they have little immediate effect on the quality of the product or on safety, but eventually the weaknesses will begin to show. BR could be forgiven for attempting to save costs, because public funds were involved, provided that safety was not unduly jeopardised. Private companies will not so easily be forgiven if shareholders' dividends and 'fat-cat' pay-offs are perceived to have priority over safety.

However, the safety record since privatisation, with the exception of Southall, has been very good and much better than might have been expected. The change in organisation and culture resulting from the handover from BR to privatised companies was huge. New, inexperienced managements might have been expected to make mistakes. But the fears have been unfounded. Why?

There was a dramatic change in the safety culture on BR during the second half of the 1980s. Before that, the British Railways Board, whilst exercising a properly responsible attitude to safety, had not found it necessary to devote a great deal of attention to the subject. There were no pressures to do otherwise; operators and engineers continued to run the railway with a proper regard for safety. Up to the mid-1980s, safety was not a separate issue; it was an integral part of every railwayman whose duties might affect safety, from the designer of rolling stock, and signal and civil engineers in drawing offices at one end of the safety chain, to those responsible for maintenance and finally to the workface — traincrews and signalmen.

However, a number of serious transport accidents in fields other than main line railways demonstrated to the Board the vulnerability of its position and it set up a Safety Directorate; not because safety standards were unsatisfactory but as a means of protection. The Safety Directorate began to change the safety culture, but it was the threat of prosecution contained in the 1974 Act which provided the real impetus so far as line managers were concerned. Staff on the ground reacted to a different stimulus.

The imprisonment of a driver following the Purley collision in 1989 had a tremendous impact on staff at the workface. Such an action was unheard of and the whole safety culture changed. Previously, safety had been taken as a matter of course; now it was a conscious affair, and safety came to the forefront. Staff felt as though a reign of terror had descended upon them. Those same staff are still operating the railways at the workface today, which is one reason why safety standards have not slipped under privatisation.

Safety now became a very high-profile subject, and a safety empire developed on the railway. It absorbed a lot of time, effort and money. Was it all really worthwhile? It is very difficult to judge; the railways were already very safe, and were becoming even safer. But events conspired to make the changes inevitable.

CHAPTER 15

Inquiries into Accidents

Since the mid-1980s, accident inquiry procedures have become extremely complex, owing to the many organisations and groups who have become more deeply involved. They are:

- The operating authority — British Rail, then Railtrack
- The Railway Inspectorate
- The police
- The coroner— if there is a fatality. (Fatal Accident Inquiry in Scotland)
- The courts — if a prosecution is undertaken
- The trade unions
- Legal representatives

NORMAL PROCEDURES UP TO ABOUT 1987

British Rail was totally responsible for safety, and it had a very detailed and efficient organisation: (1) to operate the railways safely, and (2) to investigate every accident. All accidents were reported upwards; minor ones were investigated and concluded at local level. More important ones were dealt with formally at a higher level, with witnesses being interviewed and evidence recorded. When more than one department was affected the inquiry was held jointly, with an Operating Department chairman. A full report of the inquiry, with its findings, was sent to headquarters and thence, if appropriate, to the Railway Inspectorate. The latter would decide whether the matter could be dealt with in correspondence or whether it would be appropriate to advise the Minister of Transport that a public inquiry should be held.

If BR's inquiries indicated that changes should be made, they would be instituted at once, without waiting for any action that the Railway Inspectorate might take. BR was responsible for safety, under the Transport Acts. If a public inquiry was to be held by an Inspecting Officer, it would be done within a few weeks. The public part of the inquiry would normally be completed within a day.

It might be added in passing that attendance at one of the old-fashioned public inquiries held by a Brigadier or Lt-Colonel was one of the esoteric pleasures for students of railway safety. The demeanour of witnesses under questioning spoke volumes about the man's character to the observer of human nature. How truthful was he? Could his testimony be relied on? Was he quick-witted and alert or a trifle dull? Did he know his job or did he just get by? Was he cautious in answering, as though he might have something to hide, or was he patently open and honest? It

was an exercise in human psychology, none of which is evident from the printed pages of a report.

To that extent, public inquiries had a value whose practical worth should not be overlooked, even though the audience was usually small, consisting of half a dozen railwaymen, mostly colleagues of the witnesses, half a dozen devotees of railway accident inquiries, and a couple of bored-looking reporters, but at least the day's proceedings were reported in the press and on TV and radio for millions to read, see and hear. So on balance it was worthwhile to hold public inquiries fairly often, but only for so long as the Inspecting Officer maintained a tight grip on the proceedings and finished in a day or so. Unfortunately, that type of inquiry is no longer available; it has been destroyed by events and changes in culture.

Another significant feature of public inquiries in the past was that witnesses rarely if ever declined to give evidence, either at an internal BR inquiry or at a public inquiry, even though they themselves may have been at fault. They were responsible railwaymen and recognised that the purpose of an inquiry was to learn lessons and make the railway safer; it was not to seek scapegoats. All that has changed for the worse, as we shall see shortly. The atmosphere of an inquiry has changed and witnesses may, and often do, decline to give evidence for fear of retribution. The absence of the evidence of a principal witness, or the inability to tell whether his testimony is 100% truthful and accurate, does not help in establishing the cause.

The British Transport Police needed to know the facts concerning an accident so that they could decide whether charges should be laid against anyone, and they could obtain the information they needed either from BR's inquiry report or in discussion with BR's local operating superintendent, with whom there was always close liaison. At this stage a decision could be taken on whether a person at fault should be dealt with under BR's internal disciplinary machinery or through the courts. There was also, and still is, liaison between the Inspectorate and the BT Police.

This system had worked satisfactorily for many, many years, but then there were radical changes almost overnight. What were those changes and why did they happen? Were they good or bad, desirable or unsatisfactory?

THE RAILWAY INSPECTORATE

Inspecting Officers who were ex-army men had a status and bearing that brooked no interruption at a public inquiry. They indicated quite clearly that the purpose of the inquiry was to enable them to reach a conclusion on the cause of an accident and that it was not for the purpose of establishing either civil or criminal liability. They allowed questions from the trade unions representing witnesses, but only in so far as they were relevant to the purpose of the inquiry. They stood no nonsense. Railway Officers were present to assist.

Public inquiries were followed by a public report, which contained both the findings as to the cause, and recommendations as to what ought to be done to avoid similar accidents. It was the practice for Inspecting Officers to show a draft of the report to the Railways Board so that the facts could be agreed, and any recommendations which the Inspecting Officer proposed to make were discussed at the highest level. It is greatly to the credit of both parties that there was rarely any material disagreement about the recommendations. That was the position until about 1987.

There was then a major change, which had its trigger in the extremely prolonged public inquiries following the King's Cross Underground station fire in 1987 and the Clapham accident in 1988. The Clapham Inquiry lasted for an incredible 65 days, even though the cause was known within an hour or two. It was held in the Westminster Central Hall, a huge hall, which was filled with the massed ranks of participants, each with its retinue of legal advisers. The inquiry considered over 13,000 pages of documents.

Inspecting Officers holding public inquiries were then under pressure to follow the procedures adopted during those inquiries and to allow questions more freely, not only from those representing witnesses, but also from legal representatives of injured passengers or persons bereaved. This was most ill-advised because it did not help the Inspector at all in his primary duty to establish the cause; in fact, it was a hindrance and it prolonged inquiries, often into a week or more. In order to help representatives, members of the public, and the media, to understand the facts concerning an accident it became necessary to make detailed displays using maps, plans, photographs and even video demonstrations.

The Inspectorate had unwittingly opened Pandora's box and the evils had escaped; they could not be stuffed back into the box. Only hope remained, and the answer was to reduce the number of public inquiries. There was no legal requirement for a public inquiry, but only for the publication of a report, and it became the practice for most inquiries to be held in private in the form of technical inquiries, with public inquiries being reserved for the most serious accidents.

Until recently, Inspectors' inquiries were held under the authority of the Regulation of Railways Act 1871, but the whole of that Act was repealed by the Railway Safety (Miscellaneous Provisions) Regulations 1997. Inquiries are now held in accordance with the provisions of the Health & Safety at Work Act 1974, Sec 14, and are not held in public. There is one exception — the Health & Safety Inquiries (Procedure)

Regulations 1975 (SI 1975 No 335, as amended by SI 1976 No 1246), which provides for a more formal public inquiry of the type previously held under Sec 7 of the 1871 Act into the King's Cross fire and the Clapham accident. This would appear, quite fortuitously, to have resolved the issue.

THE INVOLVEMENT OF THE POLICE
The British Transport (BT) Police Force is the competent authority for all police matters on railway premises, which in practice includes all accidents. Owing to the scattered locations in which BT police are located, and the thousands of miles of line which they have to cover, it often happens that members of local police forces arrive on the site of an accident first, which can be unfortunate because they are on unfamiliar ground and uncertain of their rights and responsibilities. This can cause over-reaction and hinder those whose duty it is to establish the cause, but as soon as BT police arrive they take charge.

The police have many responsibilities on site, and these were discussed in Chapter 6, but we are now concerned with two which arise from the accident — the decision as to whether the law has been broken and, in the case of a fatality, the reporting of the facts to the Coroner. Neither of these two objects can be achieved until the cause of the accident and the degree of blame attaching to any individual has been established. The police do not have the necessary knowledge, training and experience to do this; it is an operating department responsibility and the two organisations need to liaise with each other. Afterwards, the police can then assess whether the evidence indicates that a criminal act may have been committed. It would be wrong for the police to attempt to establish the cause of the accident themselves. Their role is limited to ensuring so far as they can that all evidence is preserved, and it is important that they do not hinder in any way those whose responsibility it is to establish the cause.

This obsession with the preservation of evidence arose from the Clapham Inquiry. It should be unnecessary for the police to be involved in this, but it indicates the working of the legal brain. It was never necessary between 1840 and 1988 and it was unnecessary as long as BR was in existence. One of the consequences of the King's Cross and Clapham inquiries was to inflate the status of the police at accident sites; this was perhaps inevitable, but circumstances have changed and it is probably desirable on the privatised railway. Huge sums of money are now at risk following a serious accident, but would any railwayman attempt to conceal or tamper with evidence to protect his own company's interests? To a traditional railwayman it would be unthinkable, but these are not traditional times.

THE ROLE OF HM CORONER
Deaths arising from a railway accident are reported to the Coroner by the police and it is then the practice for an inquest to be held. This is done in public and because the Coroner is concerned

to have all the facts put to the jury by witnesses, the proceedings are similar in many ways to a public inquiry, with the added advantage that the Coroner takes pains to ensure so far as he can that the jury understands what the witnesses are saying. Most Coroners accept the help of an Inspecting Officer, who has an official role as an assessor and may subsequently issue a public report.

Despite the Coroner's efforts to educate the jury in the finer points of railway signalling and operating, it is perhaps inevitable that there is less than 100% understanding, and it is sometimes necessary for the Coroner to give guidance to the jury. There are normally only two acceptable verdicts — accidental death or unlawful killing — and juries may find it difficult to accept accidental death if a railwayman has been negligent in any way. If the Coroner accepts a verdict of unlawful killing, the police then have to consider whether manslaughter or other charges should be brought.

The timing of the holding of Coroner's inquests in relation to any criminal proceedings is critical. If a charge has been laid against an individual, the Coroner's inquest must be deferred until the trial has been concluded. The Coroner may only hold a preliminary hearing.

COURT PROCEEDINGS

Most criminal charges arising from a railway accident are laid against a driver who has passed a signal at danger or has caused an accident in some other manner. The charge may be manslaughter (if there have been fatalities), or endangering the safety of passengers.

The courts operate on an adversarial system. It is the responsibility of the prosecution to prove its case to the satisfaction of the jury. The defence need do nothing, but will none the less be at pains to represent the defendant by exposing weaknesses in the prosecution's case and by putting forward mitigating circumstances on the defendant's behalf. The proceedings have the advantage of presenting all the facts concerning the accident and, as in the case of Coroner's inquests, the judge must be satisfied that the jury fully understands all the technical complexities, although the extent to which this is completely achievable in practice is a matter of conjecture.

THE INVOLVEMENT OF THE TRADE UNIONS

Most railwaymen who have to appear before an inquiry as witnesses (other than internal railway inquiries) choose to have the assistance of a trade union representative, who will probably be a full-time official of the union. His role is to ensure that all the facts are fully presented and that the witness receives a fair hearing. He will also intervene to protect the witness from unreasonable or unfair questioning and will advise the witness not to answer questions that may incriminate him.

The involvement of trade unions in what are akin to technical inquiries may at first sight be questionable, but trade union officers are experts in this field; unlike the witness, they know the rules of procedure and they are unlikely to be overawed by the occasion. It is becoming an increasing practice for the trade unions to employ legal representatives in the more serious cases, or where a prosecution may result. Such representation is valuable where legal procedures may be involved; less so regarding technical evidence in which the legal representative is not an expert.

THE INVOLVEMENT OF THE LEGAL PROFESSION

It is the normal practice for a defendant in a trial to be legally represented, and it is usually arranged by his trade union. Such representation is also becoming common at non-legal inquiries. This was not always the case, but has developed in recent years from what is perceived as greater police involvement in accident procedures; from the influence of the Health & Safety at Work Act, with its penal provisions; from high-profile public inquiries of the King's Cross and Clapham type; and from a general feeling among railwaymen that the balance between establishing the cause of an accident and punishing those responsible has tilted too strongly towards the latter.

Legal representatives cannot be experts in all the many and varied aspects of railway work, or indeed in any of them, and it is important that they take advice from those who who are experts in their own field. Failure to consult experts is likely to mean that representation is less effective than it would otherwise be. It is also important to remember that trade union representatives are not fully qualified in all aspects of railway work, although they may be expert in some aspects, eg signalling or driving.

There have been embarrassing occasions in recent inquiries when a lawyer has put a question to a witness, couched in the circumlocutions, introductory phrases and double negatives that lawyers are prone to use. The witness does not understand the question but, being overawed, is afraid to say so. Alternatively, he may ask for the question to be repeated, but it is likely to be rephrased in what is to him an equally unintelligible manner, so he gives an answer to what he thinks is the question. It is likely to be couched in railway jargon, because that is how railwaymen speak. The lawyer may neither fully comprehend the answer nor recognise that the witness is answering the wrong question. There is confusion all round.

This is where the chairman of an inquiry should intervene. He should ensure that the witness understands the question and that the questioner fully understands the answer. The chairman should act both as a filter and an interpreter, and he should have the necessary qualifications and experience to enable him to fulfil those roles adequately.

It is far better for embarrassing occasions to be avoided. They may be amusing to the cognoscenti, but they are also irritating.

INTERNAL RAILWAY INQUIRIES

The position which applied under BR has already been explained. It was absolutely clear cut. A formal inquiry, known as a joint inquiry, was held, and a report was submitted to headquarters, stating the conclusion of the inquiry panel on the cause of the accident. The report did not contain recommendations, because any changes that were desirable were a matter for headquarters to deal with, but they could be included in a covering letter.

The situation has changed dramatically under privatisation. Serious accidents can cost millions of pounds in damage to rolling stock and infrastructure. Compensation payments to injured passengers and the bereaved can run into millions. The line is blocked, possibly for days, with heavy loss of revenue. The exact allocation of responsibility for the accident is then a matter of supreme importance to the railway companies involved.

Whilst Railtrack is nominally responsible for the safety of operation, it would be invidious for it to take on the role of judge in its own case. A joint inquiry composed of representatives of all the companies involved would be likely to lead to adversarial conduct with much legal representation — an impossible situation. It is therefore essential that the chairman of the inquiry should be completely independent, which means that he cannot be an employee of any existing railway company. There are, at the present time, several railway officers, recently retired, who have the necessary competence, skills, experience and knowledge to undertake such a duty, and who could be expected to be impartial, but that fortunate situation will not last for ever. Eventually, the only people left will be former senior managers of one of the railway companies and their impartiality may be difficult to prove.

One solution to this problem would be to simplify the structure and combine the railway joint inquiry with the Railway Inspectorate's private technical inquiry. Both cover the same ground. No legal representation would be allowed, the trade unions would have a right to be present, not to represent witnesses, but to be satisfied that the proceedings are fair. This is fruitful territory for the simplification of post-accident procedures, but is it expecting too much? Not if the will were there.

Until 10 years ago there was the closest co-operation between BR management and the Railway Inspectorate, a relationship based on mutual trust and respect, and it is a matter of the greatest regret that such a rapport no longer exists. Those in the industry suggest that it has been seriously impaired by the Health & Safety Executive's clumsy manoeuvrings since it appropriated the Railway Inspectorate, even whilst BR was still functioning, but the situation has deteriorated further since Railtrack was privatised and resented what it regarded as high-handed interference from the HSE. Both sides are now at the 'daggers drawn' stage, as illustrated by Railtrack's misconceived, but not altogether surprising, action in instructing its staff not to co-operate with the Railway Inspectorate, an instruction that was quickly withdrawn when its wisdom (not to mention its legality) was questioned. A large measure of statesmanship is now required from both sides to restore good relations and abandon confrontation.

For the most part, the courts only become involved when a railwayman is charged with manslaughter or endangering passengers. It has been a rare event — every few years on average. Coroner's Courts only become involved when there is a fatality. That is perhaps an annual event when it concerns a fatality caused by a train accident. There is little other involvement for the police, and the main players are therefore the railway companies and the Railway Inspectorate. There is a lot to be gained by their joining forces in the cause of improved safety, a cause which is common to both parties.

(Note: there are no Coroner's Courts in Scotland. A Fatal Accidents Inquiry is held instead.)

CHAPTER 16

The Last 10 Years -
A Review of Progress

A study of the present demands a knowledge of the past, and it would be helpful, therefore, to retrace our steps and return to the beginning of our review period — 1988 — in order to see what were then the chief safety concerns, and what actions were taken to deal with them in the following 10 years. Those concerns were:

■ Drivers wrongly passing signals at danger, or failing to slow down or stop as required.

■ Drivers starting from stations and wrongly passing signals at danger, particularly where there is a single lead junction or other potential hazard immediately ahead.

■ The need to equip slam door coaches with central-locking under the control of the guard, or replace such vehicles.

■ Collisions with road vehicles at level crossings.

■ Bridges being damaged by road vehicles ('bridge bashing').

■ Vandalism.

■ A safe environment for passengers.

It is noteworthy that there were no major concerns then about the safety of the track or signalling, and none regarding the mechanical fitness of rolling stock, but the nature of the reorganisation of the railway industry following privatisation has raised a degree of uncertainty on these issues, and will need supervision by the Inspectorate.

Let us now consider the extent to which progress has been made on the safety concerns which were identified above as existing in 1988.

■ DRIVERS PASSING SIGNALS AT DANGER

This is still one of the biggest potential causes of accidents, as these pages show. Four of the six fatal train accidents that have occurred in the 1990s have been caused by drivers irregularly passing signals at danger, having failed to react to a caution signal. Such errors have the potential for multiple fatalities and should have been dealt with many years ago, but it has to be admitted that only one of the very serious train accidents in the last 30 years or so has been caused by driver error. It is instructive to list them:

■ Hither Green, Southern Region, 5 November 1967. A passenger train was derailed by a broken rail; 49 passengers were killed.

■ Hixon Level Crossing, London Midland Region, 6 January 1968. A passenger train crashed into a heavy load which was being taken across the line at an automatic half-barrier level crossing; eight passengers were killed.

■ West Ealing, Western Region, 19 December 1973. A passenger train was derailed when points were opened under the train by a loose piece of equipment on the locomotive; 10 passengers were killed.

■ Taunton, Western Region, 6 July 1978. Smouldering linen in a sleeping car caused 12 deaths.

■ Polmont, Scottish Region, 30 July 1984. A passenger train was derailed when it ran into a cow which had strayed onto the line; 13 passengers were killed.

■ Lockington Level Crossing, Eastern Region, 26 July 1986. A passenger train collided with a car at an automatic open level crossing; eight passengers were killed.

■ Clapham, Southern Region, 12 December 1988. Three trains were involved in a collision, caused by faulty wiring in a signalling equipment room; 35 passengers were killed.

■ Southall, Great Western, 19 Sept 1997. An HST collided with a freight train being shunted across its path when the driver of the HST passed a signal at danger. The AWS was isolated (ie, not in use); seven passengers were killed.

Left
The result of a fire in a sleeping car near Taunton on 6 July 1978. The fire was caused by bags of linen being placed against an electric panel heater on the wall of this vestibule. The heater was cold at the time, but warmed up during the journey and eventually overheated. *British Rail*

It needs to be emphasised that only one of these accidents was caused by a driver. Apart from the two accidents at automatic level crossings, the causes were rare, if not actually unique, and had their roots in thoughtlessness or carelessness.

However, the potential for a serious accident arising from a signal being passed at danger is substantial, as the Southall collision demonstrated, and preventive measures need to be taken urgently. Railtrack has devised the Train Protection and Warning System as an affordable and fairly effective safeguard and needs to install it without further delay. To have to record that no tangible progress has been made in the last 10 years on the crucial issue of signals being passed at danger, and that passengers are little better protected against the potential effects of such an event than they were 20 years ago, is surely a serious criticism of both BR and Railtrack. Improvements in the last 10 years have sprung from other sources. The matter is so urgent that the Inspectorate has found it necessary to seek powers to compel Railtrack to complete the installation of TPWS by the end of 2003, a situation reminiscent of 1889 when the Inspectorate had to obtain powers in similar circumstances to compel laggard railway companies to install safeguards (the Regulation of Railways Act 1889).

BR wasted several years in its failed attempt to produce a suitable Automatic Train Protection system, partly through lack of sufficient commitment, but also through the distraction of privatisation. Lack of funding was also a factor. The government stated after Clapham that the money needed to install a suitable ATP system 'would be found'. It was not, and anyone who believed that it would be was naïve. If the government required the railways to implement the recommendation of the Clapham Report regarding ATP it should have provided the necessary funds and ring-fenced them. The fact that it failed to do so indicates that the comment of lack of commitment also applies to the government.

BR's enthusiasm for ATP began to wane when the real cost and complexity of the project started to emerge, and, without a serious accident resulting in several passenger fatalities since 1989 in which a driver passed a signal at danger, the economic justification for ATP began to look very doubtful. The government agreed that it was not cost-effective, but unfortunately there was no immediately available alternative. There should have been; the possible abandonment of the ATP project was apparent for several years before the decision was finally taken. Railtrack's alternative scheme, the Train Protection and Warning System, has been a long time in gestation, which naturally arouses suspicions of a lack of enthusiasm on Railtrack's part, but HSE Regulations now require installation to be completed by 1 January 2004.

All that was needed to improve the BR Automatic Warning System was an AWS indication at a single yellow signal that was different from the indication at a double yellow signal, and which required a different response from the driver. An aspect that was different from single yellow and in greater contrast to double yellow would also have been effective. The two signals which incorporate the yellow colour are in effect working as outer and inner distant signals. Yellow (a single yellow) should have been retained for the outer distant signal; the inner distant signal should have had a different colour or combination of colours — there are several options. However, the problems of changeover would have been considerable, with tens of thousands of signals to be dealt with, and the practicable solution would have been different AWS indications at signals displaying single yellow and double yellow aspects. Railtrack has chosen to go down a different road. For the good of the industry, one must hope that that road will lead to success, and that it will be achieved quickly.

2 DRIVERS WRONGLY PASSING PLATFORM STARTING SIGNALS AT DANGER

The accidents referred to in Chapter 7 compelled BR to take further measures to deal with this problem, and these are listed in that chapter. The Train Protection and Warning System trip-stop feature will provide a more positive safeguard, but installation has yet to begin. In a separate initiative, a £3.4m project to install a simple device in driving cabs, to help prevent trains starting away from stations against a red signal, has been completed in time. It is not an automatic system, and has to be set and released by the driver, but it isolates the traction power system and prevents the driver from taking power in error. The equipment, known as the Driver's Reminder Appliance (DRA), has been installed in 4,500 driving cabs, covering all passenger trains expected to be in service beyond 2002, unless they already have a similar or better system.

Considerable progress has been made in reducing the number of accidents of this nature, and when TPWS has been installed, it will be possible to say that the problem has been more or less overcome. Single lead junctions, or other conflicting layouts just beyond stations, will no longer be such a menace.

3 PROVISION OF CENTRAL DOOR-LOCKING ON SLAM DOOR COACHES

It was expected that most slam door coaches would have been replaced by more modern designs by now, but the privatisation processes caused a lengthy hiatus in the ordering of new rolling stock, with the result that older rolling stock has had to remain in service for longer than planned. This problem will be solved in due course, but slam door stock without central door locking will be prohibited from 1 January 2005.

Almost all slam door stock which has not already been dealt with is of Mk 1 vintage, and there is a parallel problem of the crashworthiness of such coaches. However, this problem needs to be kept in perspective. The number of lives lost in collisions of trains composed of Mk 1 stock is very small and there will be fewer collisions when TPWS is in use on a sufficiently wide scale. There is no strong case for the premature withdrawal of Mk 1 stock, but HSE Regulations require such stock to be withdrawn by 1 January 2003 unless rebodied or crashworthiness-modified. Withdrawal of all Mk 1 stock is required by 1 January 2005.

4 LEVEL CROSSINGS

The potential for a serious collision at a level crossing is an ever-present concern. During the year from 1 April 1997 to 31 March 1998 there were no fewer than 24 train accidents at level crossings. No railway staff or passengers were killed in these accidents, but two occupants of road vehicles lost their lives. There needs to be a much greater deterrent to reckless behaviour by road users at level crossings, whether they cause an accident or not, and this ought to be done before the next serious accident, not after it. An analysis of collisions and fatalities of occupants of road vehicles at the main types of level crossings during the year mentioned above is as follows:

- Automatic half-barriers — four collisions, one fatality.
- Automatic open crossings, locally monitored — three collisions.
- User-worked crossings — two collisions, one fatality.
- User-worked crossings with telephones — eight collisions.
- Open crossings — seven collisions.

Automatic half-barrier crossings are sources of risk owing to the temptation to the reckless and stupid motorist to zigzag round the barriers. The Department of Transport should direct its attention to reducing the risk. BT Police have taken action at some of the more notorious level crossings by erecting video

cameras to catch offenders and the courts should support the efforts of the police by taking a more serious view of offenders, who are risking not only their own lives but also those of people in trains. Sec 34 of the Offences Against the Person Act 1861 provides that any unlawful act which endangers the safety of persons conveyed on the railway shall be punishable by imprisonment for two years. Is there any good reason why it should not be applied to those who zigzag (or bash bridges — see Section 5 following)?

Private level crossings can be hazardous. The size and weight of road vehicles and some farm vehicles is quite sufficient to derail a train following a collision, and the achievement of safety at such locations can be both difficult and expensive. It is a very long-standing problem whose solution can be costly. Who should pay? Should the cost be shared among Railtrack, the crossing user and central government? In the absence of a serious accident it is unlikely that anything other than slow progress will be made.

Right
The result of bridge bashing. The bridge was struck and damaged by a mobile digger loaded on a low-loader, distorting the track. This occurred at Oyne, between Aberdeen and Keith, on 12 May 1978. *Author's collection*

Below
The potential for derailment is obvious from this example of bridge bashing. *Author's collection*

Left
Stone arch bridges offer more resistance but are constantly being struck. *Author's collection*

height somewhat lower than the bridge clearance and connected to a flashing sign which is illuminated when the beam of the photo-electric cell is interrupted. If the driver of an overheight lorry sees the illuminated sign, and obeys it, there should be no danger either to trains or to other road users. This system has been installed at a few locations.

Bridge bashing has been a problem for many years. It is quite disgraceful that the Department of Transport has done so little about it, and surely indicates the official attitude towards road safety compared with rail safety. Unfortunately, bridge bashing appears to be considered to be a road traffic accident rather than a railway accident, and nothing much will be done until that attitude changes or there is a serious railway accident with multiple fatalities caused by the displacement of a bridge deck and the consequent buckling of the track. It is an abdication of responsibility and reflects no credit whatever upon a government department.

5 BRIDGES BEING DAMAGED BY ROAD VEHICLES (BRIDGE BASHING)

This is endemic. In the five years from 1 April 1992 to 31 March 1997 there were over 5,000 cases of bridges under the railway being struck by road vehicles which were too high to pass under them. Of this number, 231 were classed as 'potentially serious' and 42 as 'serious'. At bridges over the railway, in the same five years, there were 399 cases where there was damage to bridges that was classed as 'not serious', 81 cases classed as 'potentially serious' and 68 cases classed as 'serious'.

There is no lack of practical solutions to this problem, only the lack of will within the Department of Transport. Does the Health & Safety Executive have no powers in this direction? If not, shouldn't it have? The obvious solution, and not too expensive, at those bridges which are regularly struck, is to erect on the road approach to the bridge, a strong steel beam across the road at a height of a foot or 30cm less than the clearance of the bridge, so that an overheight lorry attempting to go through the bridge would collide with the steel beam rather than the bridge. However, the Department of Transport appears to consider such an idea to be unfair to the road user, but the danger to other road users would be no greater and the danger to trains would be removed altogether; a simple, easy and cheap way not only to improve railway safety but also to prevent the annoying delays to thousands of railway travellers and, incidentally, to other road users.

A more expensive, but less effective, deterrent is the provision of a photo-electric cell aimed across the road at a

6 VANDALISM

This is another social problem which plagues the railways and which is so difficult to combat. Railways are often distant from any type of supervision and present a natural attraction for young people, including those who are antisocial and care nothing for the consequences of their actions. They seem indifferent to the possibility of killing or injuring drivers and passengers or of blinding them with broken glass.

Some acts of vandalism pose no danger to trains or their occupants. Others do, such as placing obstructions on the line or throwing stones or other missiles at passing trains. In the 12 months from 1 April 1997 to 31 March 1998 there were 514 instances of trains being damaged, usually by windows being

Right
Vandalism near Greenock. The driver was killed when his train ran into an obstruction placed on the line, which then became derailed and crashed into a bridge abutment. The front of the train was severely damaged. *Author's collection*

broken by stones or other missiles being thrown at them. The railway line was reported as being obstructed on 351 occasions by objects being placed on it, and there were 208 acts of arson. The railway companies, especially Railtrack, assisted by the BT Police, pay a great deal of attention to the education of schoolchildren on this question, but it is a social problem outside the control of the railway industry, not helped by those local authorities whose plans result in stretches of wasteland next to the railway, which quickly become a natural play area for children who, when bored, decide to explore the railway. It is then only a short step, for certain members of the community, to stone throwing and the placing of obstructions on the line.

The black spots are well known, and there are several courses of action available to reduce the problem at such places:

1 Erect secure, unbreakable and unclimbable fencing. An expensive solution, but the costs should be shared by the government, which is at least partly responsible for social attitudes; by local authorities, whose plans often create problems; and by the railways themselves.

2 At bridges over the railway, erect barriers on the top of parapet walls, with the tops of the barriers being curved back over the pavement. This will reduce the incidence of objects being dropped on trains, and avoid the danger to children who dangle objects over the parapet wall and onto overhead live wires. Footbridges should be roofed over completely so that nothing can be thrown or dangled from them.

3 Railtrack to ensure that contractors do not leave materials and equipment lying around on or near the track which might be used by wrongdoers to obstruct the line.

4 More frequent policing. A police uniform is still the best deterrent.

Graffiti is a form of vandalism so far as the railways are concerned. It is not an art form. Graffiti degrades an environment, leading easily to other acts of vandalism and to a feeling of insecurity for passengers. It has to be tackled in two ways. Vulnerable areas such as carriage maintenance and stabling depots need to be securely fenced and patrolled. Nothing gives a worse impression than graffiti-strewn coaches. In other areas the graffiti must be erased or obliterated as soon as it appears. If not, the problem will rapidly grow worse. There is a cost to be borne, but a decent environment is more likely to attract passengers than one which is degraded and perceived to be hostile.

The Health & Safety Executive must take the initiative, and it has issued a booklet The Prevention of Trespass and Vandalism on Railways. That is fine, so far as it goes, but it is not enough. It is a typical HSE approach, as though issuing a booklet makes the problem go away. It will not. A much more vigorous approach is needed, and the HSE should establish a working party, in conjunction with the police, local authorities, and other appropriate bodies, and draw up an action plan. It is action that is needed, not talk. Here is an opportunity for the HSE to shine, to do something positive and to improve its poor public image. Local managers are already taking the initiative, but this is a national problem.

7 HOW SAFE DO PASSENGERS FEEL?

In can be unequivocally stated that passengers on trains have no fears that the train might crash. Their requirements are trains that are on time, clean and comfortable, and on which you can be sure of a reserved seat. They want good value refreshment facilities and a reasonable fare. This is demonstrated by market research. Passengers take safety for granted, but that relates to the operation of the train. They also want a safe environment within the train, and at stations and in the station car park. Busy trains and busy stations, like busy streets, are felt to be safe. When those areas are less busy, during off-peak periods and in the evenings, or when it is dark, they are perceived as being less safe and more threatening, especially by women travelling alone and by older people.

The removal of staff from smaller stations, and the removal of guards from many suburban trains under the one-man-operated train arrangement, although done for good economic reasons, impacts on the number of passengers who use the trains during quiet periods. The nationalised railway, whilst eventually recognising the problem, did little about it, because the solutions cost money which it didn't have, but the privatised railways, with the imperative to increase revenue, have quickly come to grips with the situation, employing both British Transport Police and private security firms to act as a reassuring presence on stations and, sometimes, in trains. It is the price that has to be paid for what is regarded as an increasingly violent and hostile society. It is a social problem, but the railways have to bear the cost.

Other useful actions are being taken. The use of security cameras is widespread and effective. Better lighting, especially in car parks, provides some reassurance. The elimination of dark corners helps, which is a factor now being borne in mind when stations are rebuilt and modernised, but nothing can replace the presence of a man in uniform. It also has to be remembered that a passenger's journey does not start at the station, but at home or at work, etc. The route from home to station also needs to be safe when covered on foot or by public transport, and that is a question that needs to be taken into account by local authorities. Stations are often poorly located in relation to well-lit town centres, and on the wrong side of dual carriageway roads where the need for pedestrians to use subways is a positive deterrent. Town planners, in their worship of the motor car, have a lot to answer for, and it will take a lot of money to rectify their mistakes, assuming such funds will ever be available.

The Epilogue

> 'Like one that on a lonesome road
> Doth walk in fear and dread,
> And having once turn'd round, walks on,
> And turns no more his head;
> Because he knows a frightful fiend
> Doth close behind him tread.'
>
> (S. T. Coleridge)

PRESENT SAFETY LEVELS

The first difficulty in answering the question 'How safe are the railways today?' is the establishment of meaningful standards. It is not enough to say that the number of passenger train collisions has gone up, or gone down, and it is an oversimplification to lump all collisions together as though they were all of equal severity, as though a collision at 70mph were equal to one at 10mph.

Railway safety is all about people's safety. It is not about damage to track and trains, which may be expensive but is a business consideration. Death is a very measurable condition, there are no grades of death, and the methods adopted in the operation of trains are designed to avoid killing people. It might be argued that it is the potential of accidents to kill people which is more important, rather than merely considering those that do. That is a very valid argument when considering safety investment, but it is impossible to express in numerical terms without distortion. We will therefore use statistical units which are equal — death is the great leveller.

It would be misleading to take a snapshot view of current performance, because it is not possible to make a value judgement on whether it is good or bad. One needs standards against which to measure current performance, and the most useful standards available are those which have been achieved in previous years, because that enables an assessment to be made of the degree of improvement or deterioration currently being experienced. In order to smooth out the effect of a particularly serious accident with multiple fatalities, it is preferable to consider decades rather than individual years.

The following table gives the number of passenger fatalities in train accidents in the past three decades:

1970-9	51
1980-9	75
1990-8	15 (nine years

The 1980-89 figures include Clapham, in which 35 passengers were killed. The number of passengers killed in that single accident is almost half of the number killed in the whole decade, and it indicates the distorting effect of such an accident. If Clapham had occurred a year later, the results for the 1980-9 decade would have been a creditable 40; the figures for the present decade a less-creditable 50. But we must not deal in 'ifs'. The detailed results for the 1990s, showing the number of passengers killed, are as follows:

8 January 1991	Cannon Street collision with buffers	2
21 July 1991	Newton (Glasgow) collision	2
15 October 1994	Cowden collision	2
8 September 1995	Maidenhead (fire)	1
8 August 1996	Watford collision	1
19 September 1997	Southall collision	7

Only 15 passenger deaths in nine years, during which time the railways carried approximately seven billion passengers. That's not a bad result, and one which reflects great credit on railwaymen of all grades, who have carried the day-to-day operation of trains through all the upheavals of reorganisation and privatisation.

There are two interesting points to note from the table above. The period of 1,181 days between 21 July 1991 and 15 October 1994 was the longest continuous period in the history of the main line railways during which passengers were carried without a single fatality in a train accident — an astonishing achievement. The other point of note is that five of the six accidents were caused by driver error, and that four of them involved passing signals at danger. Significantly, all four involved resignalled and remodelled layouts.

THE COST OF SAFETY

Railtrack is currently spending huge amounts on station improvements; almost certainly more than has been spent at any time since World War 1. This is splendid for the passenger, and the provision of a clean, bright, modern environment is likely to generate new business, a very worthy result. It could instead have spent at least some of the money on improvements in safety. Should it have done so?

The standard of safety on the railways is now so high that considerable amounts have to be spent to achieve even a small increase in safety. Do passengers want investment to be switched from station improvements to safety projects? There is no evidence that they do. All the pressure comes from organs of state who deal in absolutes, in black and white, and who often have an imperfect understanding of financial matters.

Those same organs of state take a considerably more relaxed view of safety regarding the railway's main competitors, the lorry and the car. Accidents on the road are tolerated with equanimity, even such disasters as major pile-ups on motorways with multiple casualties. Plenty of people voluntarily drive in an unsafe manner, travelling too fast and overtaking recklessly. Sometimes they are drunk or high on drugs. They kill and injure innocent people. Society appears to be content to pay the high price of mobility. There are double standards in the official approach to road and rail safety. Is that acceptable?

The Clapham Inquiry and its recommendations were an unjustified reaction to an isolated incident, awful though that incident was. It occurred on 12 December 1988. The previous fatal train accident from causes entirely within the railway's control was on 4 December 1984, more than four years earlier, a period of time without precedent. There was no justification for the hysteria of Clapham. It also ushered in a disagreeable change of emphasis so far as accidents were concerned, the finding of a scapegoat becoming a higher priority; someone to blame who could be punished; a culprit on whom society could take revenge. Finding the cause and taking effective action seemed to be lower down the scale of priorities.

RAILTRACK

Railtrack inherited high safety standards and procedures from British Rail. Higher standards are praiseworthy if they are cost-effective, but if they are not, such expenditure merely makes the use of rail more expensive and less competitive, both for passengers and freight. So far as the nation is concerned, it is not a sensible outcome for traffic to be transferred from the safety of rail to the less safe environment of road transport. It also conflicts with the Government's declared aim of transferring traffic from road to rail, partly as a means of reducing road congestion (a vain hope) and partly to reduce exhaust emissions (politically popular but simplistic).

However, it is important for Railtrack to do more to help the train driver and reduce the number of cases in which drivers pass signals at danger and stray beyond the safety overlap. The avoidance of casualties is only one part of the story. Damage to infrastructure and rolling stock is costly. There is a loss of revenue until the line is reopened. Thousands of passengers are delayed and may choose not to travel by train in future. Compensation has to be paid. Staff morale also suffers. These are all valid reasons for avoiding accidents. And in the background is the relatively new menace of the threat of prosecution by the Health & Safety Executive following more serious accidents.

Railtrack is the body mainly responsible for the safety of trains, but there are fears that it does not have the necessary expertise to perform that role, and that it is incapable of properly monitoring the activities of its contractors, or of designing layouts and signalling. These are fears that have existed since the beginning of privatisation, and stem from the fragmentation of the railway industry. It is a very real problem, which is not being properly addressed because much of it is hidden from view and appreciated only by those involved. The accidents at Newton, Cowden, Watford and Southall all flow from the destruction of a strong operating chain of command which started during BR days and has been further weakened by the privatisation structure. The crucial question is — Who is in overall charge of day-to-day train operations and safety? All the participating companies have their own safety cases, but who effectively monitors performance and compliance for the whole railway system? The answer is probably no one.

Railtrack is financially a very successful business, but its level of profit has attracted criticism from the government, which seems unable to comprehend that profits are essential to enable investment to be made. However, Railtrack can deflect such criticism by ensuring that the spread of investment makes adequate provision for the expected increase in the number of trains, and especially the forecast tripling of freight traffic. It would be a tragedy of the first magnitude if the railway industry had to turn away passengers and freight because there was insufficient track capacity. One appreciates that this was cut to the bone during BR days as a result of government pressure to reduce the annual deficit, but it is now just as important to provide adequate track capacity as it is to regenerate stations, and in the long run more so. Public funds are available to deal with pinch points, and one expects Railtrack to take full advantage, and to do so with the required degree of urgency. Action on this issue has not been as rapid as one hoped. Railtrack is a monopoly supplier so far as the Train Operating Companies are concerned, a monopoly which is far removed from the real customers — passengers and EWS's freight. Railway operators have long been accused of playing at trains; Railtrack must take care not to find itself similarly accused. Perhaps, therefore, the Strategic Rail Authority is a good idea. It needs teeth to ensure that the desired growth in rail traffic, especially freight, is not inhibited by lack of capacity.

PRIVATISATION

There were realistic and genuine fears that the demands of the balance sheets of the newly-privatised rail companies would lead to lower standards of safety, and that when the effect of reducing subsidy to the Train Operating Companies (TOCs) began to bite there would be a temptation to cut corners on safety. BR was not immune from such pressures, but it chose its targets carefully, with the benefit of a long experience of having to do so. TOCs may not have the same expertise, and will need close supervision by the Railway Inspectorate when the going gets tough.

It is possible that high standards of safety are being maintained because rank and file staff are reacting favourably to the evident success of privatisation in attracting more passengers and freight and in reversing the steady, morale-sapping decline that characterised BR's final years. But rail managers, who for decades have had problems of over-capacity and by reducing it have stifled the ability of the industry to expand, now have to face the consequences of a track capacity which threatens to become inadequate to meet all the aspirations of the Train Operating Companies. This is particularly relevant in the case of freight, which is seeing a remarkable increase, thanks to the drive and leadership of the former chairman of the English, Welsh & Scottish Railway, and which will require the re-laying of tracks torn up in what might be regarded as the bad old days. However, it would be quite unfair to blame BR managers for the situation. They could not have foreseen this reversal in the railway's fortunes. The blame for the problem lies fairly and squarely at the government's door for failing to have a comprehensive,

long-term transport policy. Railways are, quintessentially, a long-term industry. Government spokesmen seem unable to comprehend that.

If any proof were needed of the Government's inability to understand the inherent long-term nature of the railway, consider the criticism that is being levelled at the Train Operating Companies for their failure to produce instant improvements in performance. The attack on Virgin Rail for what is admittedly an unsatisfactory standard on the West Coast main line is a little unfair. Punctuality on that line was unsatisfactory when it was in BR's hands, and will only be improved after massive investment in both the infrastructure and the rolling stock. BR recognised

Below
The modern railway. Class 92 electric locomotive No 92024 approaches Charing on 22 February 1998 with a trainload of Rover cars destined for Brescia via the Channel Tunnel. *Brian Morrison*

Facing Page
A Class 86/2 electric locomotive No 86218 in Anglia Railways livery stands at Norwich on 29 June 1998 at the head of the 14.05 to Liverpool Street. The train is also in the new livery. *Brian Morrison*

this 10 years ago and produced plans for improvement, but the government of the day failed to provide the funds. Therefore the line continued to deteriorate, and will continue to do so until Virgin Rail's plans, in conjunction with Railtrack, come to fruition, which cannot be achieved overnight. Does the Government not understand that new rolling stock cannot be obtained off the shelf, and that improvements to track and signalling take several years to plan and implement? Perhaps it does, but is merely courting cheap popularity. The railways, despite being privatised, are still a political football.

It is ironic that the Conservative Government privatised the railways as an ideological measure, and to rid itself and the Treasury of a perennial problem. It was not done to revive a moribund nationalised concern and produce a more efficient and prosperous industry. How surprised they must be with the success of the enterprise, patchy though it may be at times, but particularly with the increase, actual and in prospect, of freight. These are heartening times for those who long to see a railway renaissance.

HM RAILWAY INSPECTORATE

What ought to be done about the Railway Inspectorate? Safety on the railways is now at a high level, but both Railtrack and the Train Operating Companies will need watching closely. The Inspectorate was formed over a century and a half ago because

the government of the day felt that some form of supervision was needed over the mass of new railway companies which were busily engaged on building new railway lines and operating them according to whatever methods they thought appropriate. Is there a parallel with the present day?

There is a very good case for removing the Inspectorate from the Health & Safety Executive, which was never its cultural home and is much more concerned with the health and safety of workers in industry generally rather than passengers on a form of public transport. There is a lack of logic in the transfer of the Inspectorate to the HSE. Does that body look after the health and safety of bus passengers, of coach passengers, of those in aircraft or on ships, or of passengers in cars? It does not. All other modes of transport report to the Department of the Environment, Transport and the Regions (DETR), and it is anomalous that the safety of railway passengers should be a responsibility of the HSE.

A government-sponsored review is currently investigating the way in which the safety of all public transport is regulated, with the possible formation of a single independent authority. That is not a good idea, because the various modes — road, rail, sea and air — are so dissimilar, and the creation of an umbrella body, still reporting to the DETR, would be a clumsy arrangement; but wherever the Railway Inspectorate should ultimately reside, it is important that it is fully staffed to carry out effectively its many responsibilities, and that its independence is not further compromised.

TO SUMMARISE

Railway passengers have never been as safe as they are today, but if that desirable state of affairs is to be maintained, both Railtrack and the Train Operating Companies will require close supervision by the Railway Inspectorate until they have demonstrated that it is no longer necessary.

The Health & Safety Executive can best assist by directing its energies and taking action against those dangers which are largely outside the railway's control — level crossing misuse, bridge bashing, vandalism and violence. These are mainly the ills of modern society and are therefore the province of government, of which the HSE is a part, but they need to be tackled so that passengers can feel safe and secure both on stations and in trains.

The Health & Safety Executive can also assist by taking a more positive and confident tone where railway safety is concerned. There have been only 15 passenger deaths in train accidents in the 1990s, which would seem to indicate that the railways today are generally very safe, but the constant dripping of criticism from the HSE, and its carping tone, serves to give the opposite impression and makes bullets for ill-informed and mischievous politicians and ministers to fire. The HSE should not be afraid to praise the railways occasionally. It is not a sign of weakness, but of strength.

However, government cannot escape a degree of blame for many of the problems during the past 10 years which have been discussed in these pages, in fact it is often the chief culprit. Consistent underfunding, both before and after 1988, is the root cause of many of those problems.

Governments have rarely been able to resist interfering in the business of railways, almost always to the latter's detriment. There have been few instances where government action has been beneficial, although one might mention the 1955 Modernisation plan, the creation of Passenger Transport Authorities in the 1968 Transport Act, and the concept of financial support to assist the transfer of freight from road to rail, embodied in the 1974 Railways Act but almost nullified until recently by lethargy and outright opposition from the Department of Transport and the Treasury. Financial support for socially desirable passenger services was a brainchild of what is now the European Union.

So far as the railways are concerned, more needs to be done to help the driver in his obedience to signals. If that can be achieved, there will be less need to worry about crashworthiness, but as the Southall accident demonstrated, there are still loopholes in the Rules and Regulations which need to be closed. The laudable and understandable desire to avoid train delays must never be allowed to compromise safety. It is an enduring truth that the price of safety is eternal vigilance, and that needs a dedicated, well-trained and experienced workforce who are proud of the railway's splendid safety record, are determined to maintain it, and who do not need supervision from outside the industry.